T0306023

A Handbook of Primary Commodities in the Global Economy

The update of this edition of the *Handbook* took place during 2019, a period of continued slow recovery in most primary commodity markets after the dramatic price falls of 2014–2015 that marked the end of the most powerful and enduring commodity boom since the Second World War. The book is intended as a guide to the ins and outs of the primary commodity universe, an increasingly crucial part of the world economy. Assuming nothing more from readers than a basic understanding of economics, the authors introduce and explain pertinent issues surrounding international commodity markets such as the global geography of raw materials, price formation, price trends, the role of commodity exchanges, the threat of depletion, cartel action, state ownership, the emerging commodity nationalism and much more.

MARIAN RADETZKI is Professor of Economics at Luleå University of Technology, Sweden, specializing through his academic career on the world of primary commodities. He has held visiting professorships at the Colorado School of Mines in the USA and the Catholic University, Santiago de Chile. The author of more than two dozen books, the most recent titled *The Price of Oil* (together with Roberto Aguilera, Cambridge University Press, 2016), Radetzki has undertaken numerous consulting assignments for industry, governments and international organizations such as the World Bank and the United Nations Development Programme.

LINDA WÅRELL is Associate Professor of Economics at Luleå University of Technology, Sweden. Her research and publications have centered on competition and public policy issues, predominantly, but not exclusively, in the minerals industries, pertaining in particular to the iron ore, steel and coal markets. Wårell is also Editor-in-Chief of *Mineral Economics*, a multidisciplinary journal focusing on economic and policy issues in the minerals industries.

A Handbook of Primary Commodities in the Global Economy

MARIAN RADETZKI
Luleå University of Technology

LINDA WÅRELL
Luleå University of Technology

CAMBRIDGE
UNIVERSITY PRESS

CAMBRIDGE
UNIVERSITY PRESS

University Printing House, Cambridge CB2 8BS, United Kingdom

One Liberty Plaza, 20th Floor, New York, NY 10006, USA

477 Williamstown Road, Port Melbourne, VIC 3207, Australia

314–321, 3rd Floor, Plot 3, Splendor Forum, Jasola District Centre, New Delhi – 110025, India

79 Anson Road, #06–04/06, Singapore 079906

Cambridge University Press is part of the University of Cambridge.

It furthers the University's mission by disseminating knowledge in the pursuit of education, learning, and research at the highest international levels of excellence.

www.cambridge.org
Information on this title: www.cambridge.org/9781108841542
DOI: 10.1017/9781108886529

First published 2021

A *catalogue record for this publication is available from the British Library.*

ISBN 978-1-108-84154-2 Hardback
ISBN 978-1-108-97091-4 Paperback

Contents

List of Figures	*page* vi
List of Tables	vii
Acknowledgments	ix
Introduction	1
1 The Historical Framework	6
2 The Geography of Commodity Production and Trade	28
3 Comparative Advantage and Trade Policy Distortions	54
4 Fossil Fuels	72
5 Price Formation and Price Trends in Commodities	91
6 Commodity Booms	116
7 Commodity Exchanges, Commodity Investments and Speculation	130
8 Sustainability and the Threats of Resource Depletion	161
9 Fears of and Measures to Assure Supply Security	184
10 Producer Cartels in International Commodity Markets	205
11 Public Ownership of Commodity Production	227
12 The Monoeconomies: Issues Raised by Heavy Dependence on Commodity Production and Exports	256
References	288
Index	308

Figures

1.1	Share of primary sector in GDP in 2017	*page* 9
1.2	Intensity of steel use in South Korea, 1970–2017	11
1.3	Regional national gas prices 2000–2018, US$/mBTU	16
1.4	Baltic Dry Index, 2000–2019	17
1.5	Developments in international seaborne trade, 1970–2017 (million tons loaded)	18
4.1	Indexes of commodity prices 1970–2018 in constant money, 1970–1972 = 100	76
4.2	US natural gas and oil production (MBOE/D)	84
5.1	Short-run price determination	92
5.2	Long-run price determination	93
5.3	World copper variable costs in 2004 and 2007 (nominal US$/ton)	96
6.1	Commodity price indices in constant US$, 1948–2018. 2000 = 100	117
6.2	Monthly commodity price indices in constant US$, 2003M1–2016M12. 2016 = 100	120
6.3	Annual growth of GDP (%)	126
8.1	US oil reserve prices 1982–2003 (constant 2003 US$ per barrel)	168
8.2	Oil resources and cost of exploitation, 2008 (US$ per barrel)	172
8.3	Cost of producing a barrel of oil in 2016 (US$ per barrel)	173
10.1	Maximization of profit and maximization of revenue	206
11.1	Proved oil reserves by company, 2010, billion barrels	230
12.1	Price stabilization with variable demand	264
12.2	Price stabilization with variable supply	264

Tables

1.1 Agriculture, mining and utilities as a proportion
of GDP (%)   *page* 8
1.2 Value (US$ per kg) at prices in 2018   10
2.1 Evolution of global exports by commodity group since
1965   33
2.2 Global export value for individual primary commodities
(billion US$)   35
2.3 World production and exports of selected primary
commodities, 2018   37
2.4 Commodity and total goods trade by region, annual
average 2015–2017 (billion US$)   39
2.5 Share of world exports for selected countries
and commodities in 2015–2017 (%)   42
2.6 Share of world exports of oil in 2018 by country (%)   44
2.7 Consumption developments for four important
industrial commodities in four regions   48
2.8 Commercial energy at the primary stage: ratio
of production to consumption   51
3.1 An illustration of tariff escalation: nominal versus
effective tariff rates   69
3.2 Tariff escalation in high-income OECD countries (%)   69
4.1 Global primary energy consumption by source   73
4.2 The importance of fossil fuels in 2018: their share
in world trade and in global GDP   75
4.3 Resource curse and oil production   82
6.1 Growth patterns during three booms (%)   118
6.2 Peaks in constant dollar commodity price indices during
three booms   120
6.3 Growth patterns during the third boom (%)   124
7.1 Futures and options volume, selected years 2001–2018
(million contracts)   131

7.2 Major exchanges in 2018 ranked by number of contracts 133
8.1 Proven reserves and R/P ratios for four minerals 165
8.2 Operating cash costs for three metals 169
9.1 Oil prices and the macroeconomy 191
10.1 Price elasticities of demand for output from a cartel (E_{DC}) that controls 60% of world supply (M = 0.6) 208
10.2 Five leading corporations' share of global production 214
10.3 Bauxite output among leading producers in the NSW 216
10.4 OPEC and world oil output (MBD) 224
11.1 State-controlled share in mining (% of world production) 233
11.2 Zambian copper industry performance 248
12.1 The monoeconomies: leading nonfuel commodity accounted for 40% or more of total exports in 2013–2017 258
12.2 The oil monoeconomies: oil and oil products accounted for more than 80% total exports in 2013–2017 259

Acknowledgments

Work on this edition of the *Handbook* was undertaken while we were both associated with the Economics Unit at Luleå University of Technology. We are grateful to our colleagues for the intellectual stimulation that enthused us and continuously fertilized our effort. Special thanks are due to Jan-Olof Edberg, chairman of Insamlingsstiftelsen Naturresursernas Ekonomi, a Swedish research foundation, and to Cambridge University Press for financially supporting the work. Finally, we wish to convey our deep appreciation for the support and encouragement to the project received from Chris Harrison, Phil Good and Matt Lloyd at Cambridge University Press, and to their staff for efficiently handling all the practicalities through the production process.

Introduction

Background

The antecedent to the present work is Marian Radetzki's book *A Guide to Primary Commodities in the World Economy*, published by Blackwell in 1990, three decades ago. In that book Radetzki presented the gist of what he had learnt over the 30 preceding years of active study and research on international primary commodity markets. The timing of that publication was clearly inopportune. Though the book received positive reviews, it aroused only limited attention. Through the 1980s and 1990s, primary commodity markets were in the doldrums. Supply conditions for most commodities were quite relaxed most of the time, and prices remained suppressed. The advanced economies were in a process of dematerialization, where declining volumes of raw materials were needed per unit of value added. This suppressed demand growth and reduced the significance of commodities in their macroeconomies. In these circumstances, security of supply assumed a low priority for users. Producers struggled with excess capacity and weak profitability. Speculators' interest was muted by the relative market calmness and declining prices. Noncommercial investors such as pension funds and mutual funds had little incentive to engage in longer-term commodity placements. These actors instead directed their capital flows to fields like information technology and sophisticated services, where markets appeared to provide a better profit potential.

Against this background, interest in commodities dwindled among public policy makers and media, but also in the academic community. Researchers found more fertile ground for their efforts in other sectors of the economy, while students' attention moved elsewhere. Commodities was simply not a rewarding career area.

This situation changed dramatically a few years into the twenty-first century, when the most powerful and unusually enduring commodity boom began. Prices of most commodities in all categories, fuels as well as minerals, food products and agricultural raw materials, exploded. Existing production capacity, dilapidated through years of negligence due to low prices, could simply not satisfy the speedy demand expansion resulting from spectacular economic advances in the emerging world, with China in the vanguard, passing through an especially commodity-intensive phase of their economic development. Earlier attitudes of complacency among consumers were replaced by worries about security of supply, with the realization that ample availability of commodities is indispensable, and that even prosperous, dematerializing economies cannot survive without safe raw-material inputs. Producers of commodities, in contrast, experienced an unexpected and extraordinary profit surge. Investments in capacity growth were stimulated by the high prices, to the extent of exhausting the immediate availability of many investment inputs.

The rising commodity prices galvanized the managers of hedge funds, pension funds and other capital portfolios to invest in commodities, both as a means of diversification and for the prospect of significant profit opportunities. Speculators also reentered the commodity markets on a large scale.

From 2005 onwards, primary commodities became truly hot stuff, with current events in the commodity markets regularly displayed on the first pages of newspapers and magazines, and figuring prominently on TV screens. In the midst of the commodity boom, 2008 was then a highly opportune time to see a new version of Radetzki's book, this time titled *A Handbook of Primary Commodities in the Global Economy* and published by Cambridge University Press (the first edition for this publisher).

The exceptional prices of most commodities persevered for a few more years after the book's publication, the constant price indexes for each major category reaching a peak around 2011. Substantial price falls were subsequently recorded, as massive new capacity, whose establishment was triggered by the boom, went into production, while at the same time the explosive global demand expansion was suppressed by a sizable downward adjustment in the economic growth pace of China and several other emerging economies. In consequence, by January 2015, the price index of all primary commodities was 40% below the peak of four years earlier.

January 2015 was also the time when Cambridge University Press approached Radetzki about a new edition of the *Handbook*. The year 2016, the planned publication date for this second edition (available in the market only in 2017), may have been slightly less exhilarating than 2008, but there is little doubt that a number of exciting stories worthy of sharing with a wider audience had emerged since the preceding edition. To mention just a few: the dominant role of China as commodity consumer had only recently been fully acknowledged; price transparency had been greatly improved by the relentless progress of commodity exchanges; resource nationalism had been on the rise, stimulated by the high prices of past years; and the emergence of shale oil and shale gas had given a new perspective to fuels markets and on sustainability and depletion.

There was dual authorship this time. Radetzki, having reached an impressive age, invited Linda Wårell, a knowledgeable and versatile fellow professor at Luleå, to share the workload, and her acceptance no doubt contributed to a broadened and refreshed problem treatment.

Content

Much of the value of the book, nowadays a true classic in the field of primary commodity analysis, consists of the wealth of data on commodities and their markets that it contains. Understanding this, Cambridge decided in 2019 to publish a third edition (to reach the market in 2020) with only limited change from the second in terms of content, but updated with the most recent numbers throughout. This time an even greater burden of work fell on Wårell, with Radetzki's role limited in the main to a scrutiny of what she delivered. No doubt she will be the sole author when a decision is taken to publish a future, fourth edition. Such a decision will unquestionably come in some years' time, given that the *Handbook* has met with hardly any competition during its 30-year life.

The text that follows provides a comprehensive overview of pertinent issues relating to primary commodities in the global economy. The basic structure of all earlier editions has been retained because we believe that it continues to be valid and appropriate. These are the major components in that structure:

- the geography of commodity production and trade;
- the distortions of production location and comparative advantage caused by protectionist trade policies;
- the institutions of price formation, the causes of short-run price instability and long-run price trends;
- the role of commodity exchanges;
- fears of and measures to ensure the importers' supply security;
- prospects for successful, monopolistic producer collusion;
- trends in and implications of public ownership;
- issues raised by a very high national dependence on commodity production and exports.

The subject of primary commodities in the global economy is vast, and not all its aspects can be treated within the confines of a single tome. In all editions, the focus of the *Handbook* has been on the economics of commodity production and trade in a somewhat narrow sense, while issues related to, for example, employment, skill creation in the sector or regional development do not receive any detailed attention.

The Readership

The subject treatment is firmly based on standard economic theory and economic logic, but we have consciously avoided technical jargon and algebra. Readers with only basic training in economics should therefore find the text fully accessible.

Despite the omissions mentioned above, the book offers a comprehensive explication of the commodity world in the international economy, and we have always been aiming at a broad readership. While experts in a particular aspect of that world will probably not gain any substantive new insights in their specialization, we are convinced that reading this book will provide them with a valuable context from which to pursue further work in their chosen field.

The following categories of readers should find the book of interest:

- students in economics, finance, business administration and related disciplines, with an interest in primary commodity markets;
- researchers that have chosen a specific commodity or a specific commodity-related issue as their area of specialization, who desire a snapshot overview of the entire commodity economics field;

- executives responsible for marketing or investment decisions in firms that produce and export primary commodities;
- executives responsible for purchase management strategies and their execution in firms whose production relies heavily on raw materials inputs;
- members of the financial community with an interest in primary commodities for the purpose of speculation or as an object for financial investment – such individuals would be found on the commodity exchanges and in organizations that manage capital portfolios, such as hedge funds, pension funds and mutual funds, but also in financial institutions, for example investment banks, that develop and market instruments for commodity placements;
- government officials in nations heavily dependent on primary commodity production and exports – Chile, Peru, Botswana, Ghana, Mongolia and Papua New Guinea provide examples, but there are many more;
- government officials in countries that rely heavily on commodity imports ought to have an equally strong interest in the analyses in this book – this country group would comprise China, the EU, Japan and the USA;
- finally, the book should find many additional readers among the broad general public concerned about rising prices and the future availability of commodities.

1 | *The Historical Framework*

This introductory chapter provides a historical framework for world commodity markets in modern times. It considers four major themes. The first theme reviews the significance of primary commodities in the overall economy at different stages of economic development. The second tracks the long-run decline in bulk transport costs, and explores the implications of this decline for the establishment of markets with a global reach for an expanding group of raw materials. The third theme focuses on the twentieth century. It demonstrates the greatly expanded role of public intervention and control in primary commodity production and trade from the early 1930s until the late 1970s, and the subsequent retreat of government involvement in favor of market forces. The fourth treats the most recent development, covering the strong economic growth in many emerging economies – especially China, which has had, and continues to have, a profound impact on the world commodity markets. This theme is only briefly introduced in the present chapter, as many of the remaining chapters will further elaborate on the subject.

1.1 Primary Commodities in the Economic Development Process

For the purpose of the present section, we derive our definition of primary commodities from national accounts of the value of output from the primary sector comprising agriculture (including hunting, forestry and fishing), mining and utilities. These are the activities that supply the unprocessed raw materials of agricultural and mineral origin, along with fuels, electricity and potable water, for use by other sectors of the economy. An alternative and somewhat wider definition, derived from foreign trade statistics, appears to be more appropriate for most of the rest of the book. This is further discussed in Chapter 2.

The significance of primary commodities in a national economy is often reduced in the process of economic development. Long historical series to vindicate this statement are hard to come by, given that national accounts were not prepared prior to the twentieth century, and reconstructions of a more distant past lack common standards. Kuznets (1966) presents the following assessment of agriculture and mining (but not utilities) as a proportion of GDP in selected countries over extended periods of time. The contraction over time in the share of primary commodities emerges starkly from his figures.

Australia	ca. 1860	36%	ca. 1940	26%
Italy	ca. 1860	55%	ca. 1950	26%
UK	ca. 1905	41%	ca. 1950	13%
USA	ca. 1870	22%	ca. 1960	5%

Data recorded on a more systematic basis did not become available until the late 1930s, and in Table 1.1 time series (including utilities from 1970 and onwards) for selected countries (for which these series are reasonably complete) are presented. As in the numbers provided by Kuznets, the primary share exhibits a dramatic decline as the economies develop over time. Table 1.1 additionally reveals far lower primary shares for rich, advanced countries such as Italy, Japan, South Korea and the USA, compared to poorer ones, for example China, India, Thailand and Turkey. Norway stands out as an exception, explained further later in the chapter.

A closer look behind the figures of Table 1.1 shows that in most cases agriculture predominated the primary sector during most of the twentieth century. In Kuznets' assessments, for instance, the agricultural sector exceeded four fifths of the primary total for the initial year, except for Australia, where the share was more than three fifths. Because of this, agriculture also dominates the recorded reduction of the primary share over time. The decline in the smaller initial share accounted for by mining is much less accentuated. In some cases (Italy, USA) that share appears to have remained relatively stable through the economic development process (Kuznets, 1966). In recent years we note that mining and utilities have come to dominate the primary sector. This can mainly be explained by the exceptionally high demand

Table 1.1 *Agriculture, mining and utilities as a proportion of GDP (%)*

	1938	1955	1970	1980	1990	2000	2010	2017
Argentina	25	19	12	10	13	10	15	12
Canada	19	14	12	16	10	11	12	11
China[1]	–	–	43	40	35	24	18	13
India	–	45	46	42	37	30	24	22
Italy	28	25	12	8	6	6	5	5
Japan	23	24	9	7	5	5	4	4
Norway	15	16	10	22	21	30	27	22
South Korea	–	46	32	20	11	8	5	2
Thailand	48	46	30	26	14	14	17	14
Turkey	48	43	33	23	17	14	14	10
USA	11	7	6	8	6	4	5	4

[1] For China, 1970–2000 data for ISIC D (manufacturing) are missing, and the numbers are therefore extrapolated based on the assumption that it represents 78% of the total ISCI C–E (based on levels after data became available).
Source: United Nations (annual a) and United Nations Statistics Division on the Internet, http://unstats.un.org/unsd/snaama/Introduction.asp.

for many mining and utilities products since the turn of the century. Chapter 2 discusses this in more detail.

Concurrent cross-section data confirm the findings derived from the time series: there is a strong reverse correlation between the level of economic development, measured by GDP/capita, and the share of the primary sector in the economy. Figure 1.1 provides a demonstration. The data show unambiguously that the dominant pattern is a decline in the primary share of the economy as nations develop. In rich market economies the primary sector seldom exceeds 10% of GDP. Exceptions to this finding require mention, and Norway is an illustrative example as it combines a very high income level with a relatively high primary sector share. The traditional importance of fishing in the country's economy explains the high weight of the primary sector until the 1960s. The subsequent development of offshore oil and gas has made Norway exceedingly rich, while expanding the primary share even more. Other exceptions to mention are Australia, Canada and New Zealand, prosperous countries with an abundant, export-oriented agriculture and a rich mineral endowment, where the primary sector

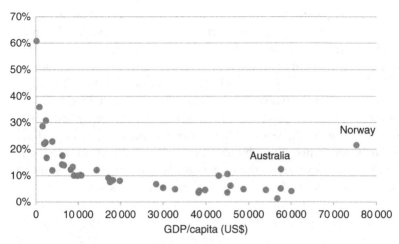

Figure 1.1 Share of primary sector in GDP in 2017
Note: 40 countries have been selected to assure a wide spread in per capita GDP. The primary sector is defined as agriculture, hunting, forestry, fishing, mining and utilities.
Source: United Nations statistics division, national accounts main aggregates database, http://unstats.un.org/unsd/snaama/dnllist.asp.formatting.output

accounts for more than 10% of overall GDP. When studying the share of the primary sector over time for these economies, a moderate increase is noted since about 2005. This corresponds to the rapid increase in primary commodity prices witnessed during this period.

The general finding that the primary sector exhibits declining importance as economies develop is not particularly surprising. Simply expressed (and abstracting from the possibilities offered by foreign trade), a key element in the economic development process is rising productivity that permits the domestic satisfaction of raw materials needs with ever lesser factor inputs. Labor and capital can then be switched to the secondary sector – that is, production of manufactures whose sophistication typically increases over time. As manufactures demand too is eventually saturated, the factors of production can migrate again, now to the service sector. The overall economy expands but the secondary and tertiary sectors more so than the primary one, leaving the latter with a declining share of the total.

With this perspective, the path of economic development can be seen as a process of dematerialization. Since all material inputs originate in the primary sector, and since this sector accounts for a shrinking share of the total, it follows that each dollar's addition to GDP will carry a material weight that declines over time. Table 1.2 illustrates what is involved. It presents the value in US$ (2018) per kilogram of a set of goods and services, listed in ascending order. The higher the value, the less primary material inputs will be needed per dollar value represented by the items. The essence of economic development is to move the center of the economy's gravity down the list, toward goods with ever higher value per kilogram. In consequence, raw materials input needs will grow more slowly than the overall economy as countries grow richer. Material savings will be further boosted by technological progress, which is typically weight reducing. It is conceivable that the need for primary materials inputs could stagnate and plausibly even shrink, as growing, rich economies become increasingly dematerialized. This finding can easily be

Table 1.2 *Value (US$ per kg) at prices in 2018*

Iron ore	0.07
Steam coal	0.11
Wheat	0.21
Crude oil	0.50
Standard steel	0.59
Copper	7.00
Motor car	15.00
Dishwasher	25.00
Jet Ski	30.00
Video game	40.00
TV set	80.00
PlayStation 4	89.00
Laptop computer	1 000.00
Large passenger aircraft	1 600.00
iPhone	5 000.00
Memory card 128 GB	20 000.00
Cloud service	∞

Source: Authors' computations.

depicted using data on primary commodity consumption and economic growth.

Figure 1.2 presents steel demand as a fraction of total GDP, at different stages of economic development in South Korea between 1970 and 2017. The figure clearly illustrates that when the economy initially expanded, the share of primary commodities (in this case represented by apparent steel use) in GDP increased, as a result of investments in infrastructure, roads, houses, factories, cars and household appliances. When the economy becomes richer and the industry sector more advanced, this increase in primary consumption will level out and eventually start to decline. Previous studies confirm that most of the developed countries have reached the income level when commodity consumption starts to decline, but this is not the case for the current emerging economies (see e.g. Wårell, 2014a).

It is easy to become complacent about the role and importance of the primary sector when its share of economic activity settles at no more than a few percentage points, as is the case in many advanced nations. Complacency may be in place so long as commodity markets function smoothly and existing needs can be satisfied without serious hurdles. Since the dawn of the present century this complacency has

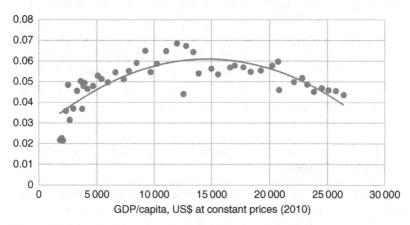

Figure 1.2 Intensity of steel use in South Korea, 1970–2017
Source: United Nations statistics division, national accounts main aggregates database, http://unstats.un.org/unsd/snaama/dnllist.asp, World Steel Association (annual).

been put in serious doubt, as a rapid rise in demand from emerging economies, such as China and India, has led to a strong boom in primary commodities markets. Income levels in China have been increasing at an unprecedented pace, and the infrastructure needed to support the expanding urban population requires large amounts of resources. The exceptional evolution in demand has fueled sharp price increases for primary commodities as supply has struggled to keep up.

More specifically, in the first decades of the twenty-first century the demand for products that contain so-called rare earth metals, such as mobile phones, computer memories, rechargeable batteries and fluorescent lightning, to name a few, exploded. Since economically exploitable resources of rare earth metals are limited and geographically concentrated, it is not surprising that widespread fears of supply shortages have been voiced by users.

At the same time, it needs pointing out that sophisticated modern economies have become masters of substitutability, permitting them to function without a particular material. But the ability to substitute will be of no help against a general constraint on supply for raw materials in aggregate, for it is overwhelmingly clear that not even the most modern economy can function without assured availability of raw materials. The population will die if food supplies fail. The manufacturing sector is critically dependent on raw materials inputs, even if the volumes needed have shrunk impressively compared to the value of manufactured output. The service sector may require quite insignificant inputs of raw materials, but it clearly cannot function if these supplies fail. Primary commodities are indispensable, just like an ordinarily inconspicuous glass of water that acquires immense value in the desert. This is easily forgotten, given the economic insignificance of raw materials in "normal" times when their availability is taken for granted.

1.2 Declining Transport Costs and the Emergence of Global Commodity Markets

Prior to the mid-nineteenth century, freight rates on long hauls were prohibitively high except for goods with very high unit prices. In consequence, global commodity trade at the time was small in volume and consisted in the main of highly valued luxuries such as coffee, cocoa, spices and precious or semi-precious metals, imported predominantly to industrializing Europe (Landes, 1980). The main subsequent changes in transport technology and transport costs for bulk materials, it seems, occurred in two spurts. The first took place in the latter half of the nineteenth century; the second began in the 1950s, but its effects came to fruition only in the 1970s. Each involved the globalization of numerous additional markets for commodities that until then had had no more than a local or regional reach. Globalization involves not only trade flows across oceans and between continents, but also, importantly, a convergence of prices across regional markets.

In the latter half of the nineteenth century, the application of steam power in transport revolutionized the economics of moving goods on land as well as across oceans. A large group of raw materials produced at increasing distances from the coast in overseas territories became economically accessible to the world's industrial centers as overland transport by oxen, horses and camels was switched to railways, and as metal steamships replaced wooden sailing vessels. This becomes dramatically evident in Paul Bairoch's (1965) numbers for the cost of shipping cotton and wheat from New York to Liverpool in constant (1910–1914) dollars per ton:

1825: 55.1 1857: 15.7 1880: 8.6 1910: 3.5

Shipping costs are akin to tariff barriers. Little trade will typically take place when the transport charges account for a major share of the delivered price. Trade will be encouraged as this share declines.

The evolution of cereal imports into (western) Europe provides vivid illustrations of the evolving impact of transport-cost decline on the widening of production sources. Odessa's short-run glory as a leading European port in the mid-1800s was based on the boom in shipping Russian and Ukrainian rye and wheat to Western Europe. Much of this trade was lost in the 1870s, first because of a flood of steam-shipped American wheat after the end of the US civil war, and then because of the extension of the Russian railways, which took over the transport of the remaining Russian cereals exports (*Economist*, December 16, 2004). At the same time, new rail connections from the prairies around Chicago to New York made US cereals even more competitive in Europe. The bulk-transport revolution continued during the following decades. Between 1880 and 1910, the transatlantic shipping cost of wheat declined from 18% to 8% of its price in the USA (Bairoch, 1965).

The 1880s also saw the introduction of refrigerated ships, permitting long distance transport of meat and fruit. The globalization of the markets for many food products speeded up European industrialization by assuring cheaper food supplies to the growing numbers of urban industrial workers. But it involved painful adjustments for European farmers, who lost out in many food products, and agricultural raw materials such as cotton and wool, to overseas supplies. The impact was profound: in the 1850s, two thirds of British bread consumption was based on domestic cereals; by the 1880s that proportion had shrunk to 20% (Dillard, 1967).

The second spurt in transport technology was far more specific, and, importantly, it was triggered by the Suez crisis in the mid-1950s. The shipping industry's response to the canal closure was to opt for huge specialized bulk carriers, along with the concomitant loading and unloading facilities in the harbors, to permit economic transport of low-value products, such as iron ore, steam coal, bauxite and oil, across vastly extended distances. The impact of the effort began to be felt only in the 1970s. The result was a further dramatic decline in the cost of shipping, particularly accentuated for the truly extended, transoceanic transport routes.

Between 1960 and 1988, the average size of the bulk carrier fleet more than doubled. In 1960, virtually all internationally traded iron ore and coal was shipped in vessels of less than 40 000 dwt, but this proportion had declined to 10% or less by 1988. Carriers in excess of 100 000 dwt did not exist in 1960, but by 1988 they accounted for 70% of iron ore and 40% of coal shipments (Lundgren, 1996). Recent developments in the world bulk carrier fleet market point toward a continued increase in average ship sizes, as carriers in excess of 160 000 dwt account for the major share of dry bulk shipments. There is also strong development of container ships (UNCTAD, annual a).

The economic impact of the new bulk-transport technology was very substantial, and especially so for the mining industries. Many European miners faced problems akin to those experienced by the farmers 120 years earlier. The freight rate for Brazilian iron ore to Europe declined from US$24 per ton in 1960 to US$7 in the early 1990s. At the same time, the cost for the much shorter shipping of iron ore from Narvik in Norway to Germany was reduced from US$8 to US$4. The geographic protection afforded to the Swedish supplies shipped through Narvik thus shrank from US$16 to only US$3 (Lundgren, 1996). The freight rate as a proportion of the total price for US coal in Western Europe was reduced from more than 30% to less than 15% in the 30-year period. The consequence was a fast evolution of global markets for these low-cost products. Long-distance maritime iron ore trade rose from 23% of world production in 1960 to 36% in 1990, and for coal from 2% to 9% (Lundgren, 1996). These shares continue to grow. In 2013, transoceanic trade in coal accounted for 17% of global output (IEA, 2014a).

The market for natural gas is one of the most recent to be subjected to the forces of globalization. Gas is an extremely bulky product with transport costs constituting a very high proportion of delivered price. Until at least the 1980s, transport by pipe was the completely dominant delivery mode. The lowest-cost gas sources had a limited geographical reach, because the transport cost was proportional to distance, and higher for piping under the sea. Three regional markets developed around the main consumption centers, viz., North America and Europe (including Russia), both predominantly supplied by pipe from internal sources, and Japan, Korea and Taiwan (more recently also China), supplied exclusively by liquid natural gas (LNG)[1] from Australia, Indonesia and Malaysia. Each of the three markets was, by and large, isolated from the others, with prices evolving along separate levels and patterns. Until the mid-1990s, the East Asian market recorded prices that were twice the level in the USA and 50% higher than in Europe (BP, annual), primarily because of the high cost of liquefaction and shipping.

Since then, however, prices in the three markets have been affected by two major, but highly opposing, developments. First, the prices became equalized for a few years, as a consequence of a combination of rising prices in piped supply and substantial cost reductions in LNG production and transport technology. These developments stimulated a fast growth of additional LNG sources, providing an extended web of long-distance supply routes, causing prices to converge. Second, the development of US shale gas production has had a profound impact on natural gas prices, especially in the USA (Aguilera and Radetzki, 2014). Figure 1.3 illustrates the development of natural gas prices in the three markets from 2000 to 2018; it shows first a period of converging prices, and then a clear pattern of divergence from about 2008. The main

---

[1] Approximately 1.4 m^3 of natural gas equals 1 kg of LNG, with prices in the range of 0.2–0.4 \$/kg. The substantial compression makes LNG economically transportable by ship.

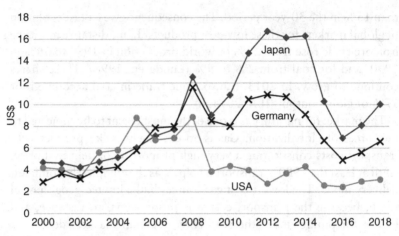

Figure 1.3 Regional national gas prices 2000–2018, US$/mBTU
Source: BP (annual).

cause for the divergence was the production of shale gas in the USA, which mainly put pressure on the national natural gas prices. This development will be further elaborated upon in Chapter 4. The price drop that is noted after 2014 in Japan and Europe is a response to the dramatic oil price fall that occurred earlier that year, since natural gas prices in the East Asian and European markets are linked to oil prices with about a 6–9 month lag. The price difference between the three markets has decreased since this collapse, but continues considerably more separated than prior to 2008. Thus, recent developments illustrate that the natural gas market still can be characterized as regional rather than international.

The successive technological revolutions have gradually reduced the transport costs of bulk commodities by a total of almost 90% between the 1870s and 1990s (Lundgren, 1996). In Figure 1.4 recent developments in transport costs for bulk commodities are depicted, and it is evident from the figure that, despite a sharp increase during the height of the commodity boom, there has been no rise between 2000 and 2019 when this is being written. This, in turn, has increased the number of globally traded primary commodities, from luxuries such as coffee, spices or precious metals before 1850 to encompass virtually all products with perceptible values in the twenty-first century. Even waste, for example scrap metal or rejects from forestry and agriculture, or

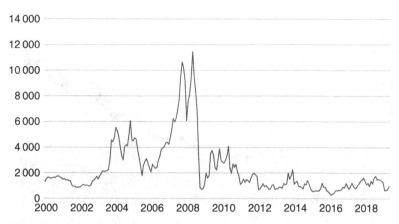

Figure 1.4 Baltic Dry Index, 2000–2019
Note: The index base year is 1985 (1000 points) and is compiled of 20 key dry bulk routes measured on a time charter basis. The index covers dry bulk carriers, carrying commodities such as iron ore, coal and grain.
Source: Bloomberg BDI, www.bloomberg.com/quote/BDIY:IND.

packaging material after use, valued as sources of energy extraction or of recycling, are increasingly subject to international trade. Chinese stone for garden decoration is being successfully marketed in Europe. An important repercussion of the globalization of primary commodity markets has been a growing dependence of the world's manufacturing centers, initially Europe, then Japan and the USA, and most recently China, on imported supply. We will revert to this subject in Chapter 2.

Some developments in maritime transportation in the early twenty-first century require mentioning. Before the financial crisis in 2008, as the world economy was still at the height of the boom, the available ships' capacity was not enough to meet the increasing import demand, especially from China. The situation on the maritime transportation market was thus one of significant shortage, leading to a sharp increase in shipping costs, especially to important ports in China, as is depicted in Figure 1.4. This development was replicated in many commodity markets where producers ultimately failed to satisfy accelerating demand, with the result that commodity prices exploded (discussed further in Chapter 5). The implications of the shipping boom were sometimes far-reaching. For instance, Wårell (2014b) stresses that the

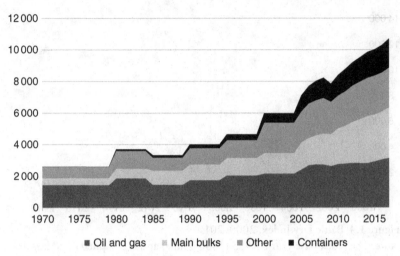

Figure 1.5 Developments in international seaborne trade, 1970–2017 (million tons loaded)
Note: Data before 2005 are for selected years (1970, 1980, 1985, 1990, 1995, 2000). Figures for 1980–2005 for main bulks also include bauxite/alumina and phosphate, as well as iron ore, coal and grain. From 2006 and onwards, these are included in other dry cargo.
Source: UNCTAD (annual a).

increase in transportation costs in 2007–2008 was a major cause of the breakdown of the iron ore pricing system.

After the financial crisis of 2008–2009, international trade volumes continued to increase mainly due to the fact that the commodity boom was still ongoing, but the volume expansion continued even after the boom came to an end about 2014. The development of international seaborne trade volumes from 1970 to 2017 is depicted in Figure 1.5, separating oil and gas from main dry bulks, other dry bulks and containers. Major dry bulk commodities, defined as coal, iron ore and grain, accounted for a major share: 42.3% of total dry cargo shipments in 2017. It is evident from Figure 1.5 that containerized cargo has had the fastest growing share for the last two decades (UNCTAD, annual a). The continued growth in international trade volumes is importantly a consequence of the low shipping costs along with reduced trade restrictions over time (see more about this below).

1.3 Public Intervention and Control in the Primary Commodity Markets

There was a clear and strong wave of far-reaching public and political intervention in primary commodity market that began in the early 1930s and lasted 50 years. Since the late 1970s, the wave has been waning, with market forces assuming increasing roles in shaping commodity market evolution, though developments since 2017, initiated by the US administration, have once again put trade restrictions on the political agenda. Before studying the content and consequences of liberalization since the 1970s, it may be instructive to ask what brought about the preceding government involvement in the first place. For if we look further back in time, say to the beginning of the twentieth century, it is clear that the government was hardly there at all.

We see four major and two subordinate factors explaining and/or motivating the deep public intervention in global primary commodity production and trade. The *1930s depression* led to a price collapse for many primary materials, so deep that it warranted public intervention to rescue the farmers and miners, mainly in the rich world. The *Second World War* created havoc in many supply lines, so worrisome that governments thought it opportune to take action aimed at restoring order. The *breakup of colonial empires* established numerous independent nations, many of which had economies dominated by raw materials production. Their governments thought it imperative to gain control over the commodity sector, especially in minerals and energy where ownership had traditionally rested in colonial or other foreign hands. The fourth factor had ideological connotations. The second and third quarters of the twentieth century were characterized by strong *beliefs in collective action* as a means to come to grips with the numerous purported fallacies of the market system (Skidelsky, 1996).

The subordinate factors comprise (a) the *ascendancy of the Soviet Union* into prominence in the international economy and its interventions in international commodity trade; and (b) the worries and concerns raised by the *emergent import dependence of the USA* on an increasing number of raw materials. Sometimes one factor worked in isolation in prompting public action. Quite often, several of these factors worked in combination and reinforced each other in complex ways in encouraging state intervention in the commodities field.

In the 1930s depression, falling prices triggered several public involvements. The governments of Canada and the USA interfered jointly in the wheat markets to cut supply from abroad to save their farmers from further price falls. Cuba collaborated with Java in launching export quotas in sugar. The colonial administrations of Malaya and Ceylon instituted export restrictions on rubber, but this scheme met resistance from consumer interests in the USA, and soon collapsed (Rowe, 1965).

In the 1945–1965 period, with the scarcities and price spikes of the Second World War and the Korean conflict still fresh in people's memories, commodity agreements were launched by the governments of exporting and importing countries to keep prices within bands that both groups would find acceptable. Export controls, sometimes combined with buffer-stock operations, were the instruments used. The markets for sugar, wheat, coffee and tin were interfered with in this manner, but after some time the efforts disintegrated, usually due to internal tensions and sometimes also because they failed to deliver the desired results (Radetzki, 1970).

The decade after the Second World War involved a painful experience for the USA, as the country became dependent on imports of a widening group of commodities of critical importance in war and peace (Paley, 1952). This prompted the government to build strategic stocks, in many cases of very significant size. On occasion, the acquisition of these stocks and their subsequent disposal created serious instability in the commodity markets. In 1962, when the International Tin Council held a buffer stock of 51 000 tons, the US government declared that its strategic stock, 350 000 tons, equal to two years' world production, was 150 000 tons in excess of what was considered US strategic needs. US disposals in 1963–1966 amounted to 69 000 tons, adding 10% to global mine supply in these years, obviously complicating the operations of the International Tin Agreement (International Tin Council, annual; monthly). In December 1973, the US government again declared substantial excess in its strategic stocks of metals and rubber, and the very sizable sales in the following year contributed to the price collapse in the international market (Cooper and Lawrence, 1975).

The early 1970s also witnessed several countries use of commodity price and export controls to assure supplies at low prices to domestic users. In the USA, price ceilings on many commodities were instituted, and export restrictions, for example for metal scrap and soybeans, were introduced to assure domestic availability (Cooper and Lawrence, 1975). The gasoline queues in the USA in 1974 were a direct consequence of the gasoline price caps. The Canadian government, for its part, implemented severe constraints on uranium exports in the mid-1970s, purportedly to assure national needs (Radetzki, 1981).

Foreign aid became common after numerous nations in Africa and Asia gained independence in the 1950s and 1960s, and since many of these nations were heavily dependent on commodity exports, schemes were launched to extend existing commodity agreements by adding elements of foreign assistance. One such extension was the "multilateral contract" with guarantees by the importing member countries to buy predetermined quantities of the commodity from exporting members at above market prices. Another was "food aid," under which huge amounts of surplus cereals, edible fats and other agricultural products were dispatched to developing countries – undoubtedly improving nutritional standards, but at the same time making life harder for farmers in developing countries (Radetzki, 1970).

Altruism was certainly not the only motivation for the arrangements; security of supply was also important. And in the case of the Coffee Agreement, the virtually explicit reason for paying the Latin American-producing countries more than the market price was to prevent the spread of noncapitalist political systems on the continent, an important issue at the time (Commodity Yearbook, 1964; Rowe, 1965).

The Soviet Union was also actively intervening in international commodity markets. It signed a number of "bilateral agreements," in a few cases involving the entire commodity export of individual developing countries for a number of years to come in exchange for manufactures, often on a barter basis. These agreements were regularly biased in favor of the commodity-exporting nation, and their implicit aim was to gain political influence. Sometimes it did not work so well for the "beneficiaries," as when the Soviet Union resold large quantities of Cuban sugar and Indian cloth in Western Europe, suppressing prices for the exporters' sales outside the "agreement" (Radetzki, 1970).

Despite this courtship of developing countries by capitalist and communist commodity importers, there was a massive wave of nationalizations of foreign-owned resource industries, primarily in the minerals and energy fields, in the 1960s and 1970s. Compensation was meager and sometimes completely absent in these takeovers. The USA and United Kingdom lost most in the process, being the largest foreign direct investors in these sectors. The Soviet Union and Japan did not suffer much from the nationalizations since their ownership positions were insignificant. The resultant state enterprises in minerals and energy brought in yet another tool for public intervention in primary commodities.

The tide of public intervention and control started to subside in the 1980s. A shift in beliefs played a crucial but by no means exclusive role in this turnaround. The confidence in the ability of markets to solve problems experienced a strong surge in consequence of the ideological revolution launched by Margaret Thatcher and Ronald Reagan. "Political failure" replaced "market failure" as the main problem to handle, according to the emerging credo.

Far-reaching consequences have followed from this ideological shift. The crumbling of the communist system in the Soviet Union and Eastern Europe is perhaps the most important result. The commodities sector has seen a wholesale privatization of state-owned positions in minerals in all parts of the world, but a contributing circumstance in this development was the disappointing performance of state entrepreneurship. In contrast, state ownership continues unabated in the oil industries of the developing countries, perhaps because of laxer performance requirements given the persistence of high oil prices and oil profits (Chapter 10).

The institution of international commodity agreements in which governments meddle, for whatever objective, has completely lost its appeal. Price stabilization is instead attempted with the help of hedging on commodity exchanges whose futures-market services have been greatly extended in time and across commodities since the 1970s. Publicly controlled strategic stocks in advanced countries in the twenty-first century are, by and large, limited to petroleum; and, at less than 5% of global annual consumption (IEA, monthly), they are trifles compared to the strategic stock ambitions of earlier decades. The use of government price controls has not been considered despite more than fourfold price increases for materials such as copper and oil between 2002 and 2008. The market is seen as an adequate instrument for establishing the value of most commodities and for assuring the satisfaction of the most urgent requirements. No queues have been seen at the petrol stations or at the strategic metal warehouses in the rich world up to now.

The governments' abdication from involvement in primary commodity markets has been quite impressive, though it is far from complete. The most important exception relates to the rich world's agricultural policies, which continue to seriously distort the markets for a number of food products (see Chapter 3). The establishment of the Common Agricultural Policy in 1962 between the EU authorities and Europe's farmers is an illustrative example. In 2018, the EU's farmer support amounted to over €58 billion, a substantial share of the total EU budget of about €160 billion (European Commission, 2019a). Japan is another rich country with a history of highly distorted agricultural policies. However, since 2013 Japan has joined the negotiations for the Trans-Pacific Partnership, putting pressure on trade liberalization, and in February 2019 the Economic Partnership Agreement between the EU and Japan came into force (European Commission, 2019b) with prospects of liberalizing commodity trade flows.

OPEC represents the other important remnant of public involvement in international commodity markets. Governments of the cartel's member countries have remained the completely dominant owners of the oil industry (the United Arab Emirates is an exception). The governments, not their companies, in most cases shape policy in terms of investments, output and prices, as well as with regard to exploration and the volume and direction of investments. The governments appoint the management, often on political merit, and they also control the financial resources available to their oil industry (for details see Chapter 4). Events in Bolivia, Russia and Venezuela in the first decade of the twenty-first century suggest that the temptation to nationalize oil and gas remains, especially when prices and profits are high.

Another, more recent reversal to commodity trade liberalization is the advance of China as a dominant player in world commodity markets. Even though China became a member of the World Trade Organization (WTO) in 2001, and since then has opened up many of its markets, the transparency is far from complete and a number of trade restrictions are still in force. In recent years, this has led to far-reaching protectionist reactions from other countries, mainly the USA. This development, which has profound effects on many primary commodity markets, will be discussed in more detail in Chapters 3 and 4.

Despite these important exceptions, it is reasonable to claim that the era of state interventionism in commodities is well past its peak and that market forces have been allowed to play a greatly increased role in the international commodity markets since the later 1980s. But one should not be too sure. The recently ascending popularity of state control in some places, as well as the recent surge of protectionist behavior, particularly in the case of the USA, may be harbingers of a new wave of nationalistic public intervention in the resource industries, after a 40-year withdrawal. However that may be, it is instructive to bear in mind the 50-year flood of state involvement between 1930 and 1980, followed by an ebb in the first decades of the twenty-first century, as the subject matter of the following chapters unfolds.

1.4 Transformation of the Resource Landscape – the Role of Emerging Asia

Since the dawn of the twenty-first century the demand for natural resources has been surging. The main driver for this is the development of large, emerging economies in Asia, especially China and India.[2] Incomes in these countries are rising at a pace that has never been seen before. China and India, whose population together in 2019 was about 2.8 billion, have been doubling their real per capita income levels every 12 and 16 years, respectively. This can be compared to the United Kingdom, which doubled its real per capita income level once during the 150-year period of the Industrial Revolution (Maddison, 2007). Considering this exceptional rise in income levels for such large populations, the effect on the world economy from the emerging economies in Asia can therefore be seen as transforming the entire resource landscape.

Demand for primary commodities (energy, minerals and agricultural products) by emerging economies increases especially fast during the period when they are in the resource-intensive phase of their economic development, as discussed in relation to Figure 1.2. The impact on demand for primary commodities from China and India is particularly strong, given their exceptional population size and pace of growth. It is

[2] Emerging Asia, as defined by the IMF, includes China, India and the ASEAN-5 (Association of Southeast Asian Nations, i.e., Indonesia, Thailand, Malaysia, Philippines and Vietnam). Other emerging economies are Brazil, Turkey, Russia and South Africa. The IMF classification for "Emerging and Developing Economies" comprises 152 countries, with 29 countries for "Emerging and Developing Asia" (IMF, biannual).

expected that in the 2020s and 2030s large proportions of the population in these economies will enter the middle class. The demand for cars, refrigerators, heating and cooling systems and other residential appliances is expected to intensify. Large amounts of resources are also required for infrastructure, as their urban populations expand. More energy is needed to accomplish growth in the household, commercial and industrial sectors. Demand for agricultural products (both food and nonfood) is also expected to increase to satisfy the higher nutritional standards of the growing middle class.

Kharas (2010) estimated that the size of the global middle class, defined as people in households with daily per capita incomes (PPP adjusted) between US$10 and US$100, would increase from 1.8 billion people in 2009 to 3.2 billion in 2020. More recent findings show that in fact the increase in the global middle class has been even faster than expected. Kharas and Hamel (2018) found that the world reached a global tipping point in September 2018, since more than half of the world's population (about 3.8 billion) had become middle class or richer. Almost all of this growth stems from China and India. It is therefore fair to assume that emerging Asia will be the leading consumer of primary commodities for many years to come. The geographical shift in primary consumption patterns in the world is further elaborated in Chapter 2.

The commodities boom early in the twenty-first century provides further evidence of the transformation of primary commodity markets as a consequence of the fast economic growth in the emerging Asian giants. World economic growth during the twentieth century took place most of the time in parallel with decreasing real resource prices. Even though demand for primary commodities increased substantially, it was easily met by expanded supply. The rise in supply was made possible by productivity increases due to technological developments that also led to lower production costs. In the twenty-first century, much like what temporarily occurred in shipping, the unprecedented rate of increase in demand for primary commodities has not been matched by a parallel increase in supply, so prices have been pushed up. The failure of supply to rise in line with demand was caused by the suddenness and strength of the demand growth, exacerbated by more challenging access to new supply sources augmenting the cost of extraction (Dobbs et al., 2013). In the middle of the 2010s the commodity boom came to an end, but the strong demand for commodities from

China continued to dominate the global markets (Desjardins, 2018). Historically, the role of emerging economies for primary commodity markets has always been important. What was exceptional early in the twenty-first century has been the fact that the emerging economies represented more than a third of the world population, while their growth rates were unprecedented. The result was an explosion in commodity demand and commodity prices. Chapter 5 provides a detailed account of the relationships sketched in this paragraph.

1.5 Conclusion

The main findings of this historical overview of some aspects of commodity markets are stated below:

1. Economic development almost invariably reduces the role played by commodities in the macroeconomy. Poor, undeveloped economies produce raw materials and consume them after only limited processing. As economies advance the scope for further and more sophisticated processing increases, as does the scope for the expansion of activities with limited raw material input needs, notably the service sector. But while, with few exceptions, the primary share of GDP shrinks as economies develop, it is essential to keep in mind that commodities are indispensable, and that no society, however economically advanced, can survive without their assured supply.

2. Historically the production and consumption of commodities was basically a national affair. Excepting expensive luxury goods, such as coffee and precious metals, commodities were simply too expensive to transport across borders and oceans. The secular fall in transport costs has greatly increased international trade in commodities, making it possible to move production to locations that offer the lowest-cost opportunities. In the twenty-first century, imports of commodities throughout the world account for a very sizable share of consumption. This holds even for cheap bulk products such as iron ore and natural gas.

3. The 50-year period between 1930 and 1980 was one characterized by deep nationalist state intervention in the resource sector. This period was preceded and followed by periods of highly liberal government attitudes, with substantial scope for market forces in commodity production and trade. Recent efforts in some countries

to increase the government's grip over natural resources and the protectionist wave in some dominant countries may be harbingers of a new wave of state involvement, but currently one cannot be sure. The efforts could alternatively be a response to the 2000s commodity boom, and could dissipate as commodity prices fall when the boom comes to an end.

4. Since the dawn of the twenty-first century, income levels in emerging Asia, especially China and India, have increased at an unprecedented pace. The demand for primary commodities generated by emerging Asia is currently dominating world demand, and is expected to continue to grow as an increasing proportion of these countries' populations enters the middle class. Despite the recent slowdown in primary commodity prices, which indicates that the resource boom has come to an end, the demand for primary commodities will remain elevated for many years to come in order to satisfy the needs of the growing middle class in emerging Asia.

2 | The Geography of Commodity Production and Trade

This chapter comprises four sections. Section 2.1 defines primary commodities and classifies them into a variety of distinct groups. These distinctions are important for some of the analyses performed in later chapters. Section 2.2 attempts to determine the significance of commodities in the international economy, both at the aggregate and the individual product level. Section 2.3 paints a broad picture of the current geography of traded commodity production and consumption. The import dependence of the major industrial regions on overseas commodity supply is explored and quantified, and the most important commodity exporting countries are identified in the process. Finally, Section 2.4 assumes an historical perspective and considers briefly the forces that have led to the increasing dependence of Western Europe, the USA and Japan and, more recently, China and India on commodity imports over the past 100 years.

2.1 Commodity Groups and Their Characteristics

The subject matter of this book is the world of raw materials, alternatively referred to as primary commodities, or, for short, commodities. A first important task is therefore to distinguish commodities from other goods. This distinction may sound straightforward and clear, but however one proceeds, substantial ambiguities remain. Some of these were briefly touched upon in Chapter 1.

The national accounts statistics of individual countries divide the GDP in accordance with the International Standard Industrial Classification (ISIC) of All Economic Activities, as designed by the United Nations Statistical Office. The GDP is obtained by aggregating the value added from the primary sector, comprising agriculture (including hunting, forestry and fishing), mining (including extraction of fossil fuels) and utilities; the secondary sector, basically manufacturing; and the tertiary sector, consisting of public and private service activities. The outputs from the primary sector can be unambiguously classed as commodities, but this definition is far narrower than the everyday concept of primary commodities. Also, the definition is ill suited for analyses of commodities in international trade, a lead theme in the present book. The point at issue is that the line between the primary and secondary sectors drawn by the ISIC is often quite early in the production process, before the product has reached its main marketable stage. For instance, meat, paper pulp and refined copper are important primary commodities in international trade, but a significant proportion of their value has been added by the manufacturing sector through the activities of slaughterhouses, pulp mills and copper smelters and refineries. For this reason, national accounts statistics are of limited use in determining the value – or volume – of commodity production and trade, as commonly understood.

The Standard International Trade Classification (SITC, also designed by the United Nations), which is employed to distinguish between different categories of goods in international trade, provides an alternative and, for our purposes, somewhat more appropriate tool for defining commodities, so we will employ the SITC in the rest of the book. Thus, the definition of commodities includes the SITC section 0, live animals and all unprocessed and processed food products; section 1, beverages and tobacco; section 2, inedible crude materials except fuels (edible oil raw materials, division 22, are also included); section 3, mineral fuels, lubricants and related materials; section 4, animal and vegetable oils and fats; division 67, iron and steel; and division 68, non-ferrous metals. This definition is statistically traceable and hence convenient. It is also shared by bodies such as the United Nations Conference on Trade and Development (UNCTAD) and the WTO. Note that this definition excludes much of the supply from the utilities sector, regarded as "primary" in ISIC, as specified in the previous paragraph. At the same time, it should be noted that the SITC definition is somewhat broader than the everyday concept of primary commodities, since it includes products such as cheese, spaghetti and chewing gum, and sheets, foils, angles and pipes made of metal.

By itself, the SITC is not particularly useful for subdividing commodities into analytical groups. Nevertheless, a major and commonly used categorization at least starts out from the SITC sections and divisions. It classes commodities into:

(a) food in a broad sense (SITC 0+1+22+4);
(b) agricultural raw materials (SITC 2–22–27–28);
(c) minerals and metals (SITC 27+28+67+68);
(d) mineral fuels (SITC 3).

Several broad characteristics based on this categorization can be identified. The distinction between (a) food, on the one hand, and (b), (c) and (d), raw materials used by industry, on the other, is of great practical significance when it comes to demand. A majority of the food items, having a more indispensable character, are likely to experience lesser variations in demand over the business cycle than the other commodity groups. Excepting foods of a luxury character such as coffee, chocolate or beef, one can also expect that food has a lesser income elasticity of demand, and hence a lower trend in demand growth in an expanding economy where consumers tend to spend decreasing shares of their income on basic necessities (Engels' Law).

The distinction between (a) and (b), agricultural products, on the one hand, and (c) and (d), mineral products, on the other, is relevant in that the supply of the former is dependent on the vagaries of the weather while that of the latter is not. The dependence on weather has had particular relevance for products such as rubber or cocoa whose output was geographically heavily concentrated, but this concentration has become less accentuated in recent decades. In general terms, one can say that the price instability of agricultural commodities is more often caused by supply-side disturbances, while that of minerals – strikes and cartels notwithstanding – is more related to variations on the demand side.

Though each of the four groups contains many different materials, the major substitutes for individual products are likely to be found within the same group. This is probably most evident in (d), the fuels group. An important implication is that prices within each group will have a tendency to move in tandem. For instance, if the price of petroleum rises, the prices of coal and natural gas will tend to rise in sympathy, but there is little presumption that such changes will have a direct influence on the price of, say, copper or wheat.

Other commodity groupings can be constructed to bring out neater but important distinctions. For instance, as discussed in Chapter 1, the unit price provides a rough measure of the transportability of commodities. Products such as cotton, coffee and tin (average prices per ton in 2016–2018, US$1830, US$3290 and US$19380, respectively) have long been globally traded, and even very long hauls involve costs that nowadays constitute only minute proportions of the price. In contrast, products such as phosphate rock, iron ore and steam coal (average prices per ton in 2016–2018, US$96, US$67 and US$87, respectively) have until recently been traded in markets that retained some regional character, on account of the high proportion of the transport cost in the total delivered price.

Commodities can also be classed into those that are easily stored and those that are not. Refrigeration and preservation have rendered all commodities storable to some extent. The hard-to-store commodities are predominantly found in the perishable agricultural groups, but there are many agricultural materials (jute, rice) that are easily stored for long periods of time. Storability affects a commodity market in at least two ways. First, it commonly provides for an increase in the elasticity of supply. Drawdown of stocks makes it possible to vary supply beyond the feasible variations of production. And second, it increases the scope for speculative activity (Chapter 7).

There are great variations among raw materials in terms of the time it takes to add to production capacity. The production of some commodities, for example bananas, sugar and wheat, can be expanded between two adjacent seasons simply by extending the area on which the crop is grown. For other commodities, such as coffee, palm oil and most minerals, several years are commonly required between the decision to increase capacity and the start-up of production from that capacity. This was witnessed on many minerals markets, where supply struggled to keep up with the sharp increases in demand for several years preceding the deep financial crisis of 2008. For example, demand for iron ore took off in about 2003 (mainly due to the growth rate in China), and it was not until 2014 that supply of this product increased substantially. Thus, even though prices of iron ore were elevated throughout this time period, and exploration and expansions of existing mines witnessed new highs, it still took many years for the supply of iron ore to catch up with the growth in demand. Typically, from exploration to actual production in a mine the time lag is about 5–10 years, and sometimes even longer. These issues are further elaborated in Chapter 5.

Even though the long-run price elasticity of supply for wheat and copper, for example, may be of the same magnitude, the short-run price elasticity of supply for copper will be much lower. This distinction makes a great difference for established producers bent on monopolistic coordination of their market. Supply cuts will seldom be worthwhile to producers of the first group of commodities, because of the speed with which additional production can be established. The second group is much more amenable to monopolistic coordination, given that the producer benefits will ordinarily be far more durable (Chapter 10).

For some materials, primary supply is supplemented by supply from secondary sources. This is important for precious metals, but also for base metals such as iron/steel, copper and lead, and for some agricultural raw materials, for example rubber and wool. The secondary supply has determinants and a cost structure that typically differ from those that apply to primary supply. The control of secondary materials is usually out of reach of primary producers. The availability of secondary supply tends to increase the overall supply elasticity for a commodity. Where such supply is important it reduces the scope for monopolistic coordination by primary producers.

The level of the price elasticity of demand constitutes yet another important distinguishing feature between commodities. The ones with many close substitutes will have high price elasticities of demand. If the price increases, demand is redirected in favor of the substitutes. This is true, for instance, of bananas and lamb, the demand for which is easily shifted toward other fruits and meats. Commodities with important uses and without convenient substitutes will usually have very low price elasticities of demand. When the use of a commodity is in some way indispensable, demand will not be much affected by a change in price. Platinum, chromium and rare earth metals are prime examples of indispensable materials with few substitutes in many uses and with very low price elasticities of demand. For a somewhat different reason, coffee too has a low price elasticity of demand. Though one can lead a comfortable life without it, a large part of humanity has become addicted to this beverage, and as a result the demand for coffee is not very sensitive to price. A low price elasticity of demand, too, is important in singling out commodities suitable for monopolistic intervention by producers.

One should note that the price elasticity of demand for any commodity is usually much higher in the long than in the short run. With time, users frequently find alternatives to a raw material whose price has become excessive. A distinction is often made between exhaustible and renewable materials, but in our view an exaggerated importance has been attributed to this distinction. For example, contrary to the claims of exhaustible resource theory, there is little empirical evidence of a difference in the determination of prices between the two commodity groups (Chapter 6).

2.2 The Importance of Commodities in the International Economy

In Chapter 1 we established an overall trend of declining commodity importance, in the macroeconomy, as nations develop. Table 2.1 confirms this tendency looking at global trade patterns over an extended period during which the global economy experienced considerable modernization. In 1965, commodities accounted for almost 50% of global goods trade, but by 2005 this share had been reduced to less than 30%. We note that the sharp reduction in the share of commodities experienced between 1965 and the beginning of the twenty-first century largely ceased after 2005. This can mainly be attributed to the commodity boom of 2005–2014 (Chapters 5 and 6).

Table 2.1 additionally reveals declining shares accounted for by food, agricultural raw materials and minerals and metals in total

Table 2.1 *Evolution of global exports by commodity group since 1965*

	billion US$		% of total goods exports			
	Total exports, all goods	Total commodities	Food	Agricultural raw materials	Minerals and metals	Fuels
1965	186	48.5	18.3	8.1	12.4	9.7
1986	1 924	39.9	10.5	3.4	7.3	18.7
2005	10 508	28.3	6.5	1.5	6.4	13.9
2018	19 451	27.8	7.9	1.4	6.2	12.4

Source: WTO (annual), www.wto.org/statistics.

goods trade over time. This observation does not imply any absolute declines, not even in constant money terms. Instead, it reflects an increasing dominance of manufactures in total goods trade. The fuels group represents an exception from this. By the mid-1980s, fuels had doubled their share of overall visible trade as oil prices, in real terms, hovered around their peak, after the oil price increases of the 1970s. The share encompassing fuels fell in the subsequent 20-year period, but in the early 2010s there was a temporary increase back to the peak level of the mid-1980s. Since then the share of fuels has decreased once again, mainly as a result of falling prices caused by an impressive expansion of shale oil and shale gas production in the USA. Nevertheless, fuels still dominate the commodity groups, and their importance provides justification for the special treatment in this book (Chapter 4).

Table 2.2 offers a more detailed insight into the performance of individual commodities over roughly the same period as that covered by Table 2.1. The 22 entries have been selected to comprise the most important commodities in the international economy, and they have been ranked according to their export values in 2016–2018. In aggregate, the 22 account for almost 57% of the total export value for commodities in the three years. We note that from the mid-1980s to the late 2010s the global export value for these commodities increased almost six times (nominal dollars). We also note that the increase in export values in the last 12 years is about as large as the rise in the preceding 20-year period, illustrating the extraordinary strength of the latest commodity boom.

Petroleum emerges at the top of the table for the four periods shown. Ever since the price increases of the 1970s, this material alone (crude and petroleum products) has accounted for about 50% of the aggregate value of the 22 items. In the early 1960s, in contrast, petroleum accounted for only one quarter of that total.

The rank of the other individual commodities differs for the four periods, depending either on shifting price levels or volume growth, or both in combination. The rank of wool has declined from 5 in the 1960s to 21 in the late 2010s, primarily because of technological developments in the textile industry, while coal and, even more, natural gas owe their recent higher ranking significantly to the opening up of international trade on a massive scale in these commodities. We also

Table 2.2 *Global export value for individual primary commodities (billion US$)*

	1963–1965	1983–1985	2003–2005	2016–2018	SITC Rev. 3
Petroleum	9.1	212.7	699.7	1 114.5	33
Iron and steel	8.6	59.9	249.3	396.5	67
Natural gas	0.2	27.2	121.3	217.6	343
Precious stones	1.0	11.8	73.9	105.3	667
Copper	1.2	5.7	34.9	61.0	2831 +6821
Hard coal	1.1	13.1	32.8	51.2	321
Iron ore	1.3	5.1	18.7	43.3	281
Wheat	2.9	15.2	17.5	42.0	041
Aluminum	0.8	7.2	29.6	39.1	2851 +6841
Coffee	1.8	9.3	9.4	39.0	0711
Timber	2.3	13.3	43.3	37.6	24
Rice	0.8	3.3	8.2	27.3	042
Maize	1.1	9.8	11.3	25.2	044
Beef	0.9	6.7	18.9	23.2	011
Sugar	0.9	4.4	11.1	19.6	0611 +0612
Cocoa	0.6	3.7	8.1	19.5	072
Zink	0.4	2.8	7.7	16.6	2875 +6861
Cotton	1.9	4.9	8.6	16.2	2631
Natural rubber	1.5	4.0	8.1	13.3	231
Tobacco	0.8	3.8	6.5	10.3	121
Wool	2.1	4.9	4.7	6.6	268
Tin	0.7	2.2	2.2	6.1	2876 +6871

Source: UNCTAD stat on the internet http://unctadstat.unctad.org/wds/ ReportFolders/reportFolders.aspx; UN COMTRADE on the internet http://comtrade.un.org/data/.

note the rising rank of iron ore and copper and the declining rank of timber and cotton.

An additional perspective on the significance of commodity trade is to compare the export values given in Table 2.2 with those for some manufactured products, even though it must be underlined that the latter are far more heterogeneous than the listed raw materials, and that this heterogeneity may add to the values they represent. In 2016–2018, the global average annual export value of passenger motor vehicles was US$738 billion, aircraft US$208 billion, footwear US$129 billion, ships and boats US$124 billion, television receivers US$84 billion, and watches and clocks US$52 billion.

The importance of primary commodity trade can alternatively be measured by weight, and when that is done a somewhat different ranking emerges (Table 2.3). Four commodities had export volumes of 500 million tons or more in 2018. These were petroleum (2263 million tons), iron ore (1640 million tons), hard coal (859 million tons) and natural gas (849 million tons). Other commodities with a large volume of exports were steel, timber and wheat. The commodities listed in the table comprise a large share of the volume of commodities in international trade. Hence, developments in these commodity markets constitute heavy determinants for the business conditions for bulk transport by sea. Many high-priced products with large export values, coffee and copper metal for example, represent very small volumes in international trade.

Table 2.3 additionally provides the volume of global production for selected commodities, and this permits an assessment of the total output that enters international trade. In some cases, a major proportion of global output is traded. This is especially so for tropical products on which the temperate rich world is dependent, for example rubber or coffee. The same applies to tin (produced in China and Indonesia) and niobium (Brazil), two minerals whose deposits are heavily concentrated in the tropics. Petroleum (the Middle East, the USA and Russia) and platinum (South Africa) are similar in this respect, in that a few countries with an exceptional resource wealth supply the rest of the world with most of its imported needs. Rare earth metals provide another example of commodities where global production is highly concentrated, considering that over 90% of all rare earth metals are produced in China (Chapter 9). This contrasts with rice and timber, two important raw materials in terms of both volume and value, where most

Table 2.3 *World production and exports of selected primary commodities, 2018*

	Production (thousand tons)	Exports (thousand tons)	Exports (% of production)
Petroleum	4 474 300	2 263 100	51
Iron ore[1]	2 493 800	1 639 520	66
Hard coal	3 916 800	858 800	22
Natural gas[2]	3 325 800	849 060	26
Steel	1 686 700	457 100	27
Timber	3 168 680	216 080	7
Wheat	763 200	181 200	24
Maize	1 034 200	147 100	14
Sugar	178 900	56 400	32
Rice	495 027	47 537	10
Phosphate rock[3]	269 000	27 379	10
Aluminum	62 536	14 817	24
Copper	20 768	13 808	66
Natural rubber	13 869	12 202	88
Cotton	25 881	9 166	34
Coffee	9 327	7 247	78
Cocoa	4 649	3 334	72
Tin	374	152	41

[1] Data for 2017.
[2] Converted from cubic meters to tons of oil equivalents by multiplication with the factor 0.90.
[3] Converted from cubic meters to tons by multiplication with the factor 0.74.
Source: BP (annual); World Steel Association (annual); UN Comtrade, http://comtrade .un.org/data; FAOSTAT, http://faostat.fao.org; USGS (annual); World Bureau of Metal Statistics (annual); USDA Foreign Agricultural Service, www.fas.usda .gov/; UNCTAD, http://unctadstat.unctad.org/wds/ReportFolders/reportFolders .aspx; World Bank (2019a).

output is domestically consumed. Taste appears to be the main explanation to the consumption patterns for rice, while timber deposits are geographically widespread, and since this material represents a low value per ton, supplies from faraway sources tend to lose competitiveness to domestic sources. Note that the traded shares probably exaggerate the importance of trade, since large quantities of the commodities listed are reexported, either in unchanged form, or after some limited degree of processing. This is obviously true for tin.

2.3 The Provenance and Destination of Traded Commodity Supply

Table 2.4 paints a broad picture of the exports and imports of broad commodity groups by major regions and countries in the 2015–2017 period.[1] Several noteworthy observations emerge from the matrix. The numbers confirm the traditional relationship in which the rich world is a net importer of commodities, even though this relationship is not as clear as it was in the past. EU28+Norway and US+Canada each recorded deficits in their commodity trade. Their fuels deficits dominated the total by far. However, the USA, Canada and Europe are net exporters of food. This is mainly a result of the protectionist policies in these markets (Chapter 3). The USA and Canada, furthermore, also record export surpluses in agricultural raw materials. A noteworthy exception of the traditional relationship of the rich world as a net importer is the Organisation for Economic Co-operation and Development (OECD) Asia Pacific region (Australia and New Zealand), where surpluses for all major commodity groups are recorded. Metals and minerals dominate this surplus, due to Australia's sizable exports of coal and iron ore.

On account of the spectacular growth in China since about 1990, the country has emerged as the world's leading net importer of commodities. While China is a net importer of all commodity groups, fuels, metals and minerals dominate total commodity imports as these are essential inputs to the expanding infrastructure in the country. The Other Asia region (excluding China) is also a net importer of commodities, even though the region is still a net exporter in food and agricultural raw materials.

Latin America (including Mexico) and Africa (south of Sahara) constitute counterpoints to the rich world in that the two regions

---

[1] Data for 2018 were unfortunately not complete when Table 2.4 and Table 2.5 were updated.

Table 2.4 Commodity and total goods trade by region, annual average 2015–2017 (billion US$)

	EU28 +Norway	USA +Canada	OECD Asia Pacific	China	Other Asia	CIS	ME +North Africa	Africa (south of the Sahara)	Latin America	Global total
Food										
Exports	544.0	182.8	51.1	66.1	205.4	43.4	59.7	42.0	209.1	1403.6
Imports	530.2	174.2	18.1	105.3	274.5	41.7	132.7	45.5	81.0	1403.2
Net exports	13.8	8.6	32.9	−39.1	−69.1	1.6	−73.0	−3.5	128.1	0.4
Agricultural raw materials										
Exports	77.6	47.1	10.3	9.4	49.7	11.2	3.8	9.9	20.9	239.8
Imports	79.0	26.0	1.8	59.9	56.1	3.8	13.5	3.4	10.1	253.5
Net exports	−1.4	21.1	8.5	−50.5	−6.4	7.4	−9.7	6.5	10.8	−13.6
Metals and minerals										
Exports	294.9	85.8	66.0	84.1	182.7	62.6	60.6	45.9	109.1	991.7
Imports	324.6	104.3	7.0	187.6	254.0	19.9	87.1	17.5	45.3	1047.3
Net	−29.7	−18.5	59.0	−103.4	−71.3	42.7	−26.5	28.4	63.8	−55.6

Table 2.4 (*cont.*)

	EU28 +Norway	USA +Canada	OECD Asia Pacific	China	Other Asia	CIS	ME +North Africa	Africa (south of the Sahara)	Latin America	Global total
Net exports										
Fuels										
Exports	324.8	186.9	55.7	30.1	308.6	243.3	512.6	102.3	104.4	1868.7
Imports	538.9	217.3	24.5	208.2	557.7	25.9	68.7	43.0	101.8	1786.1
Net exports	−214.1	−30.4	31.3	−178.2	−249.1	217.4	443.8	59.3	2.6	82.6
All commodities										
Exports	1241.3	502.7	183.1	189.7	746.4	360.4	636.7	200.0	443.5	4503.8
Imports	1472.7	521.9	51.4	561.0	1 142.3	91.3	302.1	109.3	238.1	4490.1
Net exports	−231.5	−19.2	131.7	−371.2	−395.9	269.1	334.6	90.7	205.4	13.8
All goods	5 628.7	1 905.5	238.0	2 211.5	3 702.7	478.0	1 104.2	279.8	934.1	16 482.4

Source: UNCTAD, https://unctadstat.unctad.org/wds/ReportFolders/reportFolders.aspx.

record surpluses in all but one of the categories shown. Africa has, surprisingly, emerged as a net importer of food recently, and its recorded surpluses in agricultural raw materials are small. Latin America's dominance as a net exporter of food in the world is startling. Latin America is furthermore the leading net exporter of metals and minerals.

The most noteworthy, though well-known, characteristics in the commodity trade of Middle East+North Africa and the former Soviet Union, represented by the Common Independent States (CIS), are their very sizable surpluses in the fuels trade, the former's almost exclusively the result of oil exports, while the CIS exports of oil are supplemented by sizable sales of coal and natural gas. The Middle East is a net importer of food and agricultural raw materials as well as minerals and metals, while the CIS contributes significantly to the world's need for minerals and metals.

A further point of interest regarding overall goods exports is that China, Other Asia and Europe are not only the largest importers of primary commodities; they also dominate overall goods exports. Thus, China has recently emerged as the leading importer of primary commodities, and has successfully balanced its trade account by becoming a dominant exporter of manufactures.

In contrast to the aggregate picture in terms of countries and products presented in Table 2.4, the matrix contained in Table 2.5 demonstrates the importance of a group of individual selected countries as suppliers to the world market of a set of important individual commodities. The commodities are, by and large, the same as those displayed in the earlier tables of this chapter. The countries have been chosen to include significant contributors to the world supply of at least one of the listed commodities, and have been subdivided into Latin American, Asian, African and "Western Offshoots" groups, with France and Russia added to complete the picture. The warning issued in relation to Table 2.3 that reexports may exaggerate a country's true importance as a supplier to the world market applies to Table 2.5 in equal measure. Note that the table is not exhaustive, its purpose being to provide a broad overview of the main countries and commodities.

To limit the size of Table 2.5, and given the dominance of oil in world commodity markets, the major oil-exporting countries and their importance in global export supply are displayed in Table 2.6.

Table 2.5 *Share of world exports for selected countries and commodities in 2015–2017 (%)*

	Cocoa	Coffee	Copper	Cotton	Hard coal	Iron ore	Natural gas	Natural rubber	Rice	Sugar	Tin	Tobacco	Wheat	Wool
Argentina			0.5	0.5					0.9	0.6		2.7	4.6	3.2
Bolivia							1.5				6.9			0.1
Brazil	1.5	15.1	2.5	11.8		20.3		0.1	1.3	39.1	3.9	18.6	0.5	0.5
Chile		0.1	28.0		0.1	1.1								0.4
Colombia	0.3	7.4			7.1					1.3		0.3		
Mexico	0.2	1.5	2.3	0.5				0.1	0.1	3.0		0.2	0.7	
Peru	1.3	1.9	10.2			0.5	0.3			0.3	8.2			0.6
China	0.4	4.9	1.7	0.3	0.6	0.2	0.6	0.2	2.1	0.3	0.3	5.3		11.8
India	0.3	2.3	1.9	15.0	0.1	1.2		0.3	30.3	4.8	1.6	5.8	0.2	0.7
Indonesia	6.2	4.2	4.1		26.4		4.7	36.8			29.0	1.3		
Malaysia	6.0	1.2	0.6	0.3		1	5.3	8.9	0.1	0.4	12.6	0.4		
Thailand	0.2	0.3						25.5	13.6	6.8	1.8	0.3		0.6

Vietnam							8.5	12.2	0.1	0.5	0.2		
Ghana	7.3	0.4					0.4						
Ivory Coast	25.1		1.9				5.7						
Qatar													
South Africa		0.1	0.5	0.1	5.5	15.5		0.1	0.8		0.1		6
Australia	0.3	0.2	5.7	10.9	54.7	8.6		1	0.3	2.4	0.8	11.0	38.5
Canada		1.5	4.0	2.5	4.0	4.2			0.1	0.3		13.9	
New Zealand									0.1				7.6
USA	1.9	3.0	3.3	40.9	0.9	3.3	0.9	8.9	0.4	1.6	10.3	15.0	0.6
France	4.1	2.7	0.2			0.8	0.7	0.3	4.7	0.2	1.8	9.4	0.3
Russia	0.4	0.4	3.0	13.8	1.4	15.1		0.4	0.1	0.2	0.3	12.2	0.4
Norway		0.3	0.3		0.2	13.0							0.1
Total	55.1	55.7	68.8	82.2	91	72.9	88.1	71.3	63.2	69.5	48.4	67.6	71.4

Source: UN Comtrade, http://comtrade.un.org/data.

Table 2.6 *Share of world exports of oil in 2018 by country (%)*

Russia	13.1
Saudi Arabia	12.4
USA	10.1
Other Middle East[1]	7.5
West Africa[2]	6.7
Canada	6.6
Iraq	6.1
United Arab Emirates	5.9
Kuwait	3.7
Total	72.1

[1] Includes Iran. 2. Includes Nigeria.
Source: BP (annual), sum of crude oil and products.

When studying individual countries, and focusing on shares of global exports above a 10% level, we note in the Latin American group Brazil's significance in coffee, cotton, iron ore, sugar and tobacco and Chile as a dominant exporter of copper.

A look at the Asian country group shows that China accounts for high shares of global exports of wool, and India is an important supplier of cotton and rice. Indonesia records high shares in natural rubber and tin, but it is also significant in the coal market, while Malaysia is sizable in tin. Thailand is a large exporter of natural rubber, and also a significant supplier of rice.

Australia records very high shares in the international markets for coal, iron ore and wool, exceeding 30% for all three. It accounts for more than half of global exports of iron ore, 54.7%, which is a truly exceptional proportion of world supply for a single nation. The country is also a sizable supplier in the international wheat and cotton markets. Canada is a significant exporter of wheat, while its closest neighbor, the USA, is the world's largest exporter of both wheat and cotton. The USA is furthermore an important exporter of coal, and second only to Brazil in the tobacco market.

Russia's exports of gas to Europe correspond to about 15% of world trade, and it is also a sizable contributor to the world's coal supplies.

France is a significant exporter of wheat (and a bit less so for sugar and cocoa), which is primarily due to the agricultural support policies of the European Union. Norway has a significant share of the natural gas exports.

The African and Middle Eastern country group reveals that the Ivory Coast is dominant in the cocoa market, and that Ghana is also a significant exporter of this product. We further note relatively high shares of global exports in hard coal, iron ore and wool for South Africa, even though the shares are not above the 10% threshold. Qatar is the dominant exporter of natural gas.

Those with a special interest can alternatively use the matrix table to clarify the export concentration in individual commodity markets, but we will not pursue this somewhat tedious task here (however, see Chapter 10 for a further discussion of the significance of export concentration).

Table 2.6 exhibits a relatively low concentration by exporting country in the petroleum market, when compared with the products exhibited in Table 2.5. Almost all of the 14 products listed in Table 2.5 had a lead exporter accounting for 20% or more of the global total. In petroleum, in contrast, the largest exporters, Russia and Saudi Arabia, supplied no more than 13%. A similar situation appears to prevail in the natural gas market. A further note on Table 2.6 is that in 2020 the USA is one of the top exporting countries. More on this in Chapter 4.

2.4 The Historical Accentuation of the Rich World's Dependence on Commodity Imports and the Emergence of China as a Globally Dominant Importer of Commodities

The increasing dependence of the rich world on faraway supplies of raw materials is a phenomenon that has emerged, in the main, during the twentieth century. Two factors explain the strength and timing of this development. The first is the very impressive decline in bulk transport costs, discussed in the preceding chapter. The second is the speedy pace of industrialization in the rich world, and in particular the impressive expansion of its infrastructure and heavy industries in the course of the century. These activities have absorbed huge quantities of raw materials, and foreign sources regularly offered supplies at lower costs than those of domestic producers. Our focus of attention in the development of the rich world is on Western Europe (here represented by France, Germany, Italy, Spain and the United Kingdom), the USA and Japan, and we disregard the commodity import needs of rich but thinly populated Australia and Canada, which continue to generate very sizable net commodity exports.

Several distinguishing features relating to different products and importing regions need to be brought out for a better understanding of the process. The first observation is that the consumption of tropical agricultural products, notably coffee, cocoa and tea, but also natural rubber, has always depended virtually entirely on imports. With increasing prosperity over the twentieth century, the volume of these imports has grown impressively, in line with consumption. In contrast, the prosperous regions have maintained far-reaching measures to protect domestic food production (Chapter 3). Imports of, for example, cereals, sugar, meat and fruit have therefore accounted for only limited shares of consumption.

Differences between the three regions under review in this regard should be noted. There has always been a vast difference in their population density. In 2018, population per km^2 was 349 in Japan, 185 in Western Europe, but only 36 in the USA. Abstracting from differences in climates and soils, we posit that the extent of policy measures to maintain a certain level of self-sufficiency in food must be greater where the population density is high. Agricultural protection has indeed been extreme in Japan and a bit less so in Europe, while in the USA production of most foods has been internationally competitive with little need for protective measures. In fact, the USA has been a sizable agricultural exporter since early in the twentieth century. Agricultural support has nevertheless been practiced, for instance in sugar against the more competitive cane sugar supply from the tropics, or in cotton, the latter making the country a dominant supplier to the international market (Table 2.5).

Population density should also make a difference in the ability to remain self-sufficient in mineral materials. The prospects for satisfying domestic mineral requirements should improve if there are fewer people per km^2 of potentially mineral productive land, assuming away differences in the mineral productivity of different lands. This relationship too is clearly apparent in the imports/consumption trends in the three regions, though in the mineral context the expansion of import needs is also strongly related to the timing of the major industrialization thrust.

Thus, the sparsely populated USA, which industrialized relatively early, still covered its entire needs for metal minerals in the first decade of the twentieth century, but its self-sufficiency had fallen to 70% at the time of the Second World War (Borenstein, 1954). By the middle of the century, the USA had become the world's largest importer of copper, lead and zinc, among other metals (*Resources for Freedom*, 1987). As the century ended, the USA depended on imported supply for 100% of its nickel requirements, 52% of refined copper and 40% of primary aluminum. More densely populated Western Europe, where the intensive phase of industrialization also occurred early, was reasonably self-sufficient in metals as late as the middle of the century. By 2005, however, the import dependence in copper and nickel was virtually complete. Japan industrialized much later than the other two regions. In 1950, its metal usage was only a minuscule fraction of the levels recorded in Western Europe and the USA, and could still be fully satisfied by domestic supply. However, in the course of the country's exceedingly fast industrialization and growth between 1950 and 1975, its needs for metals exploded. Japan's 1990 consumption of aluminum was 127 times the 1950 level, that of copper had multiplied 131 times and nickel 160 times, all historically truly remarkable increases over a unique 40-year period of this nation's development. Since there was little scope for increasing domestic production within the country's geographic confines, the import dependence for these and other metals had become virtually complete by the end of the century.

For the purpose of the following deliberations about the consumption developments and import needs in China (population density 151 per km^2 in 2018, i.e. somewhat below Western Europe's, and far below Japan's), a noteworthy observation is that Japan's metal consumption growth virtually ceased after 1990. Metal demand generally stagnated at about the same time in Western Europe and in the USA too, as practically all economic growth in these mature economies occurred in sectors, such as services and information technology, with insignificant metal needs. Demand stagnation is not limited to metals. The development since the 1990s shows that the stagnation in Western Europe, the USA and Japan continues, as decreasing demand is noted especially for copper but also for nickel and oil. Table 2.7 reports the consumption developments since 1950 in the major consuming regions for a set of industrial commodities.

Table 2.7 *Consumption developments for four important industrial commodities in four regions*

	Thousand tons					Average annual percentage change			
	1950	1970	1990	2005	2018	1951–1970	1971–1990	1991–2005	2006–2018
Primary Aluminum									
USA	823	3 488	4 331	6 114	4 630	7.5	1.2	2.4	-2.1
Eur5[1]	342	2 050	3 493	4 431	4 851	9.4	2.7	1.6	0.7
Japan	19	911	2 415	2 276	1 979	21.1	5.0	-0.4	-1.1
China	2	180	861	7 120	33 304	25.0	8.1	15.1	12.6
World	1 584	9 981	19 090	31 260	59 917	9.6	3.4	3.4	5.1
Nickel									
USA	91	149	128	140	136	2.6	-0.9	0.8	-0.2
Eur5[1]	28	137	219	262	245	8.2	2.4	1.0	-0.5
Japan	1	99	166	163	175	25.8	2.7	-0.1	0.6
China	n.a.	20	28	191	1 074	n.a.	1.8	13.5	14.2
World	158	709	856	1 249	2 180	7.9	1.0	2.5	4.4
Copper									
USA	1 073	1 860	2 144	2 320	1 827	2.8	0.7	0.5	-1.8
Eur5[1]	613	1 958	2 444	2 831	2 338	5.9	1.0	1.0	-1.5
Japan	12	821	1 578	1 198	1 039	23.2	3.3	-1.8	-1.1

China	5	180	580	3 830	12 482	19.0	6.0	13.4	9.5
World	2 411	7 293	10 790	16 890	23 792	5.6	2.0	3.0	2.7
Oil[2]									
USA	317	695	782	945	920	4.0	0.6	1.3	-0.2
Eur5[1]	39	451	442	459	397	13.0	-0.1	0.3	-1.1
Japan	3	200	248	244	182	23.4	1.1	-0.1	-2.2
China	n.a.	28	110	327	641	n.a.	7.1	7.5	5.3
World	505	2 253	3 140	3 837	4 662	7.8	1.7	1.3	1.5

[1] The metals data for Western Europe relate to five major countries, viz. Germany, France, Italy, Spain and the United Kingdom. 2. Oil is measured in million tons oil equivalent. Source: Metallgesellschaft (annual); Darmstadter et al, 1971; BP (annual); ICSG (annual); INSG (annual); World Bureau of Metal Statistics (annual).

The findings of the above discussion about an historical increase in the dependence on imported metal supply are corroborated by the content of Table 2.8, which tracks the changing degrees of self-sufficiency in primary energy in the three mature regions, with China and the former Soviet Union thrown in for comparison. In 1925, Western Europe, the USA and Japan had an excess of primary energy production over domestic needs, and even in 1950 they were virtually self-sufficient. But the time trend in all three has been clearly down over the entire 80-year period, with two exceptions: Western Europe in the 1980s, where the expansion of nuclear power and the rise of exploitation of fossil fuels in the North Sea led to a temporary increase in self-sufficiency; and the USA since about 2005, when the extraction of shale oil and gas has had a profound impact on the energy landscape, strongly increasing the share of the USA in world oil and gas production (Chapter 4).

China's industrialization thrust evolved in all seriousness in the 1990s, a little bit more than a decade after the economic reform of 1978 (Zhu, 2012). The country's growth since then has been unprecedented, and this has set clear marks on the consumption increase for numerous commodities intensively used in the heavy industrialization phase. Thus, in the 15-year period between 1990 and 2005, demand for aluminum, nickel and copper increased 6–8-fold, and for the 13-year period that followed the growth has continued, but at a somewhat slower pace (Table 2.7).

A possible interrelationship between stagnating or falling demand for industrial commodities in the mature, rich economies, and the very fast growth of demand in China must be elucidated. China has evolved into a leading global importer of raw materials, and a large exporter of many manufactures. Here are some figures from the twenty-first century, demonstrating the emerging role of China in the world of commodities. According to IMF (2019) China's share of global GDP (PPP-terms) on average in 2016–2018 was 18.2%, and its annual growth between 1996 and 2005 averaged 9.2%. Developments in the following ten years were equally impressive, as from 2006 to 2015 the annual growth in China averaged 9.6%. However, since 2011 GDP growth in China has decelerated, and the average growth in 2016–2018 was only 6.7%. Even if the growth has slowed down it is still impressive, especially in comparison with the rich world. In 2014, China's share of global GDP surpassed that of the USA, and in 2018 its share had risen to 18.7%, compared to 15.2% for the USA (IMF, 2019).

Previously we have noted stagnant or even falling demand for many industrial commodities since the 1990s in the rich, mature economies. At the same time, China has recently passed through a stage of its economic development that is highly commodity intensive, just as Japan did in the 1950–1975 period. Against this background, China's share of recorded global demand for a number of important commodities is truly impressive. In 2018, China's demand for copper is a staggering 52% of global demand, for coal 51%, nickel 49%, tin 46% and for steel (2017) it was 45% (World Bank, 2019a; World Steel Association, 2018). China's demand alone represents about half of global demand for a number of important commodities, which truly illustrates the country's dominance in global commodity markets. Since about 2015, growth in China's share of global demand has decelerated but considering the country's total share it will remain a dominant player on world commodity markets for many years to come.

Even after this impressive consumption growth, China's import dependence continues to be less extreme than that of Western Europe and Japan. The lesser density of China's population provides part of the explanation, but the main reason is that the country is itself one of the largest producers of many minerals and metals. Table 2.8 demonstrates that until about 2000 China was able to satisfy virtually all its needs of primary energy from domestic resources. However, we note that

Table 2.8 *Commercial energy at the primary stage: ratio of production to consumption*

	1925	1950	1965	1985	2005	2018
Western Europe[1]	1.03	0.87	0.52	0.61	0.54	0.59
USA	1.07	1.01	0.93	0.89	0.69	0.96
Japan	1.08	0.97	0.33	0.16	0.17	0.11
China[2]	0.95	1.01	1.00	1.19	0.92	0.80
Former Soviet Union	1.07	0.96	1.13	1.24	1.67	1.79

[1] EU28+Norway in 2005 and onwards.
[2] Communist Asia in 1925, 1950 and 1965.
Source: Darmstadter et al. (1971); BP (annual); Enerdata (annual).

despite the country's large endowment of coal, its fuel production is no longer able to keep up with its expanding energy needs.

The growth of raw materials demand, the intensification of commodity usage and the increasing significance of imported supply are typical of the stages of development when infrastructure and heavy industries are established. The USA and Western Europe went through similar phases of economic progress, but at a pace that was much slower than that experienced in later periods by Japan and currently by China. There are some indications of an impending slowdown in China's pace of industrialization, but even then the country's size will maintain its dominant force in the commodities world. India's economic growth and industrialization have accelerated impressively since 2003, and given this country's population size, it too is bound to play increasingly important roles in global commodity markets.

2.5 The Main Findings Summarized

Before concluding the chapter, it may be useful to summarize the main findings from the overview of the international commodity trade flows provided in this chapter:

1. Trade in commodities currently accounts for about a quarter of global goods trade, but this share has been declining. In 1965 commodities accounted for almost half of global trade in goods. The commodities boom that started in 2004, prompted by fast industrialization in emerging economies, reversed temporarily the historically falling trend. Fuels are by far the most important commodity group, measured in export values, followed by food, minerals and metals. The share of agricultural raw materials was about one tenth of that generated by fuels.

2. Oil is, without comparison, the most important traded commodity. Total oil and oil products exports in 2016–2018 represented an average value of US$1134 billion, which is far more than the entire global exports of passenger motor vehicles (US$738 billion), and about 30 times as much as the global exports of aluminum. Iron and steel (US$397 billion) and natural gas (US$218 billion) come next to oil in the ranking of commodities by export value. Oil exports are also by far the biggest when measured in tons, followed by hard coal and iron ore.

3. Asia in total records substantial deficits in its commodity trade, mainly due to the increased demand for primary commodities in fast-growing China and India. Europe as well as the USA and Canada also generate deficits in their commodity trade, while OECD Asia Pacific records surpluses due to the growing export of agricultural materials, minerals, metals and fuels, primarily from Australia. Latin America is the dominant exporting region regarding food, metals and minerals, and generates surpluses across all major commodity groups. The Middle East+North Africa along with the CIS account for a completely dominant proportion of the global exports of fuels.

4. The USA, Western Europe and Japan exhibit limited import dependence for food products. For Western Europe and Japan, this is the result of deep agricultural protection. On the other hand, all three areas have become heavily dependent on imports of industrial raw materials (minerals and metals) in the course of the twentieth century, as domestic needs erupted in response to the respective regions' industrialization. Import dependence developed earlier in the USA and Western Europe than in Japan, but there the reliance on imported supply has become far more accentuated, mainly due to its high population density. China's import dependence has grown considerably in recent years, in large part due to its impressive GDP growth, and despite the fact that the country is one of the largest producers of many minerals and metals.

5. The consumption of most industrial commodities in the three rich, economically mature regions has been stagnant since 1990, and falling in most cases since 2005. This is because their economic growth has recently been dominated by sectors with little industrial commodities needs. In contrast, heavy industrialization in China gathered pace in the early 1990s, and this country has experienced a historically unprecedented growth in the demand for industrial commodities, increasingly satisfied through imports. China has thus evolved into a dominant global importer of raw material and exporter of manufactures.

3 | Comparative Advantage and Trade Policy Distortions

3.1 Protectionism in Raw Materials: Of Great Significance, Especially Regarding Agriculture

Protection could well be the greatest deterrent to a full realization of the potential for global economic growth and its welfare yields. The main detriment of protection is that it induces production to be located in high-cost venues. Liberalization permits production to move to its lowest-cost locations, involving savings that can be very large at times. In a comprehensive study with spectacular results, Anderson (2013) measured the benefits and costs of liberalization involving removal of subsidies and barriers to trade according to the WTO's trade liberalization reform, the so-called Doha Round. The effects are assessed until the year 2100, considering both static and dynamic gains, deducting the friction costs and applying a 3% discount rate; the stunning conclusion is that the net present value of the proposed policy change ranges between US$20 000 billion and US$64 000 billion (constant 2007 dollars), half of which would accrue to the developing countries. The assessed net gains can be compared to the global and developing country GDPs in 2014, assessed using current exchange rates at US$77 300 billion and US$30 300 billion, respectively (IMF, biannual, April 2015). The proposed liberalization would have a stark impact, especially on developing countries' GDP during the period under consideration, according to the study.

Despite this knowledge, since 2016 we have been witnessing a progressive increase in the use of restrictive trade policy instruments, and a rising number of trade tensions. This development is mainly driven by a feeling in some quarters that trade is unfair, and concerns that international competition is distorted, either by market barriers or by government involvement. Disagreements between the USA and

China have been in the forefront; by 2018 they had evolved into what can be characterized as a trade war. Early in 2018 China and the USA imposed tariffs on each other's goods trade of about US$50 billion. In September, the conflict escalated as the USA introduced 10% tariffs on imports from China amounting about US$200 billion, and China responded by imposing similar tariffs on imports from the USA worth about US$60 billion. These tariffs were raised to 25% by May 10, 2019 after the USA expressed concerns that China had stalled the trade talks.

By mid-2019, the tariffs imposed by China and the USA covered in total a trade volume of US$360 billion, more than half of their bilateral trade (estimated at US$640 billion in 2017). These tariffs apply to a large number of products, most of them related to the manufactures sectors. However, some are directed to agriculture, minerals and metals, and are thus relevant for the commodities markets. The overall effects of this protectionist development are discussed in Section 3.4, but we begin by providing an historical description of trade barriers in international commodity markets, with a focus on the agricultural sector.

The agricultural sector's share of global GDP has fallen from some 10% in the 1960s to about 3% in the late 2010s (World Bank, 2019b). Despite the decline, this sector has, at least until 2016, remained in the center for most countries' trade distortion policies. For example, Anderson and Martin (2006) show that the average applied import tariffs in 2001 for agriculture and food was 17%, for textiles and apparel 10%, and for other manufactures about 3.5%. Thus, historically most of the trade distortions (and the potential gains from their removal) arise from measures to protect agriculture. It is also worth noting that about half of these import tariffs were due to agricultural protection by the rich world. Trade policies affecting agriculture are politically sensitive for a number of reasons, and it is therefore not surprising that agricultural issues caused most of the disputes in the implementation of the Doha Round.

For the reasons spelled out above, a large part of the present chapter focuses on agriculture. We consider first the national policies that affect commodity production and trade, and explore the causes for their establishment. We then provide a discussion of the increase in trade-restricting measures in the twenty-first century, both export restrictions and import tariffs, followed by a quantitative assessment of the extent of trade barriers affecting commodities in general and agricultural goods in particular. Section 3.6 looks more closely at commodity processing and explores how the location of this activity has been distorted, not only by trade-restraining policies in a strict sense, but also by a broad array of surviving colonial legacies.

3.2 What Policies, by Whom and for What Reasons?

Protection takes a multitude of forms. Not all of it is clearly visible. The original rationale for establishing protective measures has sometimes been forgotten and is often hard to establish. Importing countries account for a dominant share of the overall constraints and distortions of trade, and we begin by considering the menu of protective measures adopted to reduce commodity imports.

Traditional analyses of trade policy distinguish between tariff barriers to trade, which restrict imports by raising the domestic price, and nontariff barriers, comprising all other protection measures. It is useful to make a further distinction by subdividing nontariff barriers into the ones that restrict imports directly and those that do it indirectly by promoting domestic production. The tools to be enumerated are not exclusive to commodity trade. Most of them are equally employed to restrain manufactures trade as well.

Import tariffs, which raise the imported price and so reduce the volume of imports, constitute the classic measure for protecting domestic production from more efficient foreign competition. Tariffs can come in different forms and under different names. One form that has been frequently used in the EU and elsewhere is the *variable import levy*. Its purpose is to keep domestic production and imports stable over the price cycle in the international commodity markets. It involves the maintenance of a domestic price that is high enough to assure an adequate and stable profitability to domestic production, primarily with the help of a levy on imports that varies inversely with the international price, so as to always equate the total import price with the domestic price.

Among the nontariff barriers, a straightforward measure to restrict imports is to establish *import quotas*. Imports are then permitted only up to the level of the quota, and any remaining demand has to be satisfied from domestic output. When quotas are effective in reducing imports, their allocation among exporters regularly raises controversies, as each tries to maximize their allotment. Even when no specific limit on the imported quantity has been set, the institution of *import licenses* often involves a bureaucratic hassle that in effect leads to a restriction of the import flow. *Voluntary export restraints* are a special type of quota. The phrase is a misnomer: the restraints are typically not voluntary at all, but are adopted by the exporting country under threat from the importing government of even more severe suppression of trade. Restrictions of the import volume are often implemented with the help of *national standards*. In primary commodities, this tool would be most common for agricultural products. On health grounds, the importing country can impose a prohibition on imports of food from areas claimed to be infested by disease or where a particular insecticide has been used. Alternatively, the importing government can require elaborate and costly veterinary inspections as a precondition for import.

Instead of reducing the competitiveness or availability of imports, the protective measures can aim at inducing expanded domestic output by improving its competitiveness or by directing demand specifically toward that output. Overt subsidies involving *direct payments, concessional lending* or the *write-off of loans* will reduce domestic production costs. *Tax concessions* can have a similar effect. *Public procurement* exclusively from domestic sources will add to the demand for domestic output, to the detriment of imported supply.

Several rationales are put forth in justification of the importing countries' restrictive policies related to commodity imports. The most important is probably an urge to assure a reasonable self-sufficiency of indispensable goods, whose supply, it is felt, cannot be entrusted to foreigners. That would explain why the highest protection is afforded to food products, while the protective measures for nonfood commodities of agricultural and mineral origin are much more relaxed. Energy materials are indispensable too, but the protective measures have so far been restrained, perhaps because many importing countries have had, until the renewable boom that started to blossom from about 2015, little prospect of replacing imports by domestic supply, and where such prospects existed the expansion of output within the country was seen to be very costly.

Another rationale for protection is a concern about the labor and capital employed in existing domestic installations. Where uncontrolled imports threaten to annihilate an uncompetitive domestic commodity industry, the consequence will be an uneconomic destruction of capital and skills. In such situations, it is argued, temporary import barriers are needed so that imports are expanded only gradually, in line with the depreciation of existing assets and the ability to shift the labor force to alternative occupations. In practice, once protection is established, it tends to become a permanent feature.

In numerous industrialized countries, agricultural producers have a vocal lobby whose political support for the government in power is conditioned on continued agricultural protection. In other cases, import restrictions have been used as a way to ease a strained balance-of-payments situation. This appears to be the main motivation for the trade disputes between the USA and China, considering the large bilateral trade imbalance between the two countries. Finally, especially in developing countries, import tariffs and/or taxes on foreign trade have often been an important source of public revenue. While trade policy historically has been predominantly the preserve of the importers and invariably aimed at restricting import flows, commodity exporters, too, sometimes use policy to affect the volume of their export supply. In the first decade of the 2000s, mainly due to the price peaks for many commodities during the commodity boom (Chapter 5), there was a sharp increase in the use of export restrictions.

3.3 The Increase in Export Restrictions in International Commodity Trade

In a situation of growing global demand for raw materials, where access to the unevenly spread world resources is a priority for many countries, the use of export restrictions has increased remarkably since 2005, the beginning of the latest commodity boom. To assert control over their primary assets, many resource-rich countries turned to the use of export restrictions. In 2009, the OECD started to systematically collect data on this phenomenon as applied to primary materials (covering both industrial raw materials and primary agricultural and food commodities). The data reveal that three quarters of the documented export barriers have been introduced since 2007. A dominant proportion of the barriers was imposed by developing countries that account for a high share of natural resource supply (OECD, 2014).

This development has highlighted the need to pay attention to conditions of supply, and especially the adverse effect of restrictions on exports. Previously, governments motivated the use of export duties as a measure to boost fiscal revenue. Since about 2010, the main justifications have shifted to issues such as food security, industrial development, environmental concerns and natural resource protection.

Arguments for Export Restrictions

One important argument for imposing export barriers is related to food security. For some important agricultural products, for example wheat and rice, trade restrictions have been used temporarily in the case of failed harvests and the ensuing reduced supply in global markets. Governments in many developing countries have thus aimed at avoiding shortages and controlling sharp domestic price increases, since food represent a major share of the household budget in these countries. However, by constraining international trade, the export restrictions have on many occasions caused even stronger international price spikes. The world economy has suffered in consequence. Even though the country imposing the constraint may have benefited from lesser domestic food price rises the consequences will be particularly severe for low-income, food-deficit countries.

Another motivation for imposing export restrictions is to subsidize local industries, as this ensures that the country's industries have access to raw materials at lower prices compared to their international competitors. This motivation has been argued for some industrial raw materials (e.g. timber, fisheries and leather) which are sensitive to international competition. By the same argument, export restrictions have been used to attract investments into downstream industries. Together with higher import tariffs on processed products (see Section 3.6), export restrictions on primary goods can provide incentives to industrial development within the country.

In the case of minerals, with rare earth metals providing a striking example, many governments of exporting nations contend that production results in significant environmental harm that may be hard to rectify by environmental policy. The increases in demand for many such products, especially while the boom lasted, have resulted in strong pressures to expand output. Export restraints have then sometimes been motivated as measures to limit the environmental damage caused by the extraction activity. In a similar vein, some governments have argued that export restrictions can help avoid rapid depletion of their scarce resources.

Detriments of Export Restrictions

Domestic considerations typically motivate export restrictions, but, as noted, the effects on the global market can be severe, especially if they are imposed on products where the export market is dominated by only a few producing corporations or countries. OECD (2014) notes that maize, palm oil, rice, wheat and soya beans, among food products with heavy output concentration, have been especially vulnerable to export restrictions. In the mineral sector, supply has been particularly compromised for rare earth metals, the platinum group, tungsten, lithium and antimony, given that the top five producing countries' share is above 90%. However, severe consequences from export restrictions can also occur for more common minerals and metals such as tin, iron ore, copper and nickel.

In minerals and metals (including rare earth metals), export restrictions aroused severe trade tensions between exporting and importing nations. For rare earth metals, the importers were worried about secure supply of essential inputs to important industries, mainly high technology and green energy industries. When considering China's near monopoly position in rare earth metals production (further discussed in Chapter 9), the export restrictions imposed on these materials have led to a number of WTO disputes. In March 2012 the USA, EU and Japan jointly filed a complaint against China's export restrictions on these materials, but also on tungsten and molybdenum (WTO, 2012). The plaintiffs argued that the restrictions were highly disruptive to their industries, resulting in higher production costs, and thus provided an unacceptable competitive advantage to Chinese industries. China, on the other hand, argued that the export restrictions were primarily due to environmental concerns, as the extraction process for these materials is damaging to the ecosystem. However, these arguments were rejected by the WTO panel, which ruled against China in this case (WTO, 2014). As a result, China removed their export restrictions in January 2015. However, as the trade disputes with China and the USA escalated after 2017, there are new fears that export restrictions of rare earth metals will once again be actualized as a weapon in the trade war, at least for exports to the USA (Guardian, 2019).

Korinek and Kim (2010) analyze the effectiveness of export restrictions in bringing about desirable environmental and conservation goals. They measure effectiveness assuming that a reduction in exports actually leads to a corresponding decrease in production. Their study concludes that this connection is not guaranteed, as more production can be sold domestically (this was the case for molybdenum in China). OECD (2014) provides evidence that most governments' main motivation for implementing export restrictions (typically different kinds of domestic market failures), can be achieved more efficiently by other policy approaches that do not have negative international spillovers. In OECD (2014) it is argued that balanced taxation, efficient management of tax revenue and stable investment policies are usually more successful tools for the management of the minerals sector than the use of export restrictions. In the case of agriculture, Anderson and Nelgen (2012) argue that food security issues are better addressed by using generic social safety net policies than by using trade policy instruments.

3.4 Import Tariff Increases since 2016

Import tariffs raise the imported price to reduce the volume of imports, in an attempt to protect domestic production from more efficient foreign competition. This is indeed the main motivation to the recent political shift in US trade policy, moving from being a free-trade proponent, toward taking a more protectionist stance. The background to this political change is the growing trade deficit between the USA and the rest of the world, mainly China. In 2018, the US trade deficit with China alone reached US$419 billion, a development that started in 1985, but really took off in 2001 when China joined the WTO (US Census, 2019). The Trump administration argues that free trade leads to asymmetries, and that the emerging markets benefit to the detriment of more mature economies. The focus of this rationale is mainly on bilateral trade relationships, with the ambition to rebalance the USA in the global trading system. The argument is that trade policy in the USA should focus more on national interests, including importantly the country's national security.

National security was indeed the main justification for imposing import tariffs on steel (25%) and aluminum (10%), which were decided upon in March 2018 and implemented in June 2018. Already in his electoral campaign, president Trump announced that he had intentions to protect domestic industrial sectors against "unfair" foreign competition, as well as to rebalance US trade relationships. The tariffs on steel and aluminum were imposed after an investigation made by the Department of Commerce, which found that the imported quantities of these products were harming domestic producers, reducing US jobs and threatening national security in a broad sense. The investigation was conducted in agreement with Section 232 of the Trade Expansion Act of 1962, which historically has been used to determine the implication of imports on national security in times of crisis (US Department of Commerce, 2018).

The main implication of the tariffs has been that the prices of both steel and aluminum increased sharply in the USA relative to other countries. For example, US steel prices increased roughly 25% more than steel prices in the United Kingdom in 2018, and the price differential of US aluminum and the London Metal Exchange benchmark reached about 11% (World Bank, 2018a). Even though this can have short-term benefits for domestic producers, there is obviously a clear risk of additional costs for US consumers. The tariffs on steel and aluminum were only the starting point of the escalating trade war that followed.

Overall the imposed tariffs have caused retaliatory actions from the countries affected, mainly China, but also the EU and other countries. China responded quickly to the suggested import tariffs on steel and aluminum, and introduced similar tariffs on a variety of US products. For example, China imposed a 25% tariff on imports of US soybeans, with a significant impact on the developments of global soybean markets. Considering that China is the largest consumer of soybeans in the world, and that most of these are imported, the imposed tariff has had a large effect on trade flows. Before the tariffs, the main suppliers to China were Brazil and the USA, with about 40% supply from each country. After the tariffs, Chinese buyers have turned to other suppliers (mainly Brazil), implying that US soybean demand has fallen (World Bank, 2018a).

As demand for soybeans from Brazil has increased, due to higher demand from China, international prices have risen. This, in turn, has shifted the demand of other soybean importers toward the USA, thus partly offsetting the decrease in demand from China. However, estimates still suggest that the US export for soybeans in aggregate will nevertheless decline by about 25% in coming years, while exports from Brazil are expected to increase by some 15% (World Bank, 2018a).

The US government had already responded in July 2018 with monetary assistance ($12 billion) in farm aid to domestic farmers affected by the Chinese increase in import tariffs. They have also imposed a food purchase program, due to shrinking domestic agricultural prices, with the intention of purchasing domestically produced agricultural products to support farmers.

Overall it is noted that commodity specific tariffs cause larger price differentials between countries, leading to trade diversions, and thus affecting producers of the targeted commodity as well as its substitutes. However, the more general increase of trade tensions between major economies has potentially much more widespread effects, as concerns over weakened global trade can negatively affect global growth, and thus the potential demand for many important primary commodities. This is because tariffs negatively affect bilateral trade and significantly distort global supply chains (Nicita et al., 2018; World Bank, 2018b). The decline in many metal prices following the imposition of tariffs in 2018 illustrates that markets clearly are affected. Considering that China's importance in global commodity markets is huge, the impact on these markets from the trade tensions is likely to be considerable.

To conclude, the impact of the ongoing trade war on global commodity markets will be significant. It is noted that commodity specific tariffs (e.g. steel, aluminum and soybeans) importantly reduce and divert trade flows, due to price differentials that follow from protectionist measures. The increase in global trade tensions, and imposition of broad-based tariffs, causes fears of reduced global trade, with a negative impact on economic growth and primary commodity demand.

3.5 Measuring the Extent of Trade Restrictions in International Commodity Trade

The protectionist arsenal has undergone substantial change since the late 1980s, primarily involving a dismantling of many trade barriers, without necessarily reducing the overall impact of the barriers. Also, it needs underlining that assessments of trade policy distortions for primary commodities raise a number of methodological and practical difficulties and yield a variety of outcomes, depending on assumptions and models used, so considerable uncertainty remains about the overall impact and its change over time.

The OECD regularly publishes the level of (agricultural) Producer Support Estimates (PSEs) for its member nations and for a few important nonmember countries (OECD, 2019). PSE has become a widely used yardstick that measures the overall size of the many disparate policy instruments in support of agriculture. In 1986–1988 such support had a value of US$240 billion and corresponded to 37% of gross farm receipts (%PSE) in OECD countries. By 2016–2018, the absolute support in nominal money was roughly the same at US$235 billion, but the %PSE in OECD countries had declined to 18%. National subdivision of the numbers reveals the EU as the largest agricultural supporter in the latter period, the total amounting to US$102 billion, followed by Japan (US$42 billion) and the USA (US$38 billion). The leaders in %PSE were Norway (61%), Iceland (59%), Switzerland (55%) and Korea (52%). The %PSE was 20 in the EU and 10 in the USA. New Zealand and Australia had the lowest %PSEs at 1 and 2, respectively.

Among the non-OECD countries, China has developed into a dominant supporter for its agricultural sector, given an average PSE support in 2016–2018 of US$213 billion. In total, for the 53 non-OECD countries covered by the statistics, producer support amounted to US$440 billion. Regarding %PSE in these countries we note that the Philippines is a leader at 25%, followed by China (15%), Russia (13%) and Colombia (13%). All of these were far below the four record holders in the OECD. On average for all the 53 countries, %PSE was 5.6, thus illustrating that overall agricultural support is considerably lower in the non-OECD countries, as the average for OECD countries only is 18.

When it comes to specific commodities in OECD countries the pride (or shame) of place in percentage terms goes to rice, where total support was US$14 billion and %PSE was 55. Outside the OECD, China holds a record with total rice support of US$27 billion, and the %PSE about 30. Such high levels of protection go a long way to explain why only a minuscule proportion of global rice production is being traded (see Table 2.3). Other protected agricultural commodities among the ones reviewed in Chapter 2 comprised beef (US$19 billion, 14%), sugar (US$3.3 billion, 27%), wheat (US$2.9 billion, 5%) and maize (US$2.6 billion, 4%). Wool, on the other hand, was very lightly protected (US$19 million, 1%), while data on cotton were not provided separately in the OECD data compilations.

In a study, Anderson et al. (2013) review the literature on trends and developments of distortions in agricultural and food markets, as well as the theories that lies behind them. Using a database of agricultural distortions by the World Bank (1955–2011), which includes estimates for 82 countries that together account for about 95% of the world's population, agricultural GDP and total GDP, they analyze the evolution of trade distortions over time. The database measures the nominal and relative rate of assistance for 75 different farm products, based on the price distortions imposed by governments that create a gap between current domestic prices and the price that would exist under free markets.

Before the 1980s there is a clear tendency for a proagricultural bias in rich countries and vice versa in developing countries, that is, a tendency for a positive relation between a country's GDP per capita and its assistance to agricultural products. After the 1980s this tendency weakens, as the two country groups' average rates of assistance converge toward zero. For example, for the EU countries the relative rates of assistance reduced from an average of 77% in the 1980s to 11% in 2005–2011. However, these average results hide the fact that there are considerable differences regarding trade distortions across countries. Furthermore, there are also large distortion varieties among products even within a country. The data further reveal that there are large fluctuations from year-to-year, mainly due to the strong negative correlation between international prices and related product distortions.

In an attempt to quantify the effects of agricultural trade liberalizations since the 1980s, Valenzuela et al. (2009) analyze the net economic welfare effects from the wave of reforms in that decade. The results reveal that without the trade policy reforms implemented during the 1980s, world GDP would have been worse off by a stunning US$233 billion per year by 2004. This is a substantial figure, given that total agricultural exports in 2004 were US$783 billion (by 2017 total agricultural exports had risen to US$1736 billion). It is noted that as a share of national income developing economies gained proportionately more from the trade liberalization reforms, even though two thirds of the US$233 billion accrued to high-income countries. Dismantling all protection would permit the developing countries to increase their share of world agricultural exports from 43% to 55%, and value added in agriculture would be about 5% higher. This is more than ten times the proportional gain of just 0.4% for nonagricultural commodities from the trade liberalizing reforms.

The same study further assesses the welfare effects of the trade distorting policies that were still in place in 2004. In this thought experiment, the global welfare cost of the remaining trade distortions is estimated at US$168 billion per year, indicating that a lot of scope still remains for beneficial liberalization reforms. A closer look at the sectoral distribution of the welfare effects reveals that 70% of the welfare costs are due to agricultural policies, a striking result considering that the share of this sector in global GDP is only about 3%. An analysis of the regional distribution reveals that a dominant share, about three fifths, of the global gains from eradicating remaining agricultural protection stems from removing policies in high-income countries. Global agricultural output is shown to decline by 2.6%, a consequence of slightly higher international prices, as agricultural subsidies are discontinued. The sharpest reductions in output, both in dollar and percentage terms are recorded in the EU15 (–US$191 billion, –21%) and Japan (–US$39 billion, –23%), but Russia, the USA and the rest of Western Europe also record significant declines. The biggest gainer is Brazil (US$46 billion, 45%), while output in Australia, New Zealand and Argentina rises by some US$12 billion in each case.

The commodity boom that began in 2004, with high prices and large price fluctuations for many commodities, has amplified the research to illuminate the effects of price spikes on trade barriers (Anderson and Nelgen, 2012; Heady, 2011; Martin and Anderson, 2011; Rutten et al., 2013). The main reason is that the commodity boom led to important changes in many countries' trade restrictions. It caused a number of exporting countries to increase their export barriers (as discussed), but also food-importing countries lowered their import tariffs. Both of these changes can have an amplified effect on international food price spikes. Anderson and Nelgen (2012) find that for global grain trade the changes in trade restrictions during 2006–2008 were responsible for estimated increases in the *international* prices of rice (40%), maize (20%) and wheat (10%). They also find that the changes in trade restrictions also led to increased *domestic* price spikes across all countries. The study reveals that the trade policy reactions to food price spikes have not been an efficient instrument for stabilizing domestic prices. The other studies come to similar results, and the policy implications are collectively directed toward the benefits of further trade liberalizing reforms.

World Bank (2019a) analyzes the implications of domestic trade policies implemented during the two food price shocks in the twenty-first century. It claims that even though individual countries can benefit from imposing trade policy interventions, for example export restrictions, by insulating the domestic markets from large price swings, this can have large detrimental effects for countries that are dependent on imports. For example, the study finds that trade policies implemented during the 2010–2011 food price spike contributed 40% of the increase in the world price of wheat, and about 25% of the increase in maize prices. Thus, the combined use of trade policy measures by individual countries amplified the international price movements and increased poverty among the poorest countries.

To summarize the developments in trade policy over the past decades, here are some general conclusions. First, the use of trade-restrictive policies has declined over time on all traded goods, yielding large benefits to all countries. Trade distortions are clearly less important today than they were 40 years ago. This can be illustrated by the agricultural support to farmers in the OECD countries, measured by the %PSE, which, as noted, declined from 37% at the end of the 1980s to about 18% in 2016–2018. However, growing trade tensions in recent years resulting in increased import tariffs for many commodities illustrate that burdensome trade-restrictive policies are still in place, and substantial gains from removing them are still to be reaped.

3.6 Commodity Processing: Tariff Escalation

It was noted in Section 3.1 that dislocations of commodity production and trade due to distorting protectionist policies are mainly limited to agricultural products, and notably to food. But there is a further policy stance, widely applied to all kinds of commodities and causing considerable dislocation, that requires discussion. This is tariff escalation along the processing chain from the crude material to the finished commodity product, and its precise purpose is to assure the location of commodity processing in the country that imports the crude material.

A number of factors would determine the globally optimal location of commodity processing in the absence of trade-policy intervention.

These include transport costs, which are related to the weight reduction accomplished by the processing activity and the relative ease of transporting the crude and processed product. The weight of copper falls by two thirds as it moves from concentrates to the refined stage, thus reducing the cost of shipping. The weight of tomato concentrate may not be vastly different from that of fresh tomatoes, but it is less fragile, so the cost of shipping is reduced. In some cases, the processed product is more expensive to transport. Crude oil is predominantly shipped in highly economical, very large crude carriers, while gasoline is typically moved in specialized and much smaller ships, which are more expensive. Processing costs will not be the same in all locations. The transformation of bauxite into primary aluminum metal requires huge amounts of electrical energy. If the bauxite-producing country does not have ample and cheap power supplies, it will be economical to ship and process the bauxite elsewhere. Substantial economies of scale in processing may favor location in the raw-material-producing country in some cases, and in the consuming nation in others.

Trade policies by the commodity-importing countries have often distorted these optimal patterns in favor of location in the importing nation. A variety of arguments has been used in justification of such policies by the importers. The importing nation may be anxious, on mercantilist grounds, to reap the benefit of the value added created by commodity processing. Alternatively, it may be felt that processing is an activity of strategic importance. Such views have been put forward, for example, to motivate the refining of crude oil. Or, there may be vocal interest groups eager to defend the colonial status quo, under which virtually all processing took place in the former colonial power.

Tariff escalation is the most important, but by no means the only policy tool to accomplish these desired ends. Even in cases where the nominal tariff on the processed commodity is only modestly higher than that on the crude material, the escalation of tariffs may nevertheless provide a prohibitive deterrent against processing in the country of original production, as is apparent from the example summarized in Table 3.1. If processing increases the value of the product from US$80 to US$100 and if the nominal tariff is 10% on the crude material but 20% on the processed product, then the effective tariff imposed on the value added created at the processing stage works out at a prohibitive 60% (US$12/US$20), likely to make processing before exports an uneconomic proposition.

Table 3.1 *An illustration of tariff escalation: nominal versus effective tariff rates*

	Value (US$)	Value added (US$)	Nominal tariff (%)	Nominal tariff (US $)	Effective tariff (%)
Crude commodity	80	80	10	8	10
Processed commodity	100	20	20	20	60

Table 3.2 *Tariff escalation in high-income OECD countries (%)*

	2000	2007	2008	2009	2010	2011	2012	2013
All goods	1.0	0.1	0.1	0.1	0.1	0.2	-0.4	-0.1
Agricultural	12.6	11.2	11.8	11.2	9.8	11.2	10.0	10.5
Nonagricultural	2.1	1.3	1.4	1.4	1.2	1.2	0.3	0.3

Source: United Nations (2014).

The development of tariff escalation between 2000 and 2007–2013 in high-income OECD countries is presented in Table 3.2. The values are averages weighted by share in world import, and the table presents point differences between the applied tariffs for finished goods and the applied tariffs for raw materials, as collected by the International Trade Center at the United Nations. It must be underlined that the statistics represent rough aggregates that hide the evolution in individual cases. Nevertheless, two important insights emerge from the numbers. First, tariff escalation is mainly a concern for agricultural products; for nonagricultural commodities as a whole, tariff escalation appears to be insignificant. Second, there is a clear time trend affording a declining importance to tariff escalation as a measure to protect processing activities in importing countries. Even so, the numbers indicate that tariff escalation can still have a heavily distorting impact on trade and location of processing in agricultural products.

Instances of tariff escalation for specific agricultural products can be found, even though these aspects have been less researched. In 2009 the USA, EU and Japan applied a zero tariff on cocoa beans and unprocessed coffee. In contrast, the tariff on chocolate was 12%, 32% and 30%, respectively, and on roasted coffee 0%, 9% and 12%, respectively in the three importing regions (ITC, 2010). If processing accounts for 20% of the value of the processed products, as is the case in the example in Table 3.1, then the effective tariff will be even higher than 60% in several of the instances just quoted. UNCTAD (2003) provides data on tariff escalation in minerals, which suggest a less pronounced distortion in these commodity markets. The tariff for metal raw materials is zero for the USA, EU and Japan, but amounts to 2.2%, 2.9% and 0.9% for finished metal imports to the three regions. Trade deterrents of similar magnitude apply to fertilizers at different levels of processing.

The numbers presented above relate to tariff escalation applied by the rich world. But the sources quoted state that even more accentuated tariff escalation is practiced by many developing countries. Furthermore, other instruments are also used to protect commodity processing in rich as well as poor countries. UNCTAD (1999) recounts the sad story of how an emerging tomato-concentrate industry in Senegal, producing 73 000 tons in 1991 and generating substantial exports, was forced to contract its production levels to less that 20 000 tons by 1998, as a consequence of a package transferring US$300 million in subsidies in the EU to domestic tomato processors. Senegal was not alone in suffering. Other West African countries such as Burkina Faso, Mali and Ghana faced similar experiences as a result of the EU subsidies.

In China, value-added taxes (VAT) are used to assure domestic metal processing even beyond what is required to satisfy domestic metal consumption. Thus, a 13% VAT (recently reduced from 16%) has to be paid for refined copper and copper concentrates imports to China, but some of the VAT is returned to the Chinese smelters by the government. Chinese smelters can thus offer low processing charges to foreign suppliers for toll smelting and reexports, in consequence of the subsidies, with an ensuing expansion of the smelting industry, and a corresponding stagnation or decline in other countries – notably in Chile, the globally dominant producer of copper concentrates (private communication with Alfonso Gonzalez, Santiago de Chile).

Further location distortions arise when the raw-material-producing countries counter the tariff-escalation measures by introducing incentives for processing before export through export taxes at rates that decline with the level of processing. Indonesia dramatically introduced an export ban on unprocessed minerals in 2009 with the purpose of pressuring mineral producers to process their output before exporting.[1] In other instances, quantitative restrictions have been imposed on the export of unprocessed materials. Political pressures have also been employed as a counter measure. The involvement of foreign direct investors is regularly looked upon much more favorably by the host government, if the investments include not only the extraction and export of the raw material, but also its processing.

The impact of the distortions due to tariff escalation and other measures to protect commodity processing is hard to establish unambiguously. We have not seen any overall assessment similar to the one related to agricultural protection in general that was presented in the preceding section. There is little doubt, however, that this impact is significant, and that the world economy could reap substantial economic gains from a move toward economic optimality in the location of commodity processing.

---

[1] Marian Radetzki was one of three authors of a USAID study on the impact of this policy for the Indonesian economy (USAID, 2013).

4 | Fossil Fuels

This book does not contain separate chapters on food, agricultural raw materials or metals and minerals, which are the main commodity categories apart from the energy commodities. There are at least four reasons for affording a special prominence to energy and devoting a chapter exclusively to this commodity group.

The first is the heavy dominance of energy raw materials in the commodities universe. This is true both for trade and for the contribution they make to GDP. The second is that supply scarcities led to an extraordinary price increase for oil in the past 40–50 years, and its causes warrant an explanation. The third is that fundamental changes are occurring in oil and gas production technologies that promise to replace historical scarcity of supply and high prices with abundance. The fourth reason is the general perception that the energy system is going through a transition toward low-carbon sources, due to technical advances in nonfossil energy alternatives as well as policy efforts to hinder climate change. These reasons also provide the structure of the present chapter. Before we proceed, however, there is a need to clear up a few issues to do with definitions and delimitations of what is to be included in our discussion.

Table 4.1 provides data for global primary energy consumption, as given by BP's annual statistical compilations (BP, annual). We have combined the most recent available numbers with the oldest in this source, covering more than half a century. The complete dominance of oil, gas and coal appears clearly from the figures. In 2018, fossil fuels accounted for 84.7% of total global energy usage, down from 94.1% 52 years earlier, providing space for nuclear and non-hydro renewables. Concern for the environment, and in particular climate change, calls for a sharp reduction in the use of fossil fuels. However, in the absence of a deep climate policy (see Section 4.4) there is little reason to believe this will happen in coming decades, given the technological revolution to be described.

Table 4.1 *Global primary energy consumption by source*

	1965		2018	
	MBD	%	MBD	%
Oil	31.2	42.0	93.6	33.6
Coal	27.9	37.5	75.7	27.2
Gas	10.9	14.6	66.5	23.9
Hydro	4.2	5.6	19.1	6.8
Nuclear	0.1	0.2	12.3	4.4
Other renewables	0.1	0.1	11.3	4.0
Sum fossil fuels	70.0	94.1	235.8	84.7
Sum total	74.4	100.0	278.4	100.0

Note: Conversion factor used to convert million tons of oil equivalent (MTOE) to million barrels per day (MBD) is 49.8.
Source: BP (annual).

We have decided to exclude electricity from further deliberations in this chapter for two reasons. The present book is devoted in its entirety to physical goods in the global economy, with a heavy emphasis on trade across borders. The first reason for the exclusion of electricity is that we regard it as a service, not a good, and services are not part of the book's agenda. A further motivation is that virtually all electricity is consumed in the country of production so a very limited share of power output enters international trade. The omission of electricity implies that hydroelectricity is not included in the themes we pursue. The same applies to wind, solar and nuclear power. In the process, we have of course neglected uranium, which is used as fuel in nuclear installations. Given that the uranium trade in 2017 amounted to a total of only US$0.4 billion (UNCTAD, annual b), equal to 0.04% of global trade in crude oil, the neglect appears not overly important.

There is a conceptual problem with the "other renewables" consumption in Table 4.1, given that BP's numbers comprise only commercially traded fuels. Out of the total of 11.3 MBD given by BP, 2.7 MBD is contributed by solar and 5.8 MBD by wind (BP, annual). Remaining renewable energy forms embrace geothermal, waste and biomass. According to BP, the total for the three works out at 2.8 MBD (of which a majority represents biomass-based liquid fuels). Biofuels production, represented by ethanol and biodiesel, amounted to 1.9 MBD in 2018, a number that has increased by almost 10% yearly in the last ten years.

Attempts to go beyond the commercial categories suggest that waste and biomass comprise massive noncommercial supplies. The International Energy Agency (IEA, 2014b, p 606), for instance, evaluates overall biomass use in 2012 at 26.9 MBD, with a dominant share consumed within the households of poor countries, and we have been unable to find more recent numbers. The IEA biomass usage assessment equals one third of global coal consumption. Accepting IEA's numbers, the 2012 fossil fuel share shrinks to 81.7% of total global primary energy usage.

Like BP we are resigned to excluding noncommercial biomass and waste supply from further analysis. The quantitative appraisals of availability are vague, price information is nonexistent and the supply, though plausibly massive, does not cross borders. The following discussions, therefore, focus on the three fossil fuels. Biomass may become commercially significant in the future; in 2020, its commercial uses for the production of electricity and heat and as liquids in transport are insignificant in the overall energy picture, so we will not pursue the biomass question any further in this chapter.

4.1 The Dominance of Fossil Fuels in the Commodities Universe

As noted in Chapter 2 (Table 2.1), the aggregate of all primary commodities has recently contributed about one quarter to the overall global merchandise trade. Energy raw materials alone accounted for over 40% of this total. Table 4.2 provides detail by fuel and demonstrates the behemoth nature of the world oil market. One would have to aggregate about ten of the most important non-energy commodities to reach a value equal to oil in international trade.

A major proportion of oil output is traded across borders. The propensity to trade is much lower for coal, and even more limited for gas, where elevated transport costs reduce the economics of sales in faraway markets. Though quite small compared to oil, natural gas nevertheless is the second largest among commodities in terms of trade value, while coal ranks considerably lower.

Table 4.2 *The importance of fossil fuels in 2018: their share in world trade and in global GDP*

	World exports (million US$)	Share of global merchandise trade (%)	Global production (MBD)	Price (US $/bl)	Value of global output (billion US$)	Share of global GDP (%)
Petroleum	1261	8.6	94.7	71.3	2465	2.9
Gas	205	1.4	66.8	43.0[1]	1050	1.2
Coal	138	0.9	78.7	9.2[1]	265	0.3
Sum of three	1604	10.9	240.2		3780	4.4

[1] European import prices.
Source: BP (annual); UN Comtrade, http://comtrade.un.org/data.

The dominance of fossil fuels and of oil in particular emerges equally forcefully when measured in terms of output values, which are then compared to global GDP. This comparison, it should be noted, is relevant because the value of output in extractive industries is completely dominated by value added, their contribution to GDP. Table 4.2 shows that the value of fossil fuel output works out at some 4.4% of global GDP, with oil again the dominant material. This total is higher than the output value of the overall primary sector in many countries, as demonstrated in Table 1.1, Figure 1.1 and the text of Section 1.1.

A contributory reason for oil's dominant position among commodities is its price rise since the early 1970s. Figure 4.1 demonstrates that real oil prices rose by an astounding 780% from 1970–1972 to 2016–2018. To put this into perspective, the figure compares the oil price evolution with an index of prices for metals and minerals, a group of commodities that, like oil, are exhaustible. The latter rose not even 10%.

Figure 4.1 reveals the strong increases as well as dramatic falls in oil prices, and periods of high and low prices in between. It is noteworthy, however, that throughout the "low price" period of 1986–1999, the oil price index remained at a level about three times that of the metals and minerals price index. Even in 1998, when oil prices dipped to their lowest since 1973, the oil price index (at 251) was more than four times higher than the metals and minerals price index (at 59).

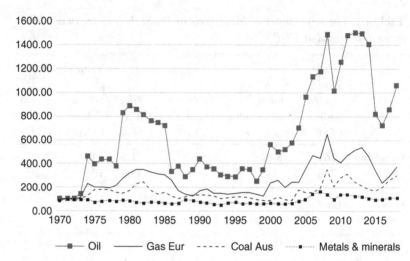

Figure 4.1 Indexes of commodity prices 1970–2018 in constant money, 1970–1972 = 100
1. The World Bank's Manufactures Unit Value (MUV) Index (US$) is used as a deflator.
Source: World Bank, www.worldbank.org/en/research/commodity-markets.

One might object to the above comparison, claiming that a broad metals and minerals index could easily hide exceptional price cases for individual products. We have therefore investigated the price histories for four of the most important individual metals and minerals materials; we found a rise from 1970–1972 to 2016–2018 of 66% for iron ore and 24% for copper, and a decline of 6% for nickel and 22% for aluminum. Looking at the entire, nearly 50-year period displayed in Figure 4.1, it is impossible to deny that oil's price performance has been extraordinary.

The figure additionally tracks the price evolution of coal (FOB in Australia) and gas (Title Transfer Facility price in Europe), the choice of quotations motivated by the difficulty to find representative price series over the extended period under scrutiny. Coal prices, it turns out, did not deviate markedly from the metals and minerals series, while gas prices rose much more strongly. There is a clear correlation between the prices of gas and oil, plausibly because gas price formation in Europe has been predominantly linked to the price of oil. Even so, the total gas price rise from 1970–1972 to 2016–2018, 204%, is 576% less than the price change attained by oil.

It is remarkable that oil was dominant among commodities even before its great price performance. In 1970–1972, when not much gas was traded internationally, oil represented an export value equal to the aggregate of the nine largest commodities next to oil (Radetzki, 1990a).

4.2 How Can the Extraordinary Oil Price Evolution Be Explained?

The price performance of oil over the past 50 years is so stupendous that it clearly warrants an explanation. The present section attends to this task. Discussion of several of the factors can be kept very brief since they are fully elaborated in later chapters of this book.

We begin by discarding three factors with little if any price impact. The first is the impact of the oil cartel. For reasons explained in Chapter 10, we do not believe that OPEC has had any significant impact on the oil price evolution. The second is depletion, a subject detailed in Chapter 8. We differ from the gospels of Peak Oil, and assert that oil resources in the ground are large and rich, so depletion cannot have affected prices in any significant way. In support, we point to the very high profitability of the oil industry throughout the period under review. To illustrate with a single example, in 2006 when oil prices hovered around US$70 per barrel, a detailed assessment set the total cost at the 90 percentile level of the world's conventional oil exploitation at US$17. At the time, US$17 was also the total cost of exploiting Canada's oil sands, while Iraqi and Saudi costs came in a range of US$1–US$3 (Aguilera et al., 2009). The third is the alleged rapid oil-consumption growth, since increases in demand have been far too moderate to generate a powerful price effect.

We see three factors in combination as responsible for oil's upward price push. The first, the inefficiencies of state-owned enterprises that have come to dominate the oil industry, is elaborated in Chapter 11, to which readers interested in the detail are directed. Here it suffices to assert that the inefficiencies have raised costs considerably and so forced prices upwards.

The second factor is excessive fiscal extraction which we refer to as government greed. It is a natural desire of governments to maximize tax revenues from natural resources. The main problem is that tax rates are typically raised dramatically when prices and profits shoot up temporarily, but are not scaled back when markets weaken. There is a collective failure to adopt a long view and base fiscal revenues on trends that assure long-run health to the industry. That myopia is exacerbated by the over-optimism of price forecasts most of the time. Such policy failures can spell disaster both to the government and to its budget as the industry shrinks under excessive public burdens, and its high profits have made oil a particular victim of the phenomenon.

A practice applied to the publicly owned oil producers in, for instance, Ecuador, Iran, Mexico and Peru (IEA, 2006) has been to credit the government budget with the entire surplus generated by the oil operations, and then to let the state-owned firm(s) apply for government funding to cover the needs for exploration and maintenance or expansion of production capacity. This practice plausibly has led to inefficiencies due to manipulated cost escalation and underreporting of profits to ensure that more financial resources remain under corporate control. Nevertheless, capacity expansion was likely slowed down or arrested, and in some cases even existing capacity was obliterated in consequence of lacking finance. Auty's (2003) description of Petroperu's noninvestment and shrinkage due to lack of finance is striking. By 1989, this state-owned oil company had been reduced to little more than a conduit for channeling oil revenues to the government, even at the expense of maintaining exploration and field development.

Between 1979 and 2005, years when global oil production capacity was employed to its full technical capability most of the time, output (and capacity) in the predominantly state-owned OPEC group had declined by 3%, while the rest of the world had expanded to produce 60% more (BP, annual). The absence of a more expansive investment drive to develop the exceptional resources in many OPEC countries could be seen as an element of cartel policy, though it is a fact that the group never applied restrictions on capacity growth. A more likely interpretation, in addition to the state-owned firms' incompetence in executing investments in capacity expansion, is that the government owners in most OPEC countries quickly raised spending for welfare programs and other social purposes after the 1970s oil price increases, and that the need to finance these programs required taxes that left the oil firms with little surplus for investments in capacity expansion.

Such destructive government behavior has in no way been exclusively applied to firms owned by the state. Policies reflecting greed have been exercised worldwide, and the privately owned industry has suffered equally from its effects. Two examples illustrate the "grab what you can now and forget about the longer term future" attitude.

The first one relates to the North Sea, where the combined output of Norway and the United Kingdom (the dominant producers) declined from 6.1 MBD in 2000 to 2.7 MBD in 2013 as increasing numbers of producers, including several international majors, exited the region. Accentuated depletion has undoubtedly made the North Sea less attractive, but tightening fiscal rules also played an important role for the production decline. In 2011, oil industry representatives in the United Kingdom complained that an exodus from the UK sector to the Norwegian one was impending as a result of a planned rise of the UK supplementary charge, originally set at 10% of profits in the early 2000s, to 32%. The industry's financial problems were exacerbated because the stiffened fiscal conditions made banks unwilling to provide investment finance (Chazan, 2011). So, how much more attractive were the fiscal conditions in the Norwegian sector? In 2013, Norway's corporate tax was reduced from 28% to 27%, but at the same time the special petrol tax was raised from 50% to 51%, making the total impositions on its North Sea sector unchanged at 78% of profits (Malkenes Hovland, 2013). Surely, the North Sea production decline since 2000 would have been far milder with less onerous fiscal conditions making it profitable for producers to invest in enhanced recovery and other technological subtleties to extract the substantial resources that remained. It is noted, though, that the North Sea has experienced a production revival since 2014, likely explained by slightly improved fiscal terms and increased industry efficiency in consequence of the sharp price decline in that year.

The second example comes from Russia (IEA, 2011). In 2010, the production cost of an undeveloped field in Siberia was assessed at US$12 per barrel, with an additional US$6 for transport to the export harbor, a seemingly highly attractive deal, given prices at US$79. But with a Russian mineral tax of US$14 and export tax of US$40, a surplus of only US$8 remained – insufficient to warrant the investment.

Little is publicly known about the highly secretive conditions offered to foreign oil firms for exploitation contracts in Middle East countries with exceedingly cheap reserves, but scattered information that has leaked out suggests the prospects for after-tax profits are as meager as suggested by the North Sea and Russian examples above.

Ambitious strategies to assure balance in the government budget when applied to the highly profitable oil industry have functioned like an international cartel, constraining capacity growth and long-run supply. The impact on prices has undoubtedly been far stronger than that of OPEC quotas and maybe of equal magnitude as the inefficiencies characterizing state-owned enterprises. Policy decisions to extract a maximum of the mineral rent and state-enterprise shortcomings in combination, then, emerge as important factors behind the extraordinary oil price developments.

We refer to the final and in our view most important factor explaining the extraordinary oil price developments as an aspect of the resource curse. The resource curse, according to its proponents (Auty, 2001; Gylfason, 2002; Sachs and Warner, 2001), is a malaise afflicting economies heavily dependent on the fossil fuels and minerals sectors. Such dependency, it is claimed, slows economic growth and social progress compared with that of other countries at corresponding levels of economic development. This finding is particularly relevant to oil, since high dependence on oil in a national economy is much more common than dependence on any other material, given the exceptional value of oil production and oil trade among commodities.

Our purpose is not to take sides in the debate about the impact of the resource curse on economic growth. Instead, we note with fascination that quite a number of nations that are heavily dependent on oil exploitation suffer from debilitating conflicts – both internal and international, and frequently with a military element – as different interest groups or nations position themselves to appropriate the oil rent. This is the aspect of the resource curse that we want to highlight in the following analysis. While individual circumstances will differ in that conflicts will also have religious, cultural and political elements, we assert that oil dominance is a common feature in most and note that the fight is importantly about the distribution of the high rents generated by its exploitation.

We have argued that, given the high profitability of oil output, the production installations in the oil industry worldwide have been used at their full technical capacity most of the time. We have also noted the absence of constraint on capacity expansion in OPEC's policy arsenal. These statements greatly facilitate the analysis which follows.

An enduring fall in output/capacity can be brought about by either of two circumstances. First, it can be caused by a combination of declines due to (a) constraints in the oil fields under exploitation that cannot be fully countered by additional investments, and (b) limitations in the resource wealth of the country under consideration that prevent the replacement of fields in decline by new ones. Both represent the classic case of depletion, like the one that occurred in the North Sea after 2000. The second cause for falling output/capacity could be circumstances above ground, for example strikes, graft, confrontational politics and military conflicts. The latter in our vocabulary are all manifestations of the resource curse that constrain the use of existing production facilities and prevent the establishment of new ones despite their prospective profitability. Capacity deteriorates quite fast if it is not looked after properly and invigorated through regular reinvestments, and such care will be difficult to maintain during disturbances like the ones just listed.

Our method of identifying and quantifying the impact of the resource curse on capacity evolution is crude and simplistic in that it is selective regarding countries and disregards many factors of potential significance. Nevertheless, we believe that the emerging orders of magnitude are reasonable.

We begin by only considering countries richly endowed with oil wealth in the ground, using the reserves/production ratio as a measurement tool, to exclude depletion as a factor plausibly limiting production. Among those countries we select five with high past production that has spectacularly declined in more recent times. We posit that in the absence of above-ground problems caused directly or indirectly by conflicts over the oil rent output would have been at least maintained, or more probably expanded, given the high oil prices and the profitability of the industry. We briefly point to the conflicts likely to have caused the production fall. Finally, we speculate about achievable output in the absence of conflict and compare it to actual current output, contending that the resource curse explains the difference.

Most of the above is contained in Table 4.3, but to complete the picture the conflicts need to be specified. This is easily done. Iran fought an extended and debilitating war in the 1980s against Iraq and has subsequently been subject to sanctions for trespassing international rules of behavior. Kuwait was an ally with Iraq during the war against Iran, but in 1990 the former ally attacked Kuwait and a bloody war, known as the Gulf War, that lasted for about six months followed. Libya's

Table 4.3 *Resource curse and oil production*

	Maximum production		Production 2018		Hypothetical production 2018
		Volume, MBD	Volume, MBD	Reduction from maximum, MBD and %	(assuming 1.5% annual growth from earlier peak, MBD and % rise)
	Year				
Iran	1974	6.1	4.7	1.4 MBD, 23%	11.7 MBD, 92%
Kuwait	1971	3.3	3.0	0.3 MBD, 9%	6.6 MBD, 100%
Libya	1969	3.4	1.0	2.4 MBD, 71%	7.1 MBD, 109%
Nigeria	1974	2.3	2.0	0.3 MBD, 13%	4.4 MBD, 91%
Venezuela	1970	3.8	1.5	2.3 MBD, 61%	7.8 MBD, 105%
Total		18.9	12.2	6.7 MBD, 35%	37.6 MBD, 99%

Source: BP (annual); IEA (monthly).

production under Gaddafi and after has been continuously plagued by international sanctions in response to his erratic rule and by internal warfare, while output in both Nigeria and Venezuela has suffered from long-term ad hoc policies related to resource nationalism that created corruption and uncomfortable uncertainties for investors. It is unlikely, in our view, that any of these events would have taken place in the absence of the five nations' economies being dominated by oil.

The results of our exercise, presented in Table 4.3, are stunning. The loss of output from the maximum year until the present, 6.7 MBD, equals almost half of overall consumption in Europe! The price impact of a production loss of such magnitude must indeed have been great. And yet, the table's last column presents even more dazzling results. In the absence of the enmities and conflicts that form the essence of the resource curse, one would have expected continuous output expansion. We assess the hypothetical current output that would arise from a modest annual 1.5% production increase from the earlier peak. Current production for the five countries would then hypothetically work out at 37.6 MBD instead of the actual 12.2 MBD, a change of more than 25 MBD! Is such a path of output expansion at all credible? We claim that it is. The hypothetical increases recorded for the five countries exceeds 100% for only two of the five countries. Compare that with the production rise between 1970 and 2018 for Brazil (1500%), Colombia (280%), Canada (250%), Mexico (325%) and Saudi Arabia (220%).

The analyses of the present section help identify the major causes of the extraordinary rise in oil prices since the beginning of the 1970s. The debilitating, capacity-destroying effect of the resource curse dominates the price impact, but the inefficiency of state ownership and government greed in combination have also constrained production capacity, and so contributed to the price rise.

4.3 The Coming Fossil Fuel Abundance[1]

A development that emerged about 2005 has since profoundly changed the US energy map, with global implications. We refer to the shale

---

[1] As production of this manuscript was being finalized in mid-April 2020, the international oil market was exposed to an historically unique upheaval caused by the Corona crisis. It is too late to present a proper analysis of the market upheaval, but we feel that this edition of our *Handbook* deserves at least a mention of what happened. The transport sector worldwide was immobilized

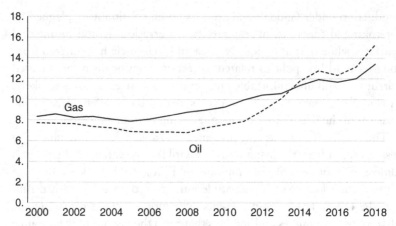

Figure 4.2 US natural gas and oil production (MBOE/D) *Source*: BP (annual).

revolution, where advances in horizontal drilling and fracking have made it possible to exploit a vast resource wealth that was not economically accessible with conventional production methods (see e.g. Aguilera and Radetzki, 2016). Though a variety of resource categories are involved, we follow the emerging convention of referring to them all as shale deposits.

Figure 4.2 shows the revolution's impact since the beginning of the century on gas and oil production in the USA. When considering the content of the figure, an essential perspective is that both gas and oil production in the country were steadily falling from their peaks in the early 1970s and virtually all the production increases shown are due to the revolution. The turnaround in gas occurred in 2005, and by 2018 output had risen by some 70%. The trend shift in oil came about three years later, but the impact was stronger: between 2008 and 2018 output increased by 125%. Interesting to note is that in 2017 the USA

---

[1] by the closure of numerous countries in an effort to limit the spread of the virus. An extraordinary abundance suddenly emerged as the demand for oil for transport vanished. Assessments of the demand shortfall suggest 30 MBD out of a global total of 100 MBD. The suddenness and size of the demand collapse made it impossible to restore market balance by reduced supply. Prices therefore shrank dramatically, temporarily even to negative numbers for the WTI quotation in the USA, where storage facilities were overfilled. The market disturbance is likely to be short-lived; the demand for oil for transport will reemerge as the pandemic subsides and countries open up. We expect substantial structural change on the supply side, however, due to widespread bankruptcies among producers.

surpassed Saudi Arabia as the world's largest producer of oil, a change that had occurred already – in 2011 – for natural gas, when production in the USA outweighed the production in Russia.

On account of high transport costs, gas is traded in relatively shielded regional markets, and the added US supply had a strong price impact: prices in the USA fell from an average of US$7.4/mBTU in the five-year period 2004–2008 to below US$4 in subsequent years. Increased oil production had no perceptible price impact on the integrated global market, and high prices persisted until the second half of 2014, when they halved from above US$100 per barrel to US$50 or below at the end of the year. Rising US supplies finally made themselves felt globally, but several other factors also contributed to the price collapse.

In the mid-2010s most US shale gas and shale oil output was economically viable at the emerging price levels. One characteristic of this infant industry has been an extraordinarily fast productivity improvement that continuously suppresses costs. Wells require ever less time to be drilled, the area covered by the horizontal extensions increases in size, while the output from each drill is incessantly expanded. Continued production increases are therefore viable in the USA and elsewhere (see below) so long as prices stay above US$2.5/mBTU at the production site for gas and US$40 per barrel for oil. In a projection for the USA that we consider overly pessimistic, the Energy Information Administration (EIA, annual, 2014) foresees a steady gas output rise of 22% between 2014 and 2035, but a peak in shale oil output already in 2020 at a level 12% above 2014.

Environmental concerns have been raised by the shale operations, and in particular by the role of fracking. Gas leakage, contamination and overuse of water, earthquakes and land degradation have been reported as the most important environmental detriments. These problems result in great measure from the "infant" character of the industry and from the "wild west" attitudes of the multitude of risk-prone firms active in the sector. We expect many of the hazards to be overcome as the industry matures and is subjected to public regulation that aims at overcoming existing hazards. There is little reason to believe that shale exploitation will involve more serious environmental impacts in the longer run than conventional exploitation of gas and oil.

While the environment has clearly been harmed by shale-related activities, the shale revolution has yielded extensive benefits to the US economy, with values far greater than the environmental damage. A study by IHS (2012) demonstrates for shale gas and oil in combination in that year investments of US$87 billion, direct and indirect employment of 1.75 million (representing 1.3% of total US employment in that year), fiscal revenues of US$31 million and a strong improvement in the current account, with shrinking oil imports and rosy prospects for exports of LNG. The lower gas prices have also strongly improved the international competitiveness of US producers of petrochemicals, fertilizer and steel, industries that make heavy use of gas. In 2014, IHS estimated an even stronger economic impact, as they found that shale oil and natural gas activities generated over two million jobs (including direct, indirect and induced), contributed over US$75 billion in fiscal revenues and added more than US$283 billion to US GDP (IHS, 2018). The oil price downturn in 2014 caused a sharp slowdown in investments, but after 2016 capital spending has bounced back as oil prices recovered somewhat and costs were reduced due to stricter cost controls and ensuing increased productivity. Thus, IHS paints an optimistic (and in our view realistic) view of future US shale industry achievements.

Several factors explain the vanguard position of the USA in the shale revolution. A long history of large-scale gas and oil exploitation has guaranteed technological prominence and a physical infrastructure that could be easily adapted to the needs of shale gas and oil. The general institutional infrastructure, needed to promote innovative entrepreneurial activities, is internationally prominent and can be readily applied to shale developments. Sparse population has reduced environmental sensitivities. US legislation that grants the landholder ownership rights to what is underground, a rule not applied by many other countries, has been another facilitating circumstance. The country's long tradition of small, adventurous exploration and production enterprises helped to speed up the revolutionary process, while the bureaucratic energy giants were late in jumping on the bandwagon. All these features help to explain why the USA took a lead in the revolution and why most other countries are lagging far behind.

But since the USA is not geologically unique the technologies of horizontal drilling and fracking are easily transferred across borders, and since shale exploitation offers important economic benefits its international spread appears to be unavoidable.

Global shale gas resources are poorly known, those of shale oil even less. The world possesses a global conventional, proved gas reserve stock of 1160 billion BOE, enough to cover 51 years of production, based on production in 2018 (BP, annual). A relatively recent study (EIA, 2013, p 2) of extractable shale gas resources covering 41 countries yields a total of 1390 billion BOE – somewhat higher than world gas reserves, though one should be clear about the difference between reserves and resources. The resources have a wide geographical spread, with China accounting for 15%, Argentina 11%, Algeria 10%, USA 9%, Canada 8%, Mexico 7%, Australia 6%, South Africa 5% and Russia 4%. Brazil, Venezuela, Poland, France and Libya are other countries with significant resource potential.

The same EIA study assesses the recoverable shale oil resources at 343 billion barrels, with Russia accounting for the largest share at 22%, followed by USA 17%, China 9%, Argentina 8%, Libya 8% and Venezuela and Mexico with 4% each. The shale oil resources identified by this study correspond to no more than one fifth of conventional oil reserves. The latter amount to 1700 billion BOE, sufficient to cover some 53 years of 2019 total extraction.

Two circumstances must be emphasized when the shale gas and oil resource numbers of the EIA study are considered. The first is the study's limited geographical coverage. Neither the Middle East nor the Caspian basin is included, so the true global quantities are bound to be considerably higher. IEA (annual, 2012), for instance, estimates the figure for global extractable shale gas at 2150 billion BOE (55% above the EIA figure), while IEA (annual, 2013) appraises extractable shale oil in the world within a range of up to 600 billion BOE (75% above the EIA figure). The IEA studies, however, do not provide national subdivisions of their numbers. The second consideration is that the share of the USA, a country which has been reasonably explored, is bound to shrink as exploration in the rest of the world gains speed.

With all the numbers collated in the present section, let us now perform a speculative, but in our opinion reasonable, thought experiment to gauge the implications for the global oil and gas markets from a maturing and globally spread shale revolution. Our starting points comprise the spectacular US ten-year achievements up to 2018, where the country's oil output rose by 125% or 8500 million barrels per day oil equivalent (MBDOE) and that of gas by 52% or 5600 MBDOE.

Virtually all of the fossil fuel rise was due to shale extraction, and we note that the country is in no way unique in its geological endowment of these resources. Consider now the quantitative consequences of a global shale-revolution spread, where, pessimistically, the rest of the world will need twice as long and attain only one half of the US achievements. With the rest of the world starting out at 79.4 MBDOE for oil (global production of 94.7 minus US production of 15.3) and 59.4 MBDOE for gas (global production of 75.6 minus US production of 16.2), our pessimistic assumptions lead to a rest-of-the-world production *rise* by 2038 of almost 50 MBDOE for oil and more than 15 MBDOE for gas. The 65 MBDOE total can be compared to the global output rise of 48 MBDOE that took place in the 20-year period between 1998 and 2018. Any further production rises in the USA should be added to the future global total.

Another revolution is seeing the light of the day, but news about it has not yet reached the media (Aguilera and Radetzki, 2016). This is the application of fracking and horizontal drilling to old and tired oil deposits to squeeze out some of the oil remaining in the well, much like standard enhanced recovery efforts, though the new technology involves lower costs and improved efficiency. The global impact of this revolution is even more speculative than the shale numbers presented in this section, but Aguilera and Radetzki's analyses point to a plausible contribution to the global oil market of some further 20 MBDOE.

Obviously, there will be a lot more oil and gas in the world as the two revolutions spread and mature, and the sources of supply for oil and gas will be more diversified than in the 2010s. Market manipulation by producers and the use of the oil weapon for political gains will be harder to apply in the emerging market conditions, but new constellations may well appear, as demonstrated by the recent strategic partnership between OPEC and Russia. Prices in the long run are unlikely to prevail above total production costs of the new supply, maybe around US$40 per barrel for oil and US$2.5/mBTU at the production site for gas. The calmer markets and the lower prices and profits will hopefully subdue the fights over oil rent and so reduce the detriments of the destructive resource curse.

Coal will face aggressive competition from cheaper and more ample supplies of gas and oil. Coal prices will decline as its producers fight to restrict market shrinkage. Even so, gas is likely to replace coal as a dominant fuel in electricity, as has already happened in the USA, and this global shift will reduce carbon dioxide emissions from the power sector. Renewables, too, will face survival threats from low-priced fossil fuels, so the cost of any climate policy to assure their maintenance and growth will have to rise to finance increasing subsidies.

4.4 Future Expectations for Renewables and Climate Policy

The emerging scenario we have painted, with increasingly ample and cheap fossil fuels as the shale and conventional revolutions mature, could be nipped in the bud by a deep and energetic climate policy that restricts the use of fossil fuels or by imposing heavy global taxes on emissions. Both could result in a large-scale cut in fossil consumption. The additional supply will then simply not be needed, and much of the stock of existing fossil fuel reserves, along with their production installations will become useless, stranded assets.

When considering the prospect of such a development occurring, it is essential to explore the likelihood of a deep climate policy being adopted. Developments in recent years point in different directions. First, we have quite strong reports from the Intergovernmental Panel on Climate Change estimating that human-induced warming reached about 1°C in 2017 (above preindustrial levels). Climate change is also frequently debated in media, and the Paris Agreement, signed in 2016 within the UN's Framework Convention on Climate Change, is the first global agreement on climate change. The agreement was a clear statement that many nations around the world are aware that actions toward climate change, reducing the use of fossil fuels, need to be taken. The agreement implies that each member has separately negotiated emission targets and is required to report its emissions to the UN.

Furthermore, the 2018 economics Nobel laureate, William Nordhaus, earned the Nobel Prize mainly for the development of the so-called DICE model, which integrates climate change and economic growth. A key conclusion from the model's applications is that a global carbon tax is the most economically efficient way to reduce carbon dioxide emissions. How likely is it then that a global carbon tax will be imposed? Recent analyses published in *Nature* find public support for such a policy (through a survey sent to citizens in Australia, India, South Africa, the United Kingdom and the USA), at least if revenues from the tax are redistributed (Carattini et al., 2019).

However, a second strand of development is questioning whether a global tax on carbon will be realized any time soon. For example, in June 2017 the US president Donald Trump announced that the USA will withdraw from the Paris Agreement, as he sees the agreement as deeply unfair to the USA. However, the withdrawal will not be effective until November 2020 at the earliest, after the US election, but the action does illustrate the political difficulty in imposing a global tax.

It should also be stressed that the transition needed to limit climate change is currently on the way in many sectors and regions around the world. The political, economic, social and technical capability of solar energy, wind energy and electricity-storage technologies has developed considerably over the last decade. Electrification, hydrogen, bio-based fuels and carbon dioxide capture, utilization and storage techniques could significantly reduce carbon emissions in energy-intensive industries. However, these options are still limited by institutional, economic and technical constraints.

Clearly, neither the main public analysts, such as the IEA or EIA, the major oil companies, such as Exxon or BP, nor the investors in future fossil production believe in a sharp decrease in fossil fuels in the medium term. All of them project continued expansion in fossil usage, even though they recognize and expect that the use of renewables will increase in the future. Without articulating any value judgment on whether a fossil fuel intensive world is preferable or not, we express agreement with the view that the introduction of a deep climate policy is unlikely any time soon and that fossil fuels are here to stay in dominant roles for the foreseeable future.

5 | Price Formation and Price Trends in Commodities

5.1 Factors Determining Price Levels in the Short and the Long Run

Commodity prices in unregulated competitive markets are basically determined at each point in time by the intersection of the short-run supply and demand curves.[1] In Figure 5.1 the price will settle at P_1 if S and D_1 represent the supply and demand schedules, respectively. There is nothing special about commodities in this regard; all unregulated competitive markets behave in this way. In the short run, the capacity to produce (or the area of land under a specific crop cultivation) is given, and the supply schedule depicts the variable cost levels in existing production units, ranked in ascending order. Natural advantage, managerial efficiency or a high proportion of fixed costs will yield low variable cost levels.

Production will continue at full capacity so long as the variable costs are covered by price. A rise in demand, demonstrated in Figure 5.1 by a rightward shift of the demand schedule from D_1 to D_2, will require the employment of additional production units, and their higher variable costs will push up the price to P_2. Such a shift could be caused by secular economic growth from one year to the next, by a cyclical upturn in business conditions that increases demand to satisfy current consumption as well as user inventories or simply by the expectation, rational or irrational, of an impending price increase, which would result in a surge in inventory demand for speculative purposes.

A similar upward push in price will result from a temporary leftward shift in the supply schedule (not shown in Figure 5.1), as part of the existing supply capacity becomes unavailable due to, for example,

---

[1] The following discussion draws heavily on Tilton (2006).

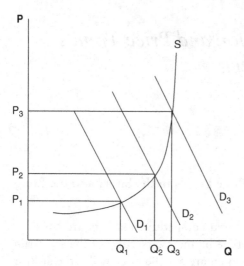

Figure 5.1 Short-run price determination

a pest- or weather-related harvest failure, or a strike or accident immobilizing an important mine or mineral-processing installation.

At low levels of capacity utilization, the short-run supply schedule tends to be relatively flat and the price elasticity of supply, defined as the percentage change of supply in response to a 1% change in price, will be high. As full capacity utilization is approached, the supply schedule will become increasingly steep and the price elasticity of supply will decline. Additional increases in demand will then be harder to accommodate by rising output, so they will result in accentuated price reactions, as shown by the move of the demand schedule from D_2 to D_3. At full capacity, the short-run supply schedule becomes vertical.

The high prices that typically arise when existing production capacity is fully used will strengthen the incentives to invest in capacity expansion. The capacity additions that will eventually emerge will extend the new short-run supply schedule to the right. Capacity change, however, is part of the long-run price determination, for the long run is defined as a period long enough to permit variations in capacity.

Figure 5.2 provides a gist of the long-run analysis. As in the short run, long-run price is determined by the intersection between the supply and demand schedules. The long-run supply schedule depicts the average total cost of marginal units at different levels of global

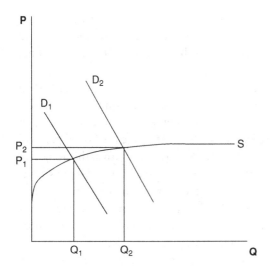

Figure 5.2 Long-run price determination

output, as capacity is allowed to vary over time, again ranked in ascending order. This curve rises at first, reflecting the limited mineral deposits and agricultural land with exceptionally low costs, but then levels off and becomes relatively flat. The rationale for the flattening is that the economically exploitable agricultural and mineral resource wealth tends to become more ample at higher cost levels.

Juxtaposed against the possible cost rise as long-run demand is expanded is a tendency for the entire supply curve to shift downward due to cost-reducing technological progress. The two forces, the rising cost as more expensive marginal resources have to be used to satisfy growing demand and cost-reducing technological progress that shifts the entire curve downwards, could well cancel each other out, making supply expansion possible at unchanged cost. History over the past 100 years suggests that technological progress has had the upper hand most of the time, so that increasing quantities could be exploited at a falling cost in the marginal project. This is reflected starkly in the long-run price trends discussed in Section 5.3 below. Furthermore, at a high enough price, the availability of a backstop resource is conceivable, permitting unlimited supply at unchanged cost. Note that a flat supply curve implies that the equilibrium price level will remain unchanged irrespective of the pace of demand growth since the long-run nature of the curve entails adequate time for capacity adjustments. Nevertheless, the supply curve in Figure 5.2 assumes, perhaps pessimistically, that a certain degree of economic depletion does occur, so that costs and prices will rise as volumes increase with economic growth over time. The depletion issues are dealt with in Chapter 8.

Actual price setting occurs only in the short run, as described in Figure 5.1. The long-run price, in contrast, is a conceptual artifice, indicating the level toward which market price is moving at each point in time. The intensity of investments in capacity expansion explains why this is so. If the market price is above the long-run equilibrium, like P_3 in Figure 5.1, investments will be strongly stimulated and the expanded capacity will in time result in a decline of prices toward the long-run equilibrium level. A boost in investments will tend to raise costs, especially if such a boost is widespread in the resource industries. This is what happened during the latest commodity boom (see Chapter 6), importantly because investment inputs became scarce and their prices were bid up. It must be underlined that this cost increase is temporary. Costs will decline as the input supply is adjusted to the higher demand growth, or as the investment bonanza subdues.

Conversely, if the market price is below the long-run equilibrium, like P_1 in Figure 5.1, investments will be restrained, capacity will expand by less than demand and prices will rise toward the equilibrium level. The greater the discrepancy between the market price and the long-run equilibrium price, the stronger the likely investor reaction and the more powerful the subsequent price adjustment.

Though there will always be market forces driving actual prices toward the long-run equilibrium, that equilibrium is unlikely ever to be reached. In practice, as discussed in Section 5.2, it is even uncertain if the level can be unequivocally identified.

More complex price determination processes are involved when production results in the output of more than one commodity.[2] This is frequently the case in the exploitation of polymetallic ore bodies (copper and nickel, lead and zinc, gold and copper), but also in agriculture where hides are produced along with beef and wool along with mutton. Where one commodity dominates the revenue, it will tend to be produced on its own merit, irrespective of the price of the byproduct. Silver is predominantly supplied as a byproduct in non-ferrous base

---

[2] Most microeconomic textbooks can be consulted for a formal treatment of joint production, e.g. Varian (2014).

metals production and its price tends to be depressed by excessive availability when demand and price for the base metals is booming. Palladium presents a similar case, because it is a byproduct in South African platinum production *and* in Russian production of nickel, and hence dependent on the conjuncture of the South African and Russian producers.

Monopolistic pricing is sometimes rewarding and is practiced in international commodity markets. Chapter 10 analyzes in some detail the price-setting issues that are involved. At this stage it suffices to note that a complete monopoly rarely, if ever, occurs in the international markets for primary materials, so formal analysis of pure monopoly has little relevance. What occurs is jointly implemented and crudely determined cuts in capacity utilization by the leading producers in markets where such action is believed to result in higher aggregate revenue and profits. In terms of Figure 5.1, an ocular inspection suffices to reveal that when demand equals D_2 and the competitively supplied quantity is Q_2 at price P_2, it would pay, at least in the short run and in total revenue terms, to reduce supply to Q_1 in order to reap price P_3.

5.2 The Blurred Nature and Instability of the Short-Run Supply Schedule

The neat conclusions from the analysis in the preceding section may be a useful guiding rod to price analysis, but its precision does not apply in practice. In the real world both demand and supply schedules will appear as ill-defined and unstable broad bands, making it hard to use them for price determination. The following discussion focuses on the short-run supply schedule and tries to explain why it is blurred and unstable, but it should be emphasized that a similar imprecision applies to the demand schedule too.

Figure 5.3 depicts short-run copper supply curves for 2004 and 2007 for profit-maximizing producers in the format regularly employed by resource industries and their consultants. The horizontal distances on the curve represent the production capacity of individual plants, while the vertical position indicates the average variable costs of production in each (cash costs, in industry parlance) in ascending order. A price decline should lead to production contraction until the lower price fully covers the variable costs. Yet, it is a common experience that production will persevere at higher levels resulting in losses for the units where

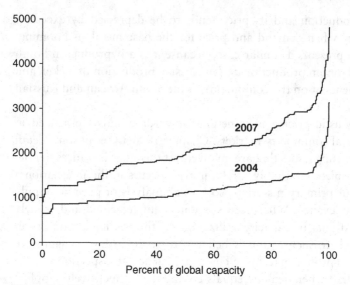

Figure 5.3 World copper variable costs in 2004 and 2007 (nominal US$/ton)
Source: Humphreys (2015), based on data generated by Wood Mackenzie.

variable costs exceed the market price. A number of reasons can explain this counterintuitive behavior.

One important explanation is that closure and subsequent reopening involve a cost. If the price depression is deemed to be short, it may be more economical to suffer temporary losses from continued operations than to incur the costs resulting from closure. There is a related ambiguity about the distinction between variable costs, which are part of the short-run supply schedule, and fixed costs, which are not, and here too the time horizon is of consequence. The cost of labor, for example, is typically assumed to vary with the level of operations but in a very short time perspective the firm may not be able to sack workers, so this cost category becomes fixed. A similar argument applies to the servicing of installations, ordinarily a variable cost category, but avoidable and hence fixed in the very short run. The greater the proportion of costs classed in the fixed category, the lesser will be the variable costs and the lower will be the supply schedule, making it economical to continue operations at depressed prices. None of the behaviors discussed so far is counter to profit maximization.

Public policy, too, may have an impact on production maintenance when prices are low. Policy actions can either shift the supply schedule downwards or induce deviations from profit-maximizing behavior. Reductions of fiscal dues, outright subsidies or devaluation of the currency, motivated by the desire to avoid production cuts, will all contribute to the public goal by instantly reducing the level of the supply schedule. Alternatively, public policy may take the form of social or political pressure exerted by public bodies on private firms to continue operations even when maintenance of production is not dictated by the profit motive.

Deviations from the profit maximization norm by the firms themselves provide a further possible explanation for continuing loss-making operations. In some firms, return on capital is only one of several criteria that guide operations. This is true of the many state-owned corporations in the minerals and energy sectors (see Chapter 11), and in the agricultural cooperatives that process raw materials supplied by their members. Goals other than profit maximization (e.g. maintenance of employment) could then motivate continued operations even when price does not fully cover operating costs. Even in firms that profess a profit-maximization goal, such deviations could nevertheless result from the managers' short-run urge to secure their own jobs.

Standard microeconomic analysis usually assumes that costs are determined independent of price, by factors such as technology, quality of the exploited land or mineral resource and scale economies, and that costs, in turn, determine prices. This view must now be qualified, for, as posited by the behavioral theory of the firm (Cyert and March, 1992), prices have a substantial influence on costs. High price and profit levels tend to push up costs and increase the organizational slack. Conversely, low prices and profits induce pressures to reduce costs.

Price developments, then, often provide a more credible reason than depletion for the evolution of cost trends. The downward real-price trend for copper from the early 1970s until the early years of the twenty-first century constituted a survival threat to many producers, and forced them to draconian measures to cut slack that had been built up during a preceding high-price period. A substantial part of the cost decreases was based on pushes for technical advance and improved managerial efficiency, factors that had been less than fully utilized while prices were high. The eventual closure of production units that were not successful in reducing their costs contributed further to the industry's cost decline. During the 1980s, the entire supply schedule for copper in the nonsocialist world declined dramatically (Crowson, 1987). The efforts of the US producers yielded particularly impressive results (Tilton and Landsberg, 1999).

Copper is not exceptional. Similar stories could be told for many other commodities. A high price relaxes the cost discipline, so costs will tend to rise. The survival threats imposed by a low price work wonders on the producers' cost performance.

Cost pressures are not alone in cementing the causal relationship between prices and costs. Rising prices make it economical to bring high-cost operations into production, while when prices fall high-cost operations are closed; all of which causes costs to go up and down as prices go up and down.[3]

The discussion in this section has brought out a number of reasons for the blurred nature of the supply schedule. We have shown that categorizations of costs tend to be fuzzy, many suppliers do not pursue profit maximization as their sole goal, public policy can alter the level of the supply curve, and price changes have an impact on costs. For all these reasons, the traditional supply schedule will be ambiguous within wide ranges. One has to proceed with great caution when using it for determining volumes supplied and prices.

5.3 Price Fluctuations in Commodity Markets and Long-Run Price Trends

Short-Run Instability

"Rapid, unexpected and often large movements in commodity prices are an important feature of their behavior" (Cashin and McDermott, 2002). This is a well-known and often-repeated statement, as is the observation that the prices of manufactures tend to be more stable. The phenomenon is regularly referred to as price volatility, and it has been observed over very long periods of time. Thus, Jacks et al. (2011) present empirical evidence from 1700 to the present revealing that commodity prices have always been more volatile than those of

---

[3] Tilton (2014) provides a detailed and fascinating analysis of how mineral production costs are affected by prices in both upward and downward directions.

manufactures. The same study finds that commodity price volatility has not increased over the long run, rather globalization and world market integration have led to less volatility compared to situations of economic isolation.

Illustrations of volatility, that is violent commodity price gyrations, up as well as down, over relatively short time spans for individual commodities are easy to produce (UNCTAD Commodity Statistics Online and World Bank Commodity Price Data; all prices are annual averages in US$ per ton): coffee (mild arabicas) went down, up, down, up and down again from 782 in 1963, 5173 in 1977, 1403 in 1992, 4385 in 1997, 1440 in 2002 and 6257 in 2011 to 3078 in 2018. Palm kernel oil prices fluctuated: 433 in 1976, 1049 in 1979, 458 in 1982, 1037 in 1984, 305 in 2001, 1654 in 2011 and 927 in 2018. Rubber prices rose from 892 in 1993 to 1648 in 1995 and then fell to 613 in 2001, they then rose again during the latest commodity boom to 4795 in 2011. Nickel prices varied from 4870 in 1987, 13300 in 1989, 5293 in 1993, an astonishing 37 230 in 2007 and down to 9595 in 2016. Copper prices varied from 1374 in 1986 to 2847 in 1989, they settled at 1559 in 2002 and then exploded to 8828 in 2011. The causes and effects of commodity booms, the phenomenon of sharp and simultaneous increases in the real prices of a broad group of commodities, is elaborated in some detail in Chapter 6.

It is equally easy to point to the main reasons for the sharp individual commodity price instability. The price elasticity of demand for raw materials is usually quite low, given that the cost of such materials typically constitutes a small proportion of the finished product price. The price of bread and car batteries will be only marginally affected by a doubling of the wheat and lead prices, so the demand for these raw-materials-absorbing finished products will remain by and large unchanged. Furthermore, a given increase in demand for finished products will regularly give rise to a more accentuated increase in the demand for the raw materials employed, as the desired inventories are augmented from the finished-product marketing stage back through the production chain. Say that there are three downstream stages in the production chain beyond the raw materials supplier, and that the desired inventories at each stage equal half of one period's sales. A 5% increase in the finished product demand will then result in an almost 17% increase in the demand for the raw material, due to the cascade of inventory adjustment at each production stage to the higher finished-product demand.[4] *Ceteris paribus*, this will result in a much larger price adjustment for the raw material than for the finished product. The same applies in reverse when the finished-product demand declines.

Fluctuations in supply, too, contribute to price instability. Weather is an important cause of supply variations in agricultural crops, even though geographical diversification of production in the twenty-first century has reduced the importance of this factor (IMF, biannual, 2006). Mineral supply may shrink due to strikes or technical accidents, but such failures would have to be widespread to significantly dent the global total. As noted in Section 5.2, the price elasticity of supply would also be quite low, at least when capacity is fully utilized, which is normally the case in competitive markets. With the exception of annual crops, it takes an extended period of time to alter the supply capacity, and in the meantime even small variations in demand will result in sharp changes in price.

The above, then, are the main explanations for the short-run price instability observed in most primary commodity markets. Such instability is believed to cause serious macroeconomic and other problems to countries that are heavily dependent on exporting one or a few commodities, and the paragraphs that follow briefly describe these problems and their common remedies.

A high level of volatility, with sharp movements up or down in the prices of individual commodities, is a concern as the price becomes increasingly unpredictable. And yet, the price level is an important signal both for producers to alter their output and for consumers to adjust their usage, and at the macro level in the determination of export revenue or import costs. When there are large movements in prices this process is hindered, as future prices become more uncertain. Pindyck (2004) thoughtfully argues that volatility affects prices, production and inventories in two ways. First, when prices move up, the uncertainty of what will come next leads to a buildup of inventories and this accentuates the price rise. Second, volatility typically reduces production levels by an increase in the opportunity cost of operating options.

---

[4] Stage 4, handling the finished product, raises its purchases by a total of 7.5% (5%, for sales, 2.5% for inventory increase). Stage 3 raises its purchases by 11.25% (7.5% for sales, 3.75% for inventory increase). Stage 2 raises its purchases by 16.9% (11.25% for sales, 5.65% for inventory increase), so the demand for the raw material at stage 1 is increased by 16.9%.

Many researchers express concern about the relationship between price volatility and economic growth. This relation is well established in the literature. Ramey and Ramey (1995) find for 92 developing and developed countries, between 1962 and 1985, that government spending and commodity price volatility are negatively related, and that countries exposed to higher volatility also experience lower economic growth. This is especially noticeable in nations heavily dependent on the production and export of one or a few commodities. Numerous other studies have noticed the negative relationship between volatility and growth performance, for instance Acemoglu et al. (2003), Fatás and Mihov (2005), Hnatkovska and Loayza (2005), Loayza et al. (2007), van Eyden et al. (2019) and Williamson (2008) .

In more general terms, volatile commodity prices cause problems of unpredictability that complicate, for example, financial planning and environmental management for the governments of commodity-producing countries. Thus, volatility often results in costly and wasteful suboptimal production and investment decisions. A common recommendation by the international community to resource-rich countries is that they should diversify their production and exports in order to avoid the problems.

The Long-Run Price Trends

Attempts to track long-run price trends for commodities in international trade have a long and confusing tradition. To be meaningful, the nominal price series have to be converted into real ones, expressed in constant money. A number of approaches can be employed to make such conversions, for example: (a) the implicit deflator of the GDPs for the OECD area as a whole, expressed in US dollars; (b) the implicit GDP deflator for the USA; (c) the US producer price index; (d) the US consumer price index; and (e) the UN's index of dollar prices of manufactured exports (CIF) from major industrialized countries (the MUV index). Each of these deflators has its advantages and shortcomings and the real price developments can differ substantially depending on which is used. One has to think carefully about the purpose of the real price series before choosing the deflator.

We have a preference for the MUV index and employ it throughout the book in our own attempts to determine commodity prices in constant money, a task of central significance in this chapter and in the discussions of commodity booms that follow in Chapter 6.

The MUV index (United Nations, monthly) seems to be more appropriate than the other indices listed above for deriving constant dollar prices of commodities. Simply expressed, it provides the (inverse) size of the basket of manufactured exports that could be obtained for US$1 at different times. It overcomes the problem of exchange-rate changes not immediately reflected in export prices that would arise with the use of a national price index. And since it relates to manufactured exports, it provides an appropriate counterpoint for measuring the price changes of raw materials in international trade. In the 1950s and 1960s, the World Bank, among others, referred to the MUV index as an "index of international inflation." In the twenty-first century the index has become less representative of global inflation trends, since it does not cover the increasingly important manufactured exports from non-OECD countries, nor prices of the sharply expanding trade in services.

Many attempts at establishing the long-run commodity price trend have been made, and they have yielded very varied results. Depending on the end points of the series, the countries whose trade is covered, the deflator used and the commodities included, the outcomes of these investigations have ranged between stagnant and substantially declining developments for real commodity prices.

Grilli and Yang (1988) at the World Bank undertook a painstaking study of real commodity prices. It covers the period 1900–1986. Though somewhat old, the study has become a classic and is still frequently quoted. The real prices are measured as an index of the dollar prices of 24 major commodities in international trade, accounting for 54% of the total nonfuel commodity trade in 1977–1979, deflated by the US index of wholesale prices of manufactures. The results reveal a statistically significant trend rate of decline of 0.59% per year, corresponding to a cumulative trend fall of some 40% over the years covered by the study. Elaborate tests in which the weights of the commodity basket are varied and the impact of the end points of the period studied are explored, confirm the stability of the negative trend and the size of the decline.

Additional insights are obtained when the material is disaggregated into major commodity groups. The annual trend decline during the 86-year period is 0.84% for metals, 0.82% for agricultural nonfood and

0.54% for food excluding tropical beverages. Tropical beverages, intriguingly, is the only group exhibiting a positive price trend. The real prices of coffee, tea and cocoa have been rising by an average of 0.63% per year between 1900 and 1986.

A more recent investigation by Cashin and McDermott (2002) covers the more extended period 1862–1999. The commodities considered include metals and minerals and agricultural raw materials, but not food and fuels. The US GDP deflator is used to convert nominal into real commodity prices. Despite the differences, the authors note a close correlation of their results with those of Grilli and Yang. The main finding of this study is a trend decline in the real price for the aggregate commodity group of 1.3% per annum for the entire 140-year period. After being somewhat stable over the first four decades, the index falls by four fifths over the twentieth century. Cashin and McDermott note that this decline is steeper than that reported by Grilli and Yang, and attribute the difference to the exclusion of food and beverages from the commodity sample under investigation.

An even more comprehensive study is performed by Jacks (2013), as he covers commodities representing US$7.89 trillion worth of production in 2011, for the extended period between 1850 and 2012. The data used are annual prices for 30 individual commodity series, from seven product categories. The price series are expressed in US dollars and deflated by the US consumer price index. Jacks' conclusion is that real commodity prices of both energy and non-energy commodities have been rising, at least from 1950 and onwards. He finds that energy products, precious metals and minerals have experienced steady increases in real prices since 1900, while grains and soft commodities represent product groups that show a decline in real prices. Compared to Cashin and McDermott (2002), a broader basket of commodities is included, and these are given weights based on their production value in 2011 (the main conclusions hold even if no weights are applied). Jacks' study thus suggests that previous literature may have been a bit over-pessimistic regarding the development of many commodity prices, even though he notes a clear distinction between commodities "in the ground," compared to commodities "to be grown."

It should be noted that even though Jacks' study uncovers real price increases for some commodities, these increases are moderate and all price series have time periods when real price decreases are recorded. Furthermore, his results are strongly influenced by the end year, 2012, when the latest commodity boom was still raging, while the two other studies quoted here ended earlier when a prolonged price suppression still reined in most commodity markets (see Figure 6.1). The choice of a different end year could plausibly reverse Jacks' conclusions about rising real prices.

How can one explain the predominant downward long-run price performance of commodities versus manufactures? It is first worth noting that the evidence of falling relative commodity price trends revealed by numerous studies, including the ones quoted here, is contrary to the theories and expectations of the classical economists. These economists postulated rising relative price trends for raw materials in consequence of the productivity-loss caused by the need to employ increasingly more meager land and mineral deposits in commodity production. Elaborating on the works of Adam Smith and David Ricardo, John Stuart Mill (1848) synthesized the classical argument for rising real commodity prices:

The tendency, then, being to a perpetual increase of the productive power of labour in manufactures, while in agriculture and mining there is a conflict between two tendencies, the one towards an increase of productive power, the other towards a diminution of it, the cost of production being lessened by every improvement in the process, and augmented by every addition to population: it follows that the exchange value of manufactured articles, compared with the products of agriculture and of mines, have, as population and industry advance, a certain and decided tendency to fall.

Notions about rising raw materials prices due to increasing pressures on land and mineral depletion remained out of vogue for a long period of time. From the early 1970s, however, they attracted intensive concern as a result of the second commodity boom (see Chapter 6) and the concurrent publication of the Club of Rome reports about an impending general depletion of resources (see Chapter 8).

Fears of price-raising scarcity were subdued in the following decades as all commodity prices resumed their long-run real declining trend, but they have resurfaced again in the proclamations of impending "peak oil," and "peak copper" for that matter, as the third boom evolved early in the twenty-first century.

The first attempts to explain the falling real commodity price trend were mounted by Singer (1950) and Prebisch (1950), who argued that there is an asymmetry in the response of prices to productivity gains between commodities and manufactures. The markets for the former are highly competitive, so any productivity improvement leads to a price decline. The monopolistic organization of the labor and capital employed in manufactures production, in contrast, enables the factors of production to reap the benefit of productivity gains in the form of higher income. The Prebisch/Singer explanation of falling commodity price trends aroused an extended debate. The critics remained unconvinced.

There are several other, less controversial, reasons that could explain the observed long-run decline in real commodity prices. First, the income elasticity of demand for most commodities (defined as the percentage change in demand due to a 1% change in income) is commonly lower than for manufactures, and so, with expanding income, the lower growth of commodity demand is likely to result in a weaker commodity price development. In fact, Singer himself used this argument in support of his theory. The second reason is that transport costs ordinarily constitute a higher proportion of the delivered price of commodities than of manufactures. The secular fall in transport costs discussed in Chapter 1 should therefore have resulted in a stronger decline in commodity price quotations. This argument would apply with particular force to bulk commodities with low prices per ton. Third, and probably most important, the manufactures price index is tricky to construct and interpret because of the continuous shifts in its product composition and the quality changes over time of individual products. The increasing size and efficiency of, say, harvesters or mine loaders during the past 50 years has involved a much greater improvement than any quality change of the cereals or ores in whose production these machines are employed. It is quite possible that the relative shifts in quality are enough to explain why manufactures prices have risen in relation to commodity prices. This is demonstrated in an interesting study (Svedberg and Tilton, 2006) that tries to adjust the consumer price index to take full account of manufactures quality change and then employs the new and lower inflation data to obtain a real price series for copper. While earlier real copper price series showed a falling price trend, the adjusted ones demonstrate a rising trend.

Finally, it seems that the classical economists exaggerated the detrimental impact on productivity resulting from the need to employ inferior lands and mineral deposits in commodity production. Improvements in agricultural productivity have assured rising global supply without the need to employ increasingly unfertile lands. On the contrary, there has been a tendency to stop using the least productive land so as to avoid burdensome surpluses. Advanced methods of exploration for minerals have not only expanded the quantity of reserves, but in some cases also ameliorated the quality of the exploited resource base over time (Chapter 8).

5.4 Alternative Trading Arrangements and Their Implications for Price Formation

A myriad of arrangements are being practiced in cross-border commodity trade, and the discussion in the present section must be selective. Our ambition is to classify the trading arrangements into a few major forms, to indicate some of the markets in which they are practiced and to point to the major implications of each form. The logical order of the classification is from the most public and transparent arrangement to the most private and opaque one.

Commodity Exchanges

Chapter 7 is devoted entirely to commodity exchanges, so they can be treated quite briefly in the present context. Commodity exchanges are markets where many buyers and sellers meet simultaneously and enter into numerous transactions relating to the products traded there. The commodities traded on exchanges are characterized by a sizable number of sellers and buyers and by relatively few quality grades. The exchange typically provides the opportunity for spot transactions, as well as futures and options trade. Transaction costs are quite low and the widespread introduction of electronic trade is lowering them further. Price determination is a key function of an exchange. The uniformity of the price facilitates transactions. The need for price haggling is virtually eliminated. The prices are monitored and published, and are regularly used to determine price levels in deals outside the exchange. The prices on the exchanges are instantaneously influenced by events in the outside world. Hence, there tends to be much greater short-run price volatility in the exchange-determined prices than under most other trading arrangements.

Commodity exchanges have proliferated, as has the number of products traded there. Reasons for this comprise declining concentration of production, more competitive market conditions and the reduction of government intervention in commodity markets. Exchange prices have added greatly to the price transparency in commodity markets.

Auctions

Auctions also commonly accommodate many sellers and buyers but unlike exchanges, which operate continuously, business is transacted only at irregular intervals. In distinction from exchanges, where the double auction principle is applied, that is, buyers and sellers are equally active in trade, the auction markets apply the principle of single auction, with a more passive role assigned to the sellers (ordinary auction) or to the buyers (Dutch auction). In ordinary auctions, the practice is to deal with the sellers consecutively, and to offer their supply one at a time. Normally, the buyers make successively higher bids, with the transaction priced at the highest bid. In Dutch auctions the procedure is reversed: the seller makes successively lower offers, with the transaction priced at the first accepted offer. As in the case of exchanges auction prices are public and transparent, but they may lack continuity if auctions are irregularly held.

A key reason for trade at auctions rather than at fully fledged exchanges is the great variety of grades, across producers and over time, in which these commodities are sold; but auctions appear to be going out of fashion in favor of exchanges as modes for commodity trade. Coffee, tea and flowers are sold at auctions in some East African countries, as is tea in Kolkata and Colombo (World Bank Commodity Price Data). Furthermore, for commodities where trading is relatively thin and does not take place on registered exchanges it can be difficult to find a continuous accurate market price. To overcome this shortcoming, developments in market design along with the use of the Internet have lately increased the use of auction-based trading platforms for many such commodities. An important trading platform for dairy products was established on the Internet in 2007, the Global Dairy Trade platform (Miller and Sapozhnikov, 2014). The use of this platform has increased tremendously over the years, and it is now influencing virtually all trade of dairy products (*Economist*, 2015, August 15, p 59).

Bilateral Contracts

This is probably the predominant arrangement in international commodity trade. It involves a pair of agents who independently agree on the terms that will apply to the trade between them. The crucial terms on which all contracts have to be explicit concern the commodity specification, the quantity, the time and place of delivery, and the price. Other than that, bilateral contracts come in many different forms. Thus, some contracts can relate to a single immediate transaction, while others concern repeated deliveries stretching over periods from a few months to a decade or more.

Bilateral contracts often employ the price levels set by commodity exchanges as a guiding rod for their price determination. Price setting becomes more tricky for commodities that are not traded on exchanges, for example alumina or copper concentrates. In principle, each bilateral pair has to negotiate and agree on the price that will apply in each contract. This is arduous and time consuming. Since prices of contractual agreements are not regularly published, the negotiations may result in a wide range of price levels at a particular point in time.

In practice, there are often conventions that simplify the procedure and help avoid blatant deviations from the average price level. For manganese, for instance, where most trade is transacted through annual bilateral contracts, a commercial practice has developed where a major supplier enters into preliminary discussions with a major customer, while the rest of the industry defers its contract negotiations. As soon as this pair reaches an agreement, all other suppliers and users adopt the agreed price as a guideline for their own negotiations. Very similar practices used to apply to the annual contracts under which a large proportion of international iron ore trade used to be transacted. Until the 1970s, the annual contractual arrangements between the Swedish iron ore exporter and the steel mills of Germany set the pace for other contract negotiations. Since then, the Brazilian company Vale (formerly CVRD) has taken the Swedish role. On the buyers' side, the lead role has been taken sometimes by European companies and sometimes by Japanese ones, but in 2007 the benchmark deal involved CVRD and Chinese Bao Steel for the first time (*Financial Times*, December 22, 2006). This shift is a result of the move within the iron ore trade from European/American/Japanese dominance to the Chinese market. From 2000 to 2011, iron ore imports to China increased almost tenfold, from 70 million tons to 687 million tons (UNCTAD, 2012a). Thus, considering that China imported over 60% of the total world imports, it should not come as a surprise that Chinese steel producers wanted a larger say in the price negotiations. In 2010, the bilateral contract arrangement on the iron ore market was abolished for more short-term spot pricing, mainly because supply could not keep up with the surging Chinese demand, shifting more and more volumes to the spot market (Wårell, 2014b).

In other cases the price transparency in bilateral contract markets is quite limited. This is true, for instance, for the international markets for sisal and jute, and for phosphates, chromite and uranium, though in all these cases there are trade associations or specialized journals which publish prices or price ranges purported to reflect the levels of actual transactions. In the case of uranium the published series relates to the small volumes sold in the spot market, while the evidence for the prices applied in the long-term contracts that dominate the uranium trade is scattered and less systematic.

In some cases the true price may not even be clearly apparent from the content of the bilateral contract. This is the case when the contracted price is preferential, to take account of the provision of long-term investment finance, or equity participation, by the buyer. Similarly, barter deals make it very hard to determine the true commodity price contained in the contract.

Especially in cases lacking transparency there is a likelihood that small parties with lesser access to information and with weaker bargaining power will get a worse deal in bilateral contracts than they would in the more transparent and impartial arrangements characterizing exchanges and auctions.

Producer-Dictated Prices

Producer-dictated prices occur in commodity markets where the number of producers is relatively small and where each sells to many customers. Producer pricing implies some degree of monopoly power; it also affords the producer a certain degree of convenience. The commodity is sold on a take-it-or-leave-it basis and, at least in theory, the need to bargain with each customer is obviated. The example par excellence is the De Beers arrangement for the sale of uncut diamonds.

Producer price quotations can coexist with prices set by commodity exchanges or the prices monitored by trade journals from bilateral contracts, but such coexistence tends to dilute the pricing power of producers. Thus, regional producer prices for copper and zinc have gone into oblivion. Producer prices typically react with a lag to market developments and alter less frequently and less violently than prices on commodity exchanges. Producers have to introduce rationing when their price is below the exchange price and are forced to offer hidden rebates when the exchange price falls below their quotations. A time series of producer prices therefore tends to give a distorted picture of transaction prices.

The pricing power in cobalt of the Central African producers was taken over in some measure by Norilsk Nickel in Russia, while Western Mining Corporation (now part of BHP Billiton) operated a mixture of producer pricing-cum-auctions on the Internet for its cobalt sales. A very large share of world molybdenum used to be produced by Amax Inc. in the United States and the company regularly announced producer prices for this material. This was discontinued as Chilean producers came to dominate production, and quotations were transferred to traders. Producer influence over price setting in cobalt and molybdenum was weakened as London Metal Exchange (LME) trade in both products was introduced in 2010. A few South African mining companies historically account for a large share of world platinum output, and traditionally set the price for their production. However, this function was effectively transferred to the New York Mercantile Exchange (NYMEX) in 1956.

In earlier times, prices set by producers could hold for extended periods of time. The proliferation of commodity exchanges has forced the price-setting producers to alter their prices more frequently and adjust more fully to the exchange quotations. The introduction of petroleum, aluminum and nickel on commodity exchanges in the 1970s and 1980s greatly reduced the relevance of the producer-price systems which traditionally dominated the trade of these products (Radetzki, 2013a).

User-Driven Prices

One could think of identical arrangements but with the roles reversed, with the buyers being few and able to dictate prices to prolific producers. Such arrangements are not very common. An old example is the military procurement of uranium by US and UK authorities, whose complete dominance of demand until the early 1960s permitted them to set the terms of their purchases. User-dictated prices prevail in some markets for food products, where heavily concentrated food processors encounter many scattered farmers.

Transfer Prices

Transfer pricing in international commodity trade occurs when the producer/exporter and the user/importer are part of the same vertically integrated corporation. The prices in such trade are internal to the firm and can be set at any level. They appear only in the accounts of the firm and are ordinarily not published. In principle, they do not affect the corporate profit before tax.

The profit-maximizing firm will have an interest in setting the transfer prices so as to minimize the sum total of profits tax, export tax and import duty. Import duties on raw materials are usually low, so ordinarily the major corporate concern is with profits and export taxes. If the transfer price is set low, profits will be shifted to the importing country. This will reduce the tax burden, if the profits tax in the importing country is lower. Governments of exporting countries who desire to maintain their tax income have instituted "posted prices" in many cases, to be applied for the purpose of tax assessment in the exporting unit of the integrated firm. These prices have sometimes been derived from production costs; in other cases they have been based on perceptions of prevailing price levels in trade between independent parties. The institution of posted prices has reduced the corporate benefit from transfer-price manipulation.

Where transfer prices dominate a market, the price transparency will usually be quite low. Even if the prices were known, it is unclear whether they would at all reflect the costs of production or the price levels that would emerge in arm's length transactions. Bauxite trade probably offers the best example of a commodity market based predominantly on transfer prices. The extent of vertical integration from bauxite to alumina and aluminum is still quite high, and a major share of the bauxite and alumina that enter international trade do so through internal corporate deals. Transfer-price arrangements account for minor shares of all international transactions in, for example, iron

ore, tea, rubber and some edible oils, where the processors in industrialized countries still own some of their sources of primary supply.
Transfer prices were far more common in the 1950s and 1960s, for
example in petroleum, iron ore, copper and many food products. Since
then, there has been a wholesale vertical disintegration of the industries
producing and processing these materials. The disintegration resulted
from the widespread nationalizations of the raw material producing
industries in developing countries. In consequence, the significance of
transfer pricing has been greatly reduced.

5.5 The Actual Price Quotations

Commodity price data may appear confusing and mystifying to the
uninitiated. The purpose of this section is to clarify some of the con-
cepts used and point to the sources where current quotations and
current and historical price series may be found.

Commodity price quotations come in many different formats, and
one has to be clear about the precise information they convey in order
to evaluate them or compare alternatives. At the most basic level, one
must be careful to note the *currency* in which the quotation is made.
The *unit of measurement* is equally important, but can be more tricky
to clarify. Tons used to come in at least three varieties, even though
metric tons have become dominant in recent times. Ounces, bushels
and gallons differ depending on country and product, so it may be
useful to refer to a handbook of weights and measures. For unprocessed
metal minerals, for example iron ore, conventions differ between quotations per unit of gross weight on the one hand and per unit of metal
content on the other. In the case of some mineral concentrates, for
example chromite, the quotation could be (a) per unit of gross weight,
(b) per unit of metal oxide (Cr_2O_3) or (c) per unit of metal content.

The *stage of processing* at which the material is sold is of course
crucial for the price. Sugar is either traded as raw or refined; uranium
comes as uranium oxide (U_3O_8) or uranium hexafluoride (UF_6), and
the additional processing costs explain existing price differences. The
quality of the product will obviously make a difference to price; one
must clarify the specific quality to which the price quotation refers.
Coffees are divided into robustas and arabicas, with the latter com-
manding a price premium. In cotton, long fibers usually command
a higher price. And the price of chrome ore is strongly influenced by

its carbon and iron content, just as iron ore also is priced based on its iron content.

The *time of delivery* is very important for the price level. When supplies for immediate delivery are ample, the prices for future delivery, quoted on commodity exchanges, will be higher than prices for spot transactions, the difference (contango) providing for the cost of carrying inventories. When the supplies for immediate delivery are scarce, spot transactions may be priced higher than deals with later delivery times, and the difference (backwardation) can be quite large.

The *delivery place* is equally important. From one extreme to the other, the place of delivery can be ex-garden, ex-mine or ex-works for agricultural products, minerals and metals, respectively; free on rail (FOR); free on board (FOB); cost, insurance, freight (CIF); and cost and freight, which is similar to CIF but insurance is not included. The price differences are most important for commodities with low values per unit of weight and long transport distances. The price of iron ore FOR in Brazil or manganese ore FOR in South Africa is much less than one half of the CIF price in the user country. Depending on the point of delivery, the price may or may not include export taxes and import duties. These range from insignificant for many commodities to very high for heavily protected agricultural products in industrialized countries. The point of physical delivery for transactions on commodity exchanges is usually from the exchange warehouses. Most of these have traditionally been located in the major industrialized countries, but this tradition is weakening.

Daily quotations from the most important commodity exchanges are regularly published by business-oriented newspapers in major business centres. The *Financial Times* (Internet edition) and the *Wall Street Journal* give a wide coverage of prices from the exchanges. To track the non-exchange commodities, one has to go to specialized journals, newsletters or government publications that provide, for example, producer and trader quotations or price ranges from bilateral deals for specific commodities. Thus, *Metal Bulletin* in the United Kingdom and *Metals Week* in the United States contain a wealth of price information on ferrous and nonferrous metals and minerals, while Platt's news service provides detailed price data on both metal minerals and energy. *Public Ledger* (UK) is the lead journal for agricultural price intelligence. The Internet is increasingly used for publishing pricing information. The US Department of Agriculture and the US Energy

Information Administration publish a variety of price data on agricultural and energy raw materials. Current quotations for many commodities are easily accessible on the home pages of the major investment banks, for example bloomberg.com and reuters.com.

More extended time series for prices of a wide range of commodities in international trade, as well as price indices for major commodity groups, are contained in IMF Primary Commodity Prices, issued monthly by the International Monetary Fund and accessed on the Internet for free, or in World Bank Commodities Price Data (The Pink Sheet), also issued monthly and accessed on the Internet for free.

5.6 Exchange Rates and Commodity Prices

A majority of the commodity price quotations in international trade are expressed in US dollars. When other currencies are used, such as the UK pound or the euro, their equivalents in US dollars at current exchange rates are often quoted alongside. An issue which has often been raised is whether suppliers to an international market reap an advantage by quoting their prices in an appreciating currency, or a disadvantage by having quotations in a currency which tends to depreciate against others. The issue may be highly relevant in less than fully competitive markets with coordinated producer pricing, or where prices are set in bilateral contracts after arduous negotiations and once established are hard to change. In such circumstances, the producers will tend to gain from having set their quotations in an appreciating euro than in a depreciating US dollar.

In contrast, when price can change flexibly, for instance when it is set on a commodity exchange, the forces of demand and supply will determine the level, with automatic adjustments for any exchange rate change of the currency in which the price is quoted so it should not matter which currency is used. The mechanics of price adjustments to exchange rate changes are subject to considerable confusion and claims are often made that suppliers will benefit by quoting in an appreciating currency, even when prices are fully flexible and changes are frequent.

To isolate the problem under scrutiny, we assume that everything else remains constant while the dollar's exchange rate shifts. At least in the short run, this is not a serious distortion of reality. Furthermore, we simplify by assuming that there are only two currencies, and that the euro is used throughout the world outside the United States.

The following proposition appears to have general validity: the greater the economic weight of the US dollar, the less US dollar prices of commodities in international trade will be affected by US dollar exchange rate changes. This is easily demonstrated by considering two extreme cases. In both, the value of the dollar is assumed to increase by 100% against the euro. In the first extreme, 99% of world economic activity takes place in the US dollar area. Given the unimportance of the rest of the world and the euro, the dollar appreciation will have an insignificant effect on global supply and demand. Hence, the dollar price of commodities will remain virtually unchanged. In the second extreme, only 1% of world economic activity takes place in the United States. A doubling of the value of the dollar will double the euro commodity price. Since virtually all production and consumption takes place in the rest of the world, the old euro price has to be restored, given that the initial demand and supply conditions for commodities have remained unchanged. Hence, the dollar price of commodities must be halved.

In the 1950s, the USA reigned supreme in international trade. Since then, the weight of the USA in the world economy has been reducing and the international significance of the US dollar has shrunk in consequence. It follows from the above argument that commodity prices in international trade, expressed in US dollars, have become gradually more sensitive to the exchange rate changes of the US currency.

6 | Commodity Booms

The phenomenon of commodity booms has lately attracted a lot of attention from academic researchers, but also from producers, industry investors and other actors with an interest in the production and consumption of primary commodities. Considering the large impact on commodity markets and, more widely, on the world economy from the booms, a whole chapter has been devoted to this phenomenon. This chapter draws heavily on Radetzki (2006; 2013b) and Radetzki et al. (2008).

6.1 Definition of Commodity Booms

Commodity booms are defined for the purpose of the present analysis as sharp simultaneous increases in the real price of a broad group of commodities. Using this definition, it is possible to detect three such booms in the period since the Second World War, beginning in 1949, 1973 and 2004 (see Figure 6.1). They were all triggered by demand shocks that were caused by unusually fast macroeconomic expansion. In all three cases, commodity producers were unable to satisfy the fast growth in commodity demand, and prices exploded in consequence.

The statement that demand is the typical cause of broad commodity-price moves should not surprise, even if analysts have attempted alternative explanations (Labys et al., 1999; Pindyck and Rotemberg, 1990). After all, alterations in supply are specific to individual commodities. Booming or slumping macroeconomic conditions, in contrast, will impact on demand across most commodity groups. We can think of two exceptions to this general rule of demand being the mover. The first is widespread crop failures caused by extreme weather events. The second is strong simultaneous additions to production capacity stimulated by a period of high prices.

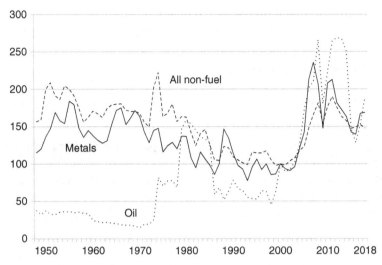

Figure 6.1 Commodity price indices in constant US$, 1948–2018. 2000 = 100
Note: The World Bank's MUV Index is used as a deflator.
Sources: IMF, UNCTAD, World Bank.

The importance of macroeconomic conditions in explaining commodity booms is clearly apparent from the numbers in Table 6.1. Note that the latest boom is presented for selected years between 2003 and 2015, and that data is provided globally, and separately for Advanced Economies[1] and Emerging and Developing Asia.[2] The latter region is of particular interest on account of its speedy growth and its substantial weight in the global economy in recent years. A common trend for all commodity booms is that the years just preceding or marking the beginning of the boom were characterized by very high growth rates in GDP and industrial production. It is also noteworthy that the first

[1] Includes 39 countries: Australia, Austria, Belgium, Canada, Cyprus, Czech Republic, Denmark, Estonia, Finland, France, Germany, Greece, Hong Kong SAR, Iceland, Ireland, Israel, Italy, Japan, Korea, Latvia, Lithuania, Luxembourg, Macao SAR, Malta, Netherlands, New Zealand, Norway, Portugal, Puerto Rico, San Marino, Singapore, Slovak Republic, Slovenia, Spain, Sweden, Switzerland, Taiwan Province of China, United Kingdom and United States.
[2] Includes 30 countries: Bangladesh, Bhutan, Brunei Darussalam, Cambodia, China, Fiji, India, Indonesia, Kiribati, Lao PDR, Malaysia, Maldives, Marshall Islands, Micronesia, Mongolia, Myanmar, Nauru, Nepal, Palau, Papua New Guinea, Philippines, Samoa, Solomon Islands, Sri Lanka, Thailand, Timor-Leste, Tonga, Tuvalu, Vanuatu and Vietnam.

Table 6.1 *Growth patterns during three booms (%)*

	1949	1950	1951	1952
North America and Western Europe				
GDP	2.6	9.2	7.2	2.1
Industrial production	-0.3	8.1	9.3	3.2
International inflation, US$	-3.5	-12.1	15.2	4.9
	1972	**1973**	**1974**	**1975**
OECD				
GDP	5.4	6.0	0.8	-0.2
Industrial production	6.5	8.1	-1.5	-4.3
International inflation, US$	9.1	16.0	21.9	11.1
	2003	**2007**	**2011**	**2015**
World				
GDP	4.3	5.6	4.3	3.4
Industrial production	3.1	5.5	4.6	1.8
International inflation, US$	5.2	6.1	11.0	-9.6
Advanced Economies				
GDP	2.1	2.7	1.7	2.3
Industrial production	1.3	3.0	1.9	0.3
Emerging and Developing Asia				
GDP	8.3	11.2	7.9	6.8
Industrial production	12.9	14.5	11.3	5.7

Note: OECD represented 68% of world GDP in 1973. In 2015 Advanced Economies represented 42.5% of world GDP, while Emerging and Developing Asia represented 30.5%, all in PPP terms. International inflation depicts the development of the UN's MUV export index, denominated in US$.
Source: IMF (biannual); OECD.stat, http://stats.oecd.org; Radetzki (1974); UNCTAD (1976); United Nations (monthly); World Bank (annual a).

two commodity booms were short and collapsed in 1952 and 1974 as the world economy experienced a sharp growth deceleration and commodity demand shrank in consequence, but that the latest boom lasted for much longer than its predecessors, importantly on account of the strong and enduring performance of Emerging and Developing Asia.

The prolonged duration of the latest commodity boom has attracted a lot of attention and discussion regarding whether it represents a so-called *super cycle* (Cuddington and Jerrett, 2008; Heap, 2005). According to this literature a super cycle is defined as a prolonged price cycle for a broad range of primary commodities, with an upward trend for roughly 10–35 years, making a complete cycle last for about 20–70 years. It is further argued that the super cycle is demand driven and that it will last for as long as the strong demand growth continues. The authors identify at least two earlier super cycles, the first at the end of the nineteenth century, driven by the expansion of the US economy, and the second between 1945 and about 1970, caused by postwar reconstruction in Europe and Japan. The proponents of the super cycle thesis see the industrialization and urbanization of China as the main cause for the current super cycle.

Our view of the prolonged duration of the latest commodity boom is rather that an extended investment cycle has been the main driver (Radetzki et al., 2008; Radetzki, 2013b). We thus argue, in line with standard microeconomic theory, that high commodity prices will prevail until sufficient capacity is installed to meet the accelerated growth in demand. When using a simplified example of different investment cycles, Radetzki et al. (2008) illustrate that a resource boom can last for 12–15 years at a maximum, due to investment lags and persisting capacity constraints. We conclude that the most recent boom definitely ended about 2015 when sizable new capacity was finally brought to the market for many important commodities, for example iron ore. The reduced demand growth caused by a slowdown in China's economic expansion in the 2010s of course also helped to puncture the boom.

Table 6.2 details the timing and level of the peak prices for broad commodity categories during the three booms. It is noted that the first two booms had peaks that basically centered on a single year, but in the latest boom two peaks occurred, in 2008 and 2011 (see Figure 6.2). The main explanation for this is the occurrence of the deep recession of 2008–2009, triggered by the financial crisis that hit the world economy in late 2008. Even though this crisis has been described as the largest setback to the world economy since the 1930s depression, it made only a short-run impression on the major commodity price indices. This is explained by the fact that the recession mainly afflicted the advanced economies, while economic growth among the recently dominant commodity consumers of Emerging and Developing Asia experienced only a brief dip followed by an impressive recovery.

Table 6.2 *Peaks in constant dollar commodity price indices during three booms*

	First boom, 1949 = 100		Second boom, 1971 = 100		Third boom, 2005 = 100	
	Peak	Date	Peak	Date	Peak	Date
Aggregate index	145	$Q_1 51$	207	$Q_1 74$	203	$Q_2 08$
Metals and minerals	134	$Q_4 51$	155	$Q_2 74$	249	$Q_1 11$
Energy	117	$Q_4 51$	326	$Q_1 74$	224	$Q_2 08$
Food	125	$Q_3 50$	140	$Q_4 74$	188	$Q_2 11$
Agricultural raw materials	187	$Q_1 51$	159	$Q_1 74$	165	$Q_2 11$

Source: IMF, www.imf.org/en/Research/commodity-prices; Radetzki (2006).

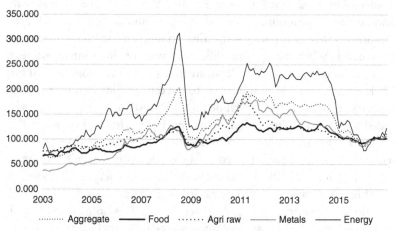

Figure 6.2 Monthly commodity price indices in constant US$, 2003M1–2016M12. 2016 = 100
Source: IMF, www.imf.org/en/Research/commodity-prices.

6.2 The First Commodity Boom

The first boom was strongly related to the Korean War, which broke out in June 1950 with an armistice reached in July 1953. The *direct* impact of the war on commodity markets arose from the insecurity felt about industrial materials supply, amplified by still-fresh memories of the painful shortages of the Second World War. This prompted a widespread buildup of strategic inventories that added to demand and pushed up prices. The *indirect* impact arose from the boost to economic growth and industrial output that resulted from the war operations.

The inflationary performance during the first boom follows a somewhat unusual path. The MUV index presented in Table 6.1 shows very little inflation for the whole of the four-year period, considering that the index increased from 23.2 in 1948 to 23.8 in 1952 (2000 = 100), a rise of only 2.6%. The details depict a far less stable price development, as we note a sharp fall in the 1950 dollar prices of manufactured exports. This is mainly the consequence of devaluations in Europe in late 1949. The prices are then adjusted to the new dollar parities, which is illustrated by a strong rise of the prices in 1951.

Agricultural raw materials and, to a lesser extent, metals and minerals carried the first commodity boom. As is apparent from Table 6.2, the first group peaked at an index of 187 early in 1951, the latter at 134 somewhat later. In contrast, the war and the macroeconomic spurt in these years had little impact on the prices of energy and food. The constant dollar index for energy never reached 120, while that for food attained 125 during two quarters of 1950. An important explanation for these weak reactions is that the major consuming countries were relatively self-sufficient in energy and food. The OPEC cartel had not yet come into existence, the USA was still a net oil exporter, while domestic coal dominated Western Europe's energy needs (Darmstadter et al., 1971). No significant harvest failures were reported at the time. The aggregate commodity price index, too, peaked early in 1951 at 145, making it the weakest of the three booms.

Neither was the boom particularly durable. By the second quarter of 1952, the price increases had, by and large, petered out as it became clear that the Korean War would not spread into a worldwide conflict and as a sharp slowdown in economic growth that year was recorded. In addition, dramatic strategic destocking added to supply, and so contributed to the ensuing price weakness (Rowe, 1965). By the end of 1952, the only remaining real impact of the commodity boom was a metals and minerals price level 20–30% higher than in 1949. All other commodity prices, measured in constant dollars, were roughly the same in 1952 as they had been in 1949. For all practical purposes, the boom was a transient phenomenon.

6.3 The Second Commodity Boom

The second boom was much stronger than the first. It was also much more pervasive. The prices of all commodity groups rose sharply. As in the first boom, a very strong macroeconomic performance during 1972 and 1973 constituted an important trigger to the rising commodity prices. But there were two additional triggers. One was that the boom had been preceded by two consecutive years of widespread crop failures. The scarcity of food led to substitution in land use, for example from cotton or jute to grains, which cut the agricultural raw materials supply. In 1973, deficient inventories both for food and agricultural raw materials were therefore recorded (Radetzki, 1974). The second trigger was unrest in the Middle East in 1973 that resulted in cut supply of oil and late in the year permitted several oil-exporting countries to declare hefty price increases that the importers could not resist. This had a strong repercussion on the aggregate commodity index given the heavy weight of oil in international commodity trade.

In contrast to the first commodity boom, very high inflation was recorded throughout the second boom. In 1971 the MUV index (2000 = 100) settled at 30.7 and in 1975 it landed at 52.5, indicating an increase in inflation for the whole boom period of an impressive 71%. The fast pace of inflation, which at times resulted in negative real interest rates, yields a sizable difference in the outcome of the boom when measured in nominal and real terms. Furthermore, not only did the period record strong price rises; these years were also characterized by large changes in the parities between major currencies. This was mainly due to the breakdown of the Bretton Woods system that determined international exchange rates. The result, after the dollar anchor had been removed, was freely floating currencies. High inflation coupled with chaos in currency markets, along with a poor performance on the stock markets in the early 1970s (Shiller, 2000), led investors to move out of bonds and shares and into real estate, art and commodities. The demand for commodity inventories as a "safe" store of value was a further contributory factor to the commodity boom (Cooper and Lawrence, 1975).

The constant dollar aggregate commodity price index reached a maximum at 207 in the first quarter of 1974. The individual commodity groups all attained their constant dollar peaks early in 1974: the energy index at about 330, all the other commodity indices around 150. In the course of 1974, under the weight of the recession, importantly prompted by the oil crisis that was manifested by disturbed oil supply and exploding oil prices, the constant dollar metals and agricultural raw materials indices fell back sharply to end the year at 100, the level at 1971 just before the beginning of the boom. Prices remained at that level through 1975, when the recession deepened. The metal prices were additionally depressed by large sales between mid-1973 and mid-1974 from the US government's strategic stockpiles, and in late 1974 from excessive commercial stocks in Japan that had been built up in the preceding year (Cooper and Lawrence, 1975). Food prices fell too, though less steeply given their lower sensitivity to the business cycle.

The energy price index stands out from the other commodity groups. Energy prices rose significantly only at the end of 1973, later than the prices of other commodities; but by early 1974 they had increased by much more than any other commodity group, and they remained 150–200% above the base year through 1975 and beyond. The supply effects of the political unrest in the Middle East explain the difference. Oil dominates the energy price index, and several oil exporters adjusted supply to the falling demand in 1974 and 1975 that was caused by the combination of deepening recession and the price shock (Radetzki, 1990a, 1990b), so the elevated oil prices persevered.

6.4 The Third Commodity Boom

The third commodity boom started about 2004 and ended about 2015, as is apparent from Figure 6.1. Like the preceding booms, it was importantly triggered by a demand shock. To illustrate, the global demand growth for oil and copper recorded in 2004 was the highest on record for over 20 years. Producers were caught unaware, with little spare production capacity, so prices in many markets exploded. As in the earlier booms, the demand shock was importantly due to fast macroeconomic expansion in the early years as is illustrated in Table 6.3.

The inflation during the period covered by the table is strikingly lower than that recorded during the second boom. When measured by the MUV Index in US dollars, international inflation works out at an anemic annual average of 1.4%. This is noteworthy, since the

Table 6.3 *Growth patterns during the third boom (%)*

	World			Advanced Economies		Emerging and Developing Asia	
	MUV index	GDP	Industrial production	GDP	Industrial production	GDP	Industrial production
2004	6.8	5.4	5.3	3.2	3.3	8.5	12.7
2005	3.1	4.9	4.0	2.8	2.1	9.3	12.2
2006	2.5	5.5	5.1	3.1	3.3	10.1	11.7
2007	6.1	5.6	5.5	2.7	3.0	11.2	14.5
2008	7.8	3.0	0.6	0.2	−2.4	7.2	10.5
2009	−6.2	−0.1	−8.7	−3.3	−14.0	7.5	7.8
2010	3.7	5.4	9.4	3.1	8.1	9.6	14.3
2011	11.0	4.3	4.6	1.7	1.9	7.9	11.3
2012	−0.7	3.5	2.7	1.2	0.2	7.0	9.3
2013	−0.4	3.5	2.7	1.4	0.1	6.9	9.0
2014	−1.4	3.6	3.4	2.1	1.9	6.8	7.5
2015	−9.6	3.4	1.8	2.3	0.3	6.8	5.7
2016	−3.9	3.4	2.0	1.7	0.1	6.7	5.8

Source: IMF (biannual, 2019); MUV index; World Bank.

13-year period displayed has been characterized by historically high global economic growth, averaging 4.0% for the world as a whole. It is clear that the third commodity boom has been forcefully driven by the Emerging and Developing Asia, and not by the more mature economies. The average yearly growth in the Advanced Economies between 2004 and 2016 has been a moderate 1.7% compared to the rampant expansion in Emerging and Developing Asia, where economic growth attained an annual average of 8.1%.

There is another reason for the dominant role of Emerging and Developing Asia in triggering and maintaining the boom. For although this area accounted for only 30.5% of global GDP in 2015, compared with the Advanced Economies' 42.5%, it has been in a development stage that is much more intensive in primary-materials use than the dematerializing, mature Advanced Economies.

If a dollar added to the GDP in Emerging and Developing Asia absorbs twice the quantity of commodities as does a corresponding dollar's growth in the Advanced Economies, the two regions would contribute about equally to commodity demand growth provided that both expanded at the same rates. But since Emerging and Developing Asia's economies expanded almost five times faster than the Advanced Economies, it follows that the region's contribution to commodity demand growth completely overwhelmed that of the Advanced Economies.

China especially stands out in this respect. The country's share of global GDP in 2015 (PPP terms) was assessed by the IMF (on Internet) at 17.1%, but its share of global demand growth between 2005 and 2016 was 37% for petroleum, 92% for aluminum and, incredibly, 116% for nickel and 124% for copper. The nickel and copper figures imply not only that all demand growth occurred in China, but that, additionally, demand shrank significantly in the rest of the world.

The aggregate monthly commodity price index experienced a steady increase from 2003 onwards and reached a peak at 203 (2016 = 100) in July 2008, just before the onset of the financial crisis. Also the energy index reached its peak in the same month at an impressive 312. However, the other major indices had their peaks in 2011, after the recession of 2008–2009. In particular the metal and mineral price index rose quickly after the financial crisis, as is evident from Figure 6.2, which supplements Figure 6.1 by providing further detail on the third boom. It is further noted that the food price index exhibits the lowest volatility over the period, in sharp contrast to the large price swings experienced by energy price index.

A closer scrutiny of the recession throws some light on its weak and brief price impact. First, on a global scale, the recession, even if it hit hard at the end of 2008, was short and not very deep, as is evident from Figure 6.3. Only in 2009 did global output contract, and in 2010 it had already bounced back to growth over 5%. Second, only mature economies were seriously afflicted, with two consecutive years of growth substantially below trend. Third, the recession was much weaker in Emerging and Developing Asia (which, as noted, has for some time dominated commodity demand growth), and in the other developing countries of the world as well.

We have asserted that accelerating and/or high economic growth has been an important trigger behind all three commodity booms. We have also suggested that near-recessionary conditions and the ensuing destocking quickly punctured the first two booms but the third boom

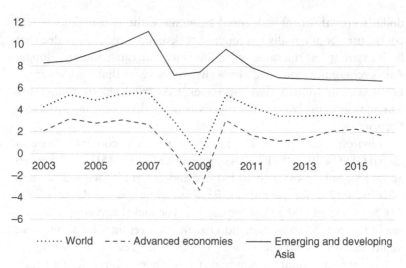

Figure 6.3 Annual growth of GDP (%) *Source*: IMF (biannual).

persevered considerably longer despite the occurrence of the 2008–2009 recession, because of continued fast growth mainly in emerging and developing Asia. Some clarification of the developments of the latest commodity boom is called for.

First, not all events of sharply accelerating macroeconomic performance give rise to booming prices in commodity markets. Other preconditions have to prevail, for example a tight production-capacity situation and relatively small inventories. Such preconditions typically emerge after prolonged periods of weak commodity prices, which discourage investments in capacity expansion and instill a sense that supply is secure and that there is limited need for inventory holding. This has clearly been the case for many primary commodities prior to the beginning of the century. Many commodity prices had been severely depressed for nearly three decades (Humphreys, 2015), and especially so for agriculture – something which is noted in Figure 6.1 but also discussed in Baffes and Haniotis (2010).

There is a common perception that it takes about five years on average for new greenfield capacity to be in place in minerals, metals and fossil fuels industries. The argument then is that five years should be enough to rectify any market imbalance caused by unexpected spurts in demand. However, this assumption has been proved wrong in the latest commodity boom. Investments are subject to a variety of perception and decision lags, comprising the time to bring together the necessary financial packages and overcome various regulatory impediments, including increasingly restrictive environmental legislation in recent times. Adding to this the time needed to overcome the investors' unpreparedness to act, due to the history of depressed prices and general lack of interest in the industry, it is clear that the latest commodity boom has lasted longer not only due to a persevering strong demand but also due to a slow response in supply. After 2015, as new supply enters many commodity markets, the fundamentals between supply and demand seem to be more in balance, thus resulting in downward pressure on the previously elevated commodity prices.

The boom in agricultural prices, though notably less accentuated compared to other commodities, clearly requires a somewhat different explanation. First, most agricultural commodities are one-year crops, so do not require greenfield investments that take five years to mature. Tropical beverages and other tree crops constitute exceptions that, like minerals, require some five years between investment and the ensuing output growth. Elsewhere, increasing production usually takes fewer years, even if it is obviously not met instantly.

In their interesting study Baffes and Haniotis (2010) discuss the causes for the 2006/2008 agricultural commodity boom. Interestingly they find no evidence that food demand growth in large emerging nations such as China and India accelerated during the food price boom. There was some evidence that the growing demand for biofuels affected the food-price spike, but considering the small share of the area under grain/oilseeds (1.5% worldwide) the authors conclude that it was not the main cause of the price spike. They then investigate the hypothesis that excess liquidity, or speculation, was the main driver of the price boom in agricultural products. The empirical evidence regarding this issue is mixed. Gilbert (2010a) comes to the hesitant conclusion that there is no evidence that speculation has been a cause of the metals and minerals price boom, but that food commodity prices have been inflated by index-based investors under the 2008 food price boom. Baffes and Haniotis (2010) conclude that a dominant cause of the 2006/2008 food-price spike was a stronger link between energy and non-energy commodity prices.

6.5 Summary and Reflections

Some of the major conclusions and reflections from the chapter are summarized below:

1. Commodity booms are defined as a major deviation from long-run equilibrium prices. Three such booms are identified in the period after the Second World War, and all have been triggered by exceptionally strong commodity-demand increases caused by fast economic growth in the world economy. Prices return closer to equilibrium when the boom ends, either because of recession and slow demand growth or because new capacity has been brought on line.

2. It is important to point out that high and steady growth of demand on its own will not normally result in a commodity boom because in such situations capacity growth will have been adjusted to even very fast expanding demand. A boom thus ordinarily occurs in a situation when demand growth *surprisingly* accelerates and it takes time to bring new capacity into production to satisfy the new demand conditions. A disequilibrium may then emerge and may be quite durable. The latest commodity boom illustrates that it can take up to a decade before new capacity is brought to the market, thus resulting in an extended period of elevated prices. However, we do not share the belief in a so-called super-cycle, where high prices remain throughout a long period of high (but steady) demand growth.

3. A reflection regarding commodity booms is that misguided beliefs regularly develop during the period of elevated prices, that is, that we now have a new, normal and much higher equilibrium price level. This belief will typically lead to overinvestment and an ensuing period of depressed prices once the excessive investments mature. This phenomenon is clearly visible in a scrutiny of historical commodity prices.

4. The chapter has revealed how China has replaced the rich Advanced Economies as a dominant force in commodity markets. China's economic growth may be slowing and its economic model shifting from emphasizing investment toward consumption, both resulting in a slowdown in the country's commodity demand. But then, other emerging economies are likely to take over China's dominant role as

fast-growing, voracious commodity consumers (Humphreys, 2015). Even though the rich countries still dominate global GDP, their influence on commodity markets will likely continue to decline. The historical shift just described may involve an increase in historical demand growth for commodities, but is unlikely to push up equilibrium commodity prices to a more elevated level.

7 | Commodity Exchanges, Commodity Investments and Speculation

7.1 Commodity Exchanges and the Commodities Traded There

Throughout this book, the concept "international commodity markets" is being used, in a very loose sense, to describe the buyers and sellers and the transactions they enter into. Commodity markets can be much more strictly defined as places where buyers and sellers of commodities meet to conduct their trade. In all countries there are many such markets of various sizes and levels of sophistication. Local rural markets provide a place for the exchange of food and other agricultural commodities. Nationwide and international markets for specific products or groups of products are also common. Spot transactions with immediate physical delivery usually dominate the trade activities of commodity markets, but there may also be forward deals, involving delivery some time in the future.

As was made clear in Chapter 5 commodity exchanges have proliferated greatly since 2000, both in terms of places where the trade is conducted and in terms of products being subject to trade. The Futures Industry Association (FIA) compiles reports on monthly volumes and options traded at some 75–80 exchanges globally. Table 7.1 presents the development of all traded futures and options contracts for selected years from 2001 to 2018, as well as of traded commodities divided into agricultural, energy and metals products. We note impressive increases in the number of all contracts traded during these years, with a peak in 2018 (reaching over 30 billion contracts). For *commodity* futures and options the increase has been even more striking. The last row in Table 7.1 reveals that the share of commodities in all traded futures and options contracts has increased from about 10% in 2001 to over 18% in 2018. Most of the increase occurred in the 2010s and in 2016 commodities constituted more than a quarter of all traded contracts.

Table 7.1 *Futures and options volume, selected years 2001–2018 (million contracts)*

	2001	2006	2011	2012	2013	2014	2015	2016	2017	2018
Number of exchanges	n/a	54	81	84	75	75	78	76	79	82
All contracts	4 281	11 862	24 946	21 129	21 567	21 853	24 801	25 220	25 199	30 282
Agricultural	156	489	997	1 254	1 211	1 388	1 640	1 932	1 306	1 488
Energy	167	386	814	902	1 311	1 161	1 411	2 214	2 171	2 238
Metals	109	218	777	874	1 080	1 244	1 598	2 189	2 020	1 814
Share of commodities	10.1%	9.2%	10.4%	14.3%	16.7%	17.4%	18.7%	25.1%	21.8%	18.3%

Source: FIA (annual).

Commodity exchanges are distinguished from other types of markets by the particular features they have developed in response to a variety of specific needs. They exhibit several distinct characteristics:

- Trade is exclusive to a limited membership, but the members of the exchange can conclude deals both on their own behalf and on behalf of their clients. The latter are usually far more important.
- Trade used to take the form of open outcry, but since the turn of the century most exchanges have adopted electronic trading. The price of bids to buy is gradually raised and that of offers to sell reduced, until a commonly agreed price is reached.
- There is a strict standardization of trade practices with regard to, for example, volumes, qualities, delivery times, margins and payment terms. Some exchanges stipulate a maximum permitted price change from the previous day.
- Futures transactions with a high degree of transferability dominate trade. Physical trade has a subordinate position, as a majority of the futures contracts are liquidated through the issue of opposite contracts before delivery falls due.
- A clearing house, established and financially guaranteed by its members, is regularly attached to the exchange. All futures contracts issued by the members have the clearing house as the opposite party. The net position of the clearing house for a particular commodity and delivery date must always be zero.

During most of the twentieth century, the dominant exchanges were located in London, New York and Chicago, but that dominance is gradually being reduced as a result of activities on emerging commodity exchanges in China, India and Japan. In fact, in the first six months of 2019 over 40% of all contracts traded (both futures and options) were traded in the Asia-Pacific market. Table 7.2 ranks the 15 most important exchanges, specifies their country of origin and commodities traded, and provides information about volumes of trade in 2018. It covers the volume of trade in *all* futures and options combined, as data for trade exclusively in primary commodities are difficult to obtain. However, exchanges that do not trade commodities directly often cover them indirectly through trade in indices as well as other exchange-traded products. The exchanges that have been considered as the most important regarding commodities are NYMEX, LME, Chicago Mercantile Exchange (CME), Chicago Board of Trade and

Table 7.2 *Major exchanges in 2018 ranked by number of contracts*

Rank	Exchange	Traded commodities	Volume (2018)	Share (%)
1	**CME Group (USA)**		4 844 856 880	16.0
	Chicago Mercantile Exchange	Agricultural	2 259 630 942	
	Chicago Board of Trade	Agricultural, Energy, Metals	1 778 590 729	
	NYMEX	Energy, Metals	652 470 369	
	Commodity Exchange	Metals	153 713 320	
	Eris Exchange		451 520	
2	**National Stock Exchange of India (India)**	Energy, Metals	3 790 090 142	12.5
3	**B3 (Brazil)**	Agricultural, Energy	2 574 073 178	8.5
4	**Intercontinental Exchange (USA)**		2 474 223 217	8.2
	ICE Futures Europe	Agricultural, Energy	1 276 090 376	
	NYSE Arca		460 113 644	
	NYSE Amex		389 866 979	
	ICE Futures US	Agricultural, Energy, Metals	342 613 160	
	ICE Futures Canada	Agricultural, Energy, Metals	2 973 036	
	ICE Futures Singapore	Energy	2 566 022	
5	**CBOE Holdings (USA)**		2 050 884 142	6.8
	Chicago Board Options Exchange		1 283 269 272	
	BATS Exchange		422 706 669	
	C2 Exchange		150 923 570	
	EDGX Options Exchange		118 429 304	
	CBOE Futures Exchange		75 555 327	
6	**Eurex (Germany)**		1 951 763 081	6.4
7	**Nasdaq (USA)**		1 894 713 045	6.3
	Nasdaq PHLX		724 170 578	

Table 7.2 (*cont.*)

Rank	Exchange	Traded commodities	Volume (2018)	Share (%)
	Nasdaq Options Market		428 650 957	
	International Securities Exchange		402 504 406	
	International Securities Exchange Gemini		205 043 832	
	Nasdaq Exchanges Nordic Markets		87 272 887	
	Nasdaq NFX	Energy	22 012 655	
	Nasdaq Boston		17 424 846	
	International Securities Exchange Mercury		5 982 457	
	Nasdaq Commodities	Agricultural, Energy	1 650 427	
8	**Moscow Exchange (Russia)**	Energy	1 500 375 257	5.0
9	**Korea Exchange (South Korea)**	Agricultural, Metals	1 408 257 756	4.7
10	**Shanghai Futures Exchange (SHFE) (China)**		1 201 898 093	4.0
	Shanghai Futures Exchange	Energy, Metals	1 175 388 670	
	Shanghai International Energy Exchange	Energy	26 509 423	
11	**BSE (India)**		1 032 693 325	3.4
	BSE	Agricultural, Metals	1 022 757 747	
	India International Exchange	Energy, Metals	9 935 578	
12	**Dalian Commodity Exchange (DCE) (China)**	Agricultural, Energy	981 927 369	3.2
13	**Zhengzhou Commodity Exchange (ZCE) (China)**	Agricultural, Energy, Metals	817 969 982	2.7

Table 7.2 (*cont.*)

Rank	Exchange	Traded commodities	Volume (2018)	Share (%)
14	Hong Kong Exchanges and Clearing		480 966 627	1.6
	Hong Kong Exchanges and Clearing	Metals	296 183 076	
	LME	Metals	184 783 551	
15	Miami International Holdings		421 320 501	1.4
	MIAX Pearl		220 609 083	
	MIAX Options		200 711 418	

Source: FIA (annual).

Intercontinental Exchange Inc. (ICE). However, as more and more commodities are traded in Asia exchanges there have grown in importance greatly. For example, in 2018 the top five contracts for metals were traded at the Shanghai Futures Exchange and the Dalian Commodity Exchange.

Some of the exchanges have operated for over a century, others are of more recent vintage. The specialization in terms of commodity coverage, usually the result of historical accident, varies considerably. Some exchanges predominantly serve the nation where they are located, while others are truly international in character.

Traditionally, trading on commodity exchanges took place in so-called open outcry systems, which involve traders in a pit shouting their bids or offers to other traders in the pit. This has changed: in the last two decades electronic trading has speedily and almost completely taken over the outcry system on most exchanges. In July 2006 less than 5% of total monthly soybean futures trade at the CME Group was transacted electronically but 18 months later the figure had risen to 80%. By 2011, the CME Group reported only 7% of all contracts traded in open outcry systems (Irwin and Sanders, 2012). Similar shifts have occurred in many other commodity markets. On December 17, 2004, the Winnipeg Commodity Exchange (since 2008 known as ICE Futures Canada), which began trading in 1887, switched to electronic trading; it was the first agricultural exchange to fully abandon the outcry system.

Irwin and Sanders (2012) see the move in commodity trading to electronic platforms as a structural change of the commodity futures markets. They argue that this change could be an explanation for the coincident increase in trading activity. The main motivation for the shift is that electronic trading leads to lower trading costs and better information flows for involved parties. For empirical evidence of this see, for example, Ates and Wang (2005), Frank and Garcia (2011) andShah and Brorsen (2011). Access to the futures markets also improved considerably when electronic trading took over, both through easier and more direct access to the markets, but also through development of new financial tools (discussed further in Section 7.3).

The move toward electronic trading, along with a standardization of the bidding process, has led to a trend where many exchanges have been bought by specialized and truly global exchanges. An example is the fully electronic ICE, which, by acquiring other exchanges since it started in 2000, has become the fourth largest exchange in the world.

Not all commodities are suited for trade on exchanges. A number of conditions must be satisfied for futures markets in a commodity to function well:

- There must be many buyers and sellers providing sufficient liquidity for continuous market quotations.
- There must be preparedness among those who trade the physical commodity to use the market for hedging, and speculators must provide matching deals.
- The inherent price variability in the commodity must be considerable; that is, its supply and demand schedules should experience a significant instability and have a low price elasticity.
- The commodity must be easy to grade, or else it will be difficult to specify the quality covered by futures contracts.
- The commodity must be storable so that a comprehensible relationship between spot and futures prices can be established. With the development of preservation and refrigeration, virtually all commodities have become storable.

For successful introduction on an exchange, it is important that the contract specification suits the needs of those who buy and sell the physical commodity. At the same time, the contract should be attractive to the speculators and investors whose business provides continuity and liquidity to the market. For example, the size of the contract, and hence the margin payments, should not exceed the financial capacity of individual investors.

The group of commodities traded on the exchanges is being continuously widened. Important new arrivals on the exchanges since the 1970s comprise gold (1975), nickel and aluminum (1979), crude oil (1983), steel (2006), molybdenum, cobalt and crude palm oil (2010), steam coal (2011), and coking coal and iron ore (2013). Among metals and minerals the top three commodity futures traded in 2018 were steel, iron ore and nickel. Lead positions in energy were, not surprisingly, taken by oil, natural gas and coal, while soybean meal, rapeseed meal and apple led the futures trade volumes among agriculturals (FIA, annual).

A number of commodities are still not traded on the exchanges. There are several different reasons behind their exclusion:

- Standard grades are hard to establish. This applies to tea and ferrochrome.
- A dominant producer maintains a high degree of market control and can dictate prices. This was true for aluminum and nickel until a few decades ago, and is still true of, for example, chromium and niobium, the latter with an extremely concentrated world supply.
- The inherent price fluctuations may be small, or else a price stabilization scheme may be operated by major importing or exporting governments, reducing the producers' and consumers' incentive to hedge. The large stockpiles and price-support schemes for groundnuts and tobacco that have been maintained by the US government over a long period of time (see the US Farm Service Agency and the US Commodity Credit Corporation home pages on the web) are an important reason why these products are not traded on the exchanges.[1]

---

[1] The same argument applies to trade in currencies, where there was no futures trading until the exchange rates started to fluctuate after the breakdown of the Bretton Woods system in 1971.

7.2 Instruments and Functions

Broadly, commodity exchanges have the following functions:

- They constitute authoritative mechanisms for price determination.
- They usually establish a physical trade outlet.
- They provide an opportunity for hedging.
- They greatly facilitate both highly speculative and very safe investments in commodity inventories and commodity-related trade instruments.

Before discussing what the exchanges do, however, it is necessary to describe the instruments that help them perform their roles. The present discussion of the instruments and functions, as well as the following one on the exchange actors and their behavior, is no more than a brief introduction that aims to bring out the bare bones of what is involved. The activities going on at and around commodity exchanges involve a plethora of derivatives tailored to specific needs, with high levels of complexity and sophistication. Readers interested in further detail are referred to Chevallier and Ielpo (2013).

There are basically two instruments, namely futures contracts covering a continuum in time and options on such contracts. These are treated in turn.

Futures Contracts

A *futures contract* is an agreement to buy or to sell a specified quantity of a commodity for the agreed price, with delivery at a particular future time. The quantities covered by a contract and the periods when futures contracts fall due are determined by the trade practices of the exchange and vary across commodities and exchanges. A few examples will illuminate the contract volumes and number of contracts on leading commodity exchanges in 2018: soybean meal futures on DCE, 10 tons, 238 million contracts; rapeseed meal futures on ZCE, 10 tons, 104 million contracts; Brent oil on Moscow Exchange, 10 barrels, 441 million contracts; steel on SHFE, 10 tons, 531 million contracts; iron ore on DCE, 100 tons, 236 million contracts. The standard features of futures contracts make them highly liquid. The owner of a contract can sell it at any time at the going price for that commodity and delivery month.

It is important to distinguish futures contracts from *forward contracts*. The latter involve a wider concept that comprises futures contracts. Any contract that stipulates delivery in the future is a forward contract. Forward contracts need not have standardized provisions regarding quantities, grades and dates when they fall due. Since each forward contract is unique, it is much less easy to trade. A transfer of a forward contract is dependent on finding a party interested in its particular specifications.[2]

A member of the exchange entering into a futures contract to buy does not need to pay for their purchase at the time, but they are required to provide a *margin*, usually representing 10–20% of the purchase value, as their commitment to the deal. This margin is held by the clearing house of the exchange, formally the opposite party to the contract. If the price declines after the buyer has signed the contract, a need may arise to top up their payments, so that the margin always stays at some 10–20% of the current contract value. Suppose that the buyer has committed to purchase a commodity for $10 000 and has paid a margin of $1500. If the price falls by 20% before the stipulated delivery time, the buyer will have no incentive to fulfill the contract. It will be financially preferable to them to lose the margin and buy the commodity at the lower price, for $8000. Hence, to ensure contract execution, the buyer will be asked to make additional margin payments before their margin has been depleted by the price fall. Failing such additional payments, the contract will be liquidated. This will take the form of issuing a futures sales contract to the buyer with the same delivery date but at the going, lower price. The two contracts will cancel out each other, and the loss, amounting to the difference between their values, will be recovered from the original margin payment. If, on the other hand, the price rises, payments can be made to the futures buyer, since they are not required to hold margins above the 10–20% level. Analogous conditions apply when members of the exchange enter into futures contracts to sell.

In any normal circumstances, the margins will provide a complete financial guarantee for the commitments entered into by the clearing house. In principle, therefore, commodity futures trade involves no risk

---

[2] The distinction between the tradability of the two contract forms is akin to the distinction between trade with the use of money and barter trade.

that the opposite party defaults. This adds considerably to the fungibility of futures contracts.

The tin debacle on the LME in 1985 is a spectacular though rare instance of futures contract holders defaulting on their obligations, but it should be added that the LME did not have any clearing house at the time. The defaulter was no less than the International Tin Council, dominated by its producing country members and operating through a combined use of buffer stocks and export restrictions. Through a series of events in the early 1980s, the council came to defend a price substantially above long-run equilibrium, applying export restrictions and yet forcing the buffer-stock manager to buy increasing quantities of the metal. To stretch the financial resources available for the purpose, the manager employed the stock, which had grown to an enormous size, as collateral for loans that were then used for margin payments in futures transactions. By October 1985, the manager's resources had been completely exhausted so he ceased operations, defaulting on his futures purchase commitments and leaving behind a total debt in excess of US$1 billion, a huge sum at that time. Tin trade on the LME was suspended, and when it reopened in June 1989 the price settled very substantially below the level before the default. The debacle led to a fundamental reorganization of the LME, including the establishment of a clearing house.

In practice, the existence of a clearing house does not offer an iron-clad guarantee against default. When price movements are very fast, the call for additional margin payments may not be speedy enough to assure that margins are positive on all contracts at all times. The possibility of default will be there as soon as margins reach a zero level.

Today's quote for future delivery is usually not the same as today's spot price. Depending on current market conditions and expectations about the future, there will ordinarily be a difference between the two. The term *contango* refers to a situation where the futures price exceeds the spot price, while *backwardation* involves a futures price below the spot level. We return to a further discussion of this distinction later in this section.

The majority of futures contracts are entered into for the purpose of hedging, speculation or investments, with no intention to provide or take physical delivery at the contract's expiry. In fact, some exchanges do not offer any facilities at all for physical trade. A major proportion of the futures contracts are voluntarily liquidated through the procedure described above, before delivery falls due. The liquidated futures purchase transaction will yield a loss if the price for the contracted delivery date has fallen between the issuance of the original contract and liquidation. The transaction will yield a profit if the price has risen. The reverse will be true for futures sales transactions.

Options

The *options* traded on commodity exchanges are directly related to the futures contracts. One must distinguish between the *issuers* and *holders* of options, since their involvements are highly asymmetrical. There are *call* and *put* options. A call option gives the holder the right (but not the obligation) to buy a futures contract at a predetermined price, the *strike price*, at any time until the option's expiry. Analogously, a put option gives the holder the right to sell a futures contract at a predetermined price. The issuer of the option is obliged to comply with the holder's rights.

Options are freely transferable. The price of the option is called the *premium*. This is what the issuer charges when they first issue the option and what the holder is paid when they transfer the option to another holder.

Options have a limited life and lapse on their expiry. The life can extend over several years. The premium will fluctuate through the life of the option in a pattern determined by two factors: the "time value," which depends on the remaining time until expiry (the shorter the remaining time, the lower the value), and the "intrinsic value," which depends on the relationship between the strike price and the underlying futures contract price. The intrinsic value will fluctuate in parallel with the futures price development. At the time of expiry, the time value will be zero and the intrinsic value will represent the entire premium.

The option holders' only obligation is to pay the premium. To them, options are distinctly different from futures contracts, in that they do not carry any responsibility for taking or making deliveries. From the issuers' point of view, the option carries a strong resemblance to a futures contract in that their obligation is precisely to issue such a contract whenever the option holder chooses to exercise their right.

The holder will reap a profit if the option premium rises from the time they acquired it and until they exercise their right. They will lose if there is a decline in the premium. The holder's loss cannot exceed the premium they paid, for they can always choose to do nothing and let the option lapse. The issuer's gains and losses are opposite to those of the holder. The gains are limited to the initial premium received, but the potential losses are infinite.

As in the case of futures contracts, the issue of options is guaranteed by the clearing house of the commodity exchange. Also, in a majority of cases, the option rights to acquire futures contracts are not exercised. Instead, the options are sold at the going premium when it is positive or not exercised at all when the premium is zero.

A Physical Trade Outlet

Most exchanges do offer a convenient facility for physical trade to the buyer or seller who needs it, for instance because they have no developed trading connections. The exchanges always stand ready, in principle, to absorb and release the commodity on a spot basis, at the going price. The importance of this function, though quite limited compared to futures and options trading, should nevertheless not be underrated. In 2018, physical deals on the LME involved about 1.16 million tons of aluminum (about 2.2% of total global aluminum production), 775 000 tons of copper (about 3% of global copper production) and some 240 000 tons of nickel (about 3.6% of global nickel production). Physical trade, as defined here, is the material that flows out of inventories (private communication with Phillip Crowson). However, one should keep in mind that all materials going out of the warehouses held by an exchange is not necessarily used directly by consumers.

Socialist countries used to be particularly important users of the exchanges for their physical trade. Much of the somewhat irregular supply of USSR aluminum and nickel was disposed of in the 1970s and 1980s through the LME. Similarly, Chinese requirements for metal imports were for a long time importantly satisfied through purchases on the LME. Producers who for some reason have been unable to place their entire output directly with clients are known to dispose of their marginal supplies on the exchanges. The inventories held by the exchanges provide a convenient supply of last resort when other supply sources dry up.

After dealing with futures, options and physical trade facilities, we now proceed by exploring the role of the exchanges as mechanisms for setting commodity prices, arguably their most important function.

Price Formation

The following several paragraphs clarify the dominant role played by exchanges in setting the prices for physical transactions in the commodity industries. Two circumstances must initially be clarified. First, as noted, only a limited part of the trade that takes place on the exchanges is physical trade. Most of the action involves paper transactions in which physical material never changes hands. Second, a predominant proportion of physical trade occurs outside the exchanges, in transactions directly between the producers and users of the commodity. The point to be elucidated is that this predominant physical trade regularly occurs at prices tightly related to those that prevail in spot and futures transactions on the exchanges.

Whenever an international commodity exchange succeeds in establishing a broad-based and continuous trade in a commodity, the price quotation in that trade is usually adopted, with required modifications, throughout the commodity industry. The price-setting mechanisms on the exchange are of course far from perfect in reflecting market fundamentals. For instance, where the market is thin, a few transactions may unduly influence the price developments in an ad hoc manner. With a thin market, there is also the likelihood that gaps will occur in the time series of futures prices, because there are no contracts expiring in some of the months covered by the trading period.

An interesting question, then, is how much trading is needed for an efficient representative price to be established. According to Holder et al. (1999), a monthly trading volume of more than 10 000 transactions is a criterion to define a futures contract as successful. However, data from the largest CME reveal that between 40% and 78% of traded commodity futures in August 2019 did not reach this threshold.[3] Does this imply that efficient prices are not reached in these markets? In their

---

[3] About 40% metal futures did not reach this threshold, 42% of agricultural products futures and 78% of energy futures. It should though be noted that the number of energy futures are much higher compared to metal and agricultural futures.

study, Adämmer et al. (2015) investigate two thinly traded futures contracts, hog and piglet at the Eurex in Frankfurt, and come to the somewhat surprising conclusion that even a few transactions per week can be enough to provide reliable price information for producers and traders of physical commodities.

Different prices may be quoted when a commodity is traded on several exchanges. Ordinarily, the prices will run in parallel. Also, the possibilities for arbitraging will prevent the price difference from widening beyond what is warranted by differences in the specified quality that is traded and to reflect the transport costs from the point of delivery to the major consuming centers.

Claims are sometimes made that the price quotations on commodity exchanges are distorted through intentional manipulation, including attempts to corner the market, such as occurred in silver in the Hunt Brothers' episode of 1979, and in copper during the Sumitomo scandal in 1996 (Gilbert, 1996). These shortcomings of commodity exchange prices notwithstanding, it should be underlined that the alternative price-setting mechanisms suffer from other, often more serious deficiencies, so the influence of commodity exchange quotations on the prices at which trade takes place in a commodity industry is not surprising.

A great attraction is that the prices set by the exchanges are instantaneously available and widely published. This contributes significantly to the influence they carry in trade and industry. Where trade in a commodity has been successfully established on an exchange, its prices tend to replace other price quotations and dilute the price-setting power of producers. From the late 1950s, *Metal Bulletin* regularly quoted a price for aluminum in Europe, entitled "Certain Other Transactions," which at times differed substantially from the dominant Alcan (producer) quotation. After the introduction of aluminum on the LME in 1979, the *Metal Bulletin* price became superfluous and was discontinued (Crowson, 1998). In the course of the 1980s, the LME quotation was generally accepted as the authoritative reference price. Developments have been similar in the case of nickel. Oil used to be Platt's or Argus, but is now Brent on ICE or WTI on NYMEX, while quotations for steel futures introduced on the LME in 2006 have replaced the trader prices hitherto published by *Metal Bulletin*.

The OPEC oil producers ceased posting their sales prices after crude oil trade was introduced, first on NYMEX in 1983 and then on ICE in

London in 1988. With the lively oil trade on the exchanges, the cartel's ambitions have been shifted to the defense of a price band, with the desired prices to be attained not through producer dictate but through market forces on the exchanges and the actions of the cartel limited to adjustments in supply.

Producers find it hard to exceed the widely quoted exchange price levels for long and by more than the narrow margins that buyers are prepared to pay for the increased convenience and security offered by a long-standing trade relationship. Where producers continue to quote their own prices, these quotations tend to change much more frequently and more tightly in line with the market once an exchange starts to provide a pricing rod; and in the end the producer quotes tend to become an irrelevance.

The exchange prices are influenced instantaneously by events both in the commodity market and in the outside world. Their daily fluctuations can therefore be considerable, and sometimes they are claimed to be seriously exaggerated by speculation (discussed in more detail in Section 7.3). Prices in transactions outside the exchange tend to be more stable, either because producers maintain their own quotations for much longer than a day or an hour or because they employ, for example, monthly averages of exchange quotes when they sell to their customers. Price stability may of course be desirable, but such stability can gloss over pent-up imbalances which could cause severe disruptions in the market once they become visible. Instantaneous price adjustment to emerging market fundamentals instituted by trade on the exchanges can help avoiding such disruptions.

Contango and Backwardation

Just like the instruments of futures contracts and options, the relationship between the spot and futures prices (contango and backwardation) provides considerable scope for rewarding commodity engagements by the financial community. It is appropriate, therefore, to discuss this relationship in some detail before venturing in the next section into the involvements of the financial community in commodity markets.

A contango market results from an abundance of immediate supply relative to the expected future supply. The current abundance will depress the price for immediate delivery, as compared to delivery in the future. Notice, however, that the possibility of arbitrage limits the level of the contango to the cost of storing the commodity between now and the time of future delivery. For example, the 12-month futures price cannot exceed the spot price by much more than 7% when the cost of physical storage, including deterioration, is 3% per year and the rate of interest is 4%. A higher contango will make it profitable to buy spot, take physical delivery and incur the cost of storage while immediately making a 12-months futures sale. Such action will increase spot demand and raise spot prices until the contango declines to just above the 7% level.

The contango is a blessing to producers in oversupplied markets, for it provides a neat mechanism for financing excess inventories without risk to the investors. This investment opportunity has been regularly employed by banks and other financial agencies. Strictly speaking, the deals represent long hedges. However, the different nature of the agents and of the basic purpose for their action warrants their classification as investors, not as hedgers.

A market in backwardation indicates a shortage of immediate supply and a perception of more ample supplies in the future. In contrast to the contango, there is in theory no maximum in the difference between spot and futures prices when the market is in backwardation, since arbitrage is not possible. A shortage today can cause spot prices to explode, irrespective of what is expected of the future. The futures price could remain at only a fraction of the inflated spot price, despite the knowledge that the current shortage will soon be overcome, for example because new production facilities are being opened up. In practice, inventories almost always establish a tie between the high spot price and the low, backwardated futures price, and it has to do with the convenience yield of inventory holdings. Inventories typically exist at many levels through-out the production–processing–wholesale–retail chain, and they yield a benefit to the holders through the convenience of being immediately available, should a need for their use arise. The inventories will be held so long as this benefit is valued more than the net gain from selling spot at the high price, buying futures at the low price and accepting the inconvenience of doing without until the futures purchases are delivered. At some level of backwardation, the inconvenience is overwhelmed by the gain from an inventory release. This constitutes a link between the spot and futures price, and a cap to the extent of backwardation.

7.3 The Actors and Their Objectives

We distinguish between three categories of actors on the exchanges, each characterized by the pursuit of a separate objective in their deals on the exchange. The first category, the hedgers, comprises those who depend on the commodity as such for their livelihood, primarily its producers, processors and users. They do not necessarily seek to profit from their transactions on the exchange. The livelihood of this group may be threatened by unexpected price fluctuations, so their primary interest is to avoid the price risk and they do it through hedging, a kind of price insurance. The second category, the speculators, come to the exchange with no initial risk. On the contrary, they seek to assume the price risk for the purpose of profit. So, when hedgers enter the futures market to assure themselves of the prevailing price, speculators enter that market on the opposite side, thereby providing the liquidity without which hedging would not be possible. The third category of actors on the commodity exchanges embraces the investors, who place money in commodities either because such placements offer a safe rate of return or as a means of portfolio diversification, but nevertheless with the expectation of a return. The latter type of investors operates with a far longer time perspective than that typically assumed by the speculators. The distinction between speculators and investors is not always crystal clear.

Hedgers

The general principle of hedging is to open a futures position opposite to that confronting the hedger in the physical market at a future time. The hedger is interested in safeguarding against one of two fundamental price risks. The first is that the value of unsold products will decline if the commodity price falls; the second is that the cost of future commodity purchases will increase if the commodity price rises.

The Value of Unsold Products Will Decline If the Commodity Price Falls

An owner of a commodity inventory (wholesaler, processor) can be assured against the risk of price decline by making a *short hedge* at the time they acquire their inventory, that is by futures sales involving quantities and due dates that correspond to the planned disposal of their physical holdings. In this way they are assured of the current commodity price on the futures market for these future disposals. When a physical disposal comes due, the owner will buy a corresponding amount spot on the exchange. The initial futures and later spot transactions on the exchange cancel out each other. If the price has fallen in the period between physical acquisition and disposal, there will be a loss from the physical transactions, but a compensating gain from the futures purchase and spot sale on the exchange. If the price has risen, the exchange transactions loss will be compensated by the gain in the physical trade. The cost of this hedge will be the interest on the margin payment and the brokerage fee plus any contango or minus any backwardation that prevails in the market at the time the futures contract is signed.

The wholesaler can alternatively acquire a put option with a strike price close to their physical purchase price and expiry about the time of their planned physical sale. If the price falls, the wholesaler will compensate their physical loss by the gain on the option premium. If the price rises, there will be a gain from the physical trade, but the premium of the option may fall to zero. The cost of these transactions will be the premium paid for the option and the brokerage fee for its purchase and sale.

The specific circumstances of each case will determine which of the two hedges provides the best and cheapest price insurance. The futures hedge will involve an expanded financial cost of additional margin payments, and an ensuing temporary need for more cash if a loss is incurred in the exchange transaction. The options hedge can yield a speculative gain if rising prices result in a profit from physical transactions that is larger than the premium initially paid for the option.

Commodity producers often make short hedges when they consider the current price quoted in futures transactions to be attractive. The commodity exchanges provide them with a means to lock in that price for their future output. Metal producers are known on occasion to have sold their entire anticipated output over several years into the future, thus securing the price of that output. New gold mines have sometimes used such extensive futures sales as collateral for loans to finance the development of the mine, as did CODELCO, the state-owned Chilean copper corporation, with the anticipated output of Gaby, a new mine (*Platt's Metals Week*, 2006, February 27), and more recently, shale-oil producers in the USA, to protect themselves against impending oil price falls in 2014.

The Cost of Future Commodity Purchases Will Increase
If the Commodity Price Rises

A direct user of a commodity or a manufacturer of goods with a high content of the commodity might avoid the risk of a forthcoming price rise by locking in the current prices in the futures market through a *long hedge*. This involves futures purchases on the exchange timed to coincide with their physical commodity needs in the future, cancelled through spot sales on the exchange at the time of the physical purchase. Alternatively, a call option can be acquired to make a long hedge. The assurance against price risk as well as the cost of the transaction and the relative merits of the futures versus options instruments are analogous to those in the short hedge. Users could alternatively make a long hedge to secure an uncertain physical availability.

The possibility of hedging a specific commodity is not entirely contingent on it having a developed futures market. An imprecise, but often satisfactory hedge can be attained with the help of a closely related commodity whose price is likely to move in parallel with the one on which the hedger is dependent. An edible oil that is not traded on any exchange can be approximately hedged through the futures market of another closely related edible oil. Arabica coffee futures can in most cases provide a satisfactory hedge for robustas, while crude oil is a reasonably close hedging substitute for bunker oil. The natural-gas futures contracts provide acceptable hedging facilities for deliveries in geographical markets out of the reach of the exchanges.

Speculators in Commodity Markets

The high level of standardization and the ensuing liquidity of the futures contracts and options makes it very easy to move funds in and out of commodity markets. This characteristic is a precondition for the widespread interest of the financial sector in commodity placements. As noted earlier in this section, there are two different actors, each with their distinctly different investment objective, and the instruments employed on commodity exchanges can be used to provide the satisfaction of either. The next several paragraphs explore the behavior and objectives of the commodity speculator. We subsequently turn to the investors, who see the commodity markets primarily as an additional asset class providing prospects for both inherently safe placements with returns only marginally above the "normal" and riskier but profitable investments, with the added benefit of offering means for portfolio diversification.

Speculation is a broad and amorphous concept. In the context of commodities, and in the broadest sense, it involves all actions that aim at profiting from a move in commodity price. Buying a futures contract on the exchange or prematurely filling a half-full automobile tank, both in anticipation of an impending price rise, can be classified as speculative activity, even though the latter action is undertaken by a commodity consumer (the car driver). A narrower definition in which the speculators have no intrinsic interest in the commodity as such is common. According to the *Shorter Oxford English Dictionary*, speculators buy and sell "in order to profit by the rise or fall in the market value, as distinct from regular trading or investment."

Speculators' typical objective is to reap very high profits in return for taking very high risks. With the narrower definition, the difference between hedgers' and speculators' behavior can be explained either by a difference in risk aversion or by the greater ability of speculators to diversify their positions. The role of speculation can therefore be seen as a means for the transfer of risk among agents with different preferences.

Commodity exchanges provide speculators with attractive opportunities for highly geared investments. The limited margin payments on futures contracts stretch the speculators' money at least by a factor of five, as compared with speculation in physical commodity deals. The potential return – and loss – for a given investment is multiplied in equal measure. The issue of options involves speculators in a risk of unlimited losses. But although there is an upper limit on the gains from the issue of options, these gains can be massive in relation to the small capital that needs to be committed.

Combinations of futures contracts and options permit the speculator to set the degree of risk in accordance to their desire. For example, they can enter a futures contract to sell if they expect prices to decline. If, instead, prices rise, they will lose, and there is no limit to the size of their loss. Such a limit can be established at, say, 50% of the value of the contract by the speculator acquiring a call option with a strike price 50% above the futures sales price.

Since the clearing house of a commodity exchange must maintain a balanced position in any commodity for any future date, the minimum role that the speculators must play is to establish futures contracts that fill the imbalance between short and long hedges (Ghosh et al., 1987). Because, by definition, they do not hold any offsetting positions on these minimum investments, the speculators carry the entire risk of loss or potential for gain from price movements.

Speculators are always there to respond to hedgers' needs regarding volume and timing of futures and options – at a price. Ordinarily, however, their actions go far beyond the satisfaction of hedgers' requirements. A large part of the positions they assume constitute bets against other speculators. In these ways, speculation improves the continuity and increases the liquidity in commodity exchange trade.

The expanded speculative activity has raised concerns about a possible upward price push and the creation of price bubbles for commodities by speculators. This issue is further discussed in Section 7.4.

Financial Investors in Commodity Markets

The first decade of the twenty-first century saw a phenomenal growth in commodity investments by institutions, hedge funds and individuals, who buy and sell futures and options without an ensuing physical transaction. Globally, commodity assets under management by financial investors increased in value from about US$13 billion in 2003 to an astounding US$450 billion in 2011. Despite a subsequent decline as the boom ended, these volumes still reached some US$350 billion in 2013 (FCA, 2014). Since then, financial investments in commodities have continued to increase, as is evident in Table 7.1.

The expansion of electronic trading over that period stimulated the emergence of many new financial tools that facilitate investors' commodity engagements. These were initially developed by investment banks. They comprise commodity index funds, over-the-counter swap agreements and many others. All are related to one or other established commodity price index. Goldman Sachs was one of the first to establish a commodity index fund and to launch its trading on the exchanges (Goldman Sachs, 2005). The Standard and Poor's Goldman Sachs Commodity Index (S&P GSCI) is one of the most widely tracked, and considered an industry benchmark. The GSCI is heavily weighted in energy. The major alternatives comprise the Bloomberg Commodity Index and the Commodity Research Bureau

Index, the latter having been in existence since 1957. All the financial instruments provide indirect exposure to a specific commodity or a group of commodities in futures markets, traded on exchanges. With many variations, investments in these instruments are expended on buying commodity futures, which are rolled over at maturity, that is sold just before expiry, with a matching purchase of new futures.

Special mention is warranted of exchange traded funds (ETFs), the most common among the new financial products. ETFs offer investors the possibility to pool their money into a fund to gain exposure in commodity assets. The launching financial institution invests in futures contracts in the chosen commodities and then sells shares in the fund to individual investors.

The development of these exchange traded instruments has provided market access to institutions and individuals who might otherwise have been prohibited by law, or reluctant for other reasons to participate in financial trading in commodity markets. It should be added that the exchange traded instruments generate considerable brokerage fees, hence they are favorably viewed by the launching investment banks (Irwin and Sanders, 2012).

The phenomenal growth of the new instruments was strongly stimulated by the findings in some analyses presented to promote commodity investments. Calculating the performance of hypothetical investments in the futures of these indexes several decades back in time yields remarkable conclusions: both the total returns and the risks to investors in these instruments would have been on a par with those on equity investments and much higher than those from investments in bonds. There is little correlation in the annual return from equities and commodities, so the addition of commodity investments stabilizes the overall diversified portfolio performance. Furthermore, commodity investments are claimed to provide a better protection against inflation than do investments in equities and bonds, and they are far superior in terms of returns to investments in physical commodities or in the equity of commodity-producing firms (Center for International Securities and Derivatives Markets, 2006). Even more remarkably, there are numerous academic papers that reach similar conclusions (Bodie and Rosansky, 1980; Conover et al., 2010; Erb and Harvey, 2006; Gorton and Rouwenhorst, 2006; Greer, 1994).

We are somewhat skeptical about these findings. Could the more recent of the studies just cited be unduly dependent on the impact of rising prices during the commodity boom of 2004–2011? And how would the results be altered if the price falls between 2011 and 2015 were included in the analysis? Our skepticism is strengthened by the more recent contribution by Bessler and Wolff (2015) which concludes that the benefits of adding commodities to a portfolio are considerably smaller than suggested in earlier work. Furthermore, their results suggest that the investment returns vary with type of commodity. There are more benefits from industrial materials, precious metals and energy, and hardly any positive portfolio effects at all for food commodities.

An obvious question to ask is how and why so many studies conclude that hypothetical investments in futures commodity indexes would have performed so well even in the face of a period of long-run commodity price decline (for over two decades before the most recent commodity boom), as depicted in Figure 6.1.

Iwarson (2006) provides a plausible explanation by revealing a methodological fallacy in the approaches to calculating the yield. It goes beyond mere numbers by subdividing the backdated returns from 1970 to 2005, yielded by hypothetical investments in the Goldman Sachs index, into several components. When measured in nominal SEK (Swedish currency), the total annual average return over this 35-year period works out at an impressive 15%, compared with a 17% annual return on the holding of Swedish equities and 10% on the holding of Swedish bonds (however, the commodity futures index investment would have slightly outperformed a portfolio of US equities, measured by the S&P 500 index). The commodity futures index returns consist of the following components:

- An annual average 6% return on rising spot prices of commodities, primarily an effect of the heavy dominance of oil in the Goldman Sachs index, and the strongly appreciating oil prices over the period,[4] so it cannot be precluded that an equally weighted index would have shown a zero or even negative yield on this count;
- A roll return of 2% per year, implying backwardation most of the time for most of the commodities comprised in the index;
- A collateral return: since investments in the futures commodity index require no more than a small margin payment, most of the

---

[4] The numbers underlying Figure 6.1 point to a total increase in real oil prices of 540% over the 35-year period 1970–2005. This corresponds to an annual average of 15%, and much higher in nominal prices.

committed capital can be used to purchase treasury bills, with the interest received attributed to the commodity investment. This collateral return has averaged 7%, almost one half of the total return.

In a more recent study, Yan and Garcia (2017) analyze the usefulness of commodities in a portfolio comprised of stocks and commodities, using price data from three different commodity indices and 15 individual commodity futures, between 1991 and 2015. They separate the results between three different "generations" of commodity indices, where the first generation indices are passive (hold long positions in contracts close to maturity), the second generation indices select contracts along the futures curve (e.g. if the market is in contango they select contracts at the end of the curve) and the third generation indices are active and based on strategies (e.g. they can take short positions in downward markets and long positions in upward markets – so-called momentum strategy). Their main findings are that including most individual commodity products futures (except live cattle) does not significantly improve the portfolio performance. The same result is found for first and second generation commodity indices. However, for more active commodity indices, that is third generation, there is some evidence that portfolio performance is enhanced. The general conclusion appears to be that commodities are seldom the cause of improved portfolio performance.

In our view, the claim that the total return on investments in commodity index futures is on a par with that of holding stocks is fallacious and greatly exaggerates the attractiveness of commodities versus stocks as investment classes. This fallacy arises from the comparison of investments in commodity index futures, which benefit from a large collateral return, with investments in holding stocks, which do not. The correct comparison should be with investments in stock index futures (substantially increasing the investors' risks), where both instruments benefit from collateral returns. We have not seen such a comparison presented by those who have marketed investments in commodity index futures, but given the significance of the collateral return investments in commodity futures are unlikely to match investments in stock futures.

Despite the fallacy identified above, investments in commodities are likely to prevail. Investment banks continue their eager promotion of commodity investments, while the public may like some involvement in an alternative to the dominant equity market.

7.4 Impact on Price Formation and Other Influences

How is a commodity market, and for that matter a commodity industry, affected by the introduction of exchange trade for that commodity? The impact attracting the greatest attention is that on prices, caused by the ease of entry for speculators to the exchanges. The following paragraphs are predominantly devoted to this issue. Several other plausible impacts may follow from exchange trade, and these will be mentioned briefly, as the chapter ends.

A problem running throughout the present discourse is the direction of causality: particular features characterizing the commodities traded on the exchanges may be the consequences of exchange trade; but these characteristics may equally likely be inherent to the commodity markets, and be the very reason for the introduction on the exchanges. Unreflected belief that exchange trade has always been the cause of the characteristics that can be observed must be avoided.

Impact on Prices

Speculators make their bets on the futures markets. Their purchase of futures pushes up the futures price, and this will impact on spot prices too, through the possibility of arbitrage if the market is in contango and through the convenience yield in backwardated markets. Liquidation of speculators' long positions will have an analogous depressing impact on futures and spot prices, as will an initial speculator entry through futures sales. Given the huge volumes in the futures markets, the speculators' positions would have to be very sizable to make a dent on these markets. But then, it is important to realize that the resources of the financial markets potentially available to speculators are huge too, and that the limited margin payment requirements provide for a considerable stretch of these resources. Also, the speculators' impact can be greatly augmented by a focus on selected markets, and not necessarily the biggest ones.

The basic theoretical presumption is that, under normal circumstances, speculation will even out price variations (Telser, 1981). After harvest, when the price is low, speculators will bid up futures prices until the contango is sufficient to make investments in inventory holdings worthwhile. The demand for inventories will strengthen the spot price level. At the height of an industrial boom, speculators will bid down futures prices, and so make stockholding unprofitable. The liquidation of stocks will reduce the inflated spot price. In this way, speculator foresight, stretching across seasons or phases of a business cycle, generates profits to their actions and at the same time this foresight evens out the inherent commodity price instability.

The theoretical analysis may seem to be contradicted by the observation that commodities traded on the exchanges tend to have less stable prices than commodities which are not. But then, the causality could be the other way round. Exchanges perform especially valuable functions for commodities with inherently volatile prices, and their services are simply not needed for materials whose prices are stable. We noted in Section 7.1 that the stabilization schemes maintained by the US government in the groundnut and tobacco markets are the probable reason why these commodities are not traded on the exchanges. Exchange traded commodities can in fact constitute a kind "adverse selection" insofar as price stability is concerned.

Speculators' activities would destabilize commodity markets only if their forecasts proved persistently wrong. Say that the industrial boom and the high industrial commodity prices of agricultural or mineral origin were not followed by a recession and low prices, but by a strike and even higher prices. Then, the depletion of existing inventories caused by erroneous speculator expectations would amplify the ensuing price rise and the speculators would lose wholesale from their investments.

If, in fact, speculators lose on average and so destabilize prices, there may nevertheless be a positive consequence of their activity in that the losses would correspond to a lowering of the average price paid by users and/or an increase in the average price received by producers (Friedman, 1969). The net social effect of such destabilizing speculation would depend on whether this benefit is greater or smaller than the discomfort of greater price instability. It may be that producers would feel the need to insure themselves against the higher price volatility, and that the cost of the measures would absorb their price gain.

Even if commodity speculation were to normally yield a gain, and so to stabilize prices most of the time, this does not preclude the existence of speculative bubbles that on occasion could drive prices to extreme highs or lows. Bubbles have to do with the fact that speculators are often more interested in what others believe and do (herd behavior) than in the fundamentals of the commodity market. Keynes (1936) distinguished between large, professional and well-informed speculators, on the one hand, and small amateur speculators, on the other. It could be that the former profit from speculation, while the latter lose. Speculators who are successful become large and those who are not leave the market and are replaced by other small speculators. This distinction provides an interesting mechanism for the emergence of speculative bubbles.

Commodity markets are occasionally invaded by amateur speculators. Their entry results in a strong price boost, even when the fundamentals for higher prices are not there. The professionals will then tend to follow the amateurs and amplify the price increase in the confident belief that they can profit from the price moves. Once the amateur money inflow has been exhausted and the price ceases to rise, the professionals sell out and the bubble bursts. In such circumstances, profitable speculation by the professionals will have a destabilizing impact on prices (Stein, 1981).

Analyses of the impact of speculation on prices have recently been greatly facilitated by more systematic data collection. The Commodity Futures Trading Commission (CFTC) in the USA makes an ambitious effort to collect detailed data on the composition of open interest across commodity futures and options contracts in the USA, in the so-called Commitment of Traders (COT) report. The data covers 22 commodity products (agricultural, energy and metals) and are made available to the public, both in a short and long format, at an aggregate and disaggregated level. The disaggregated COT data were first introduced in October 20, 2009 but available numbers go back to June 13, 2006. In the short report, open interest is separated both in reportable and non-reportable positions. For reportable numbers, short positions are provided for commercial and noncommercial traders, regarding holdings, spreading, changes from previous report, number of traders and percent of open interest by category. The long report additionally divides the data by crop year (if applicable) and identifies concentration of positions held by the four and eight largest traders. Supplemental reports provides futures and options positions for commercial, noncommercial and index traders altogether in 12 agricultural commodities.

In an early study on the effects of speculative activity on commodity prices Cooper and Lawrence (1975) found that speculation was an important factor behind the sharp increase in commodity prices in 1972–1975. However, in this time period the amount of financial capital in commodity markets was only a fraction of what it is today. As noted in Section 7.3, the presence of financial investors not directly related to commodities increased substantially in commodity futures markets from about 2003 and onwards. About the same time commodity prices started to increase, and it would not be surprising if the new financial investors were attracted to commodities by the possibility of high earnings. However, since the increase in financial involvements coincided with large movements in commodity prices, the belief that speculation had a real impact on commodity prices emerged. The hedge-fund manager Michael Masters was a strong proponent of this view, which he presented several times to the US Congress and CFTC. In Masters (2008) he argues that the substantial increase of institutional investors in commodity markets, with nearly US$30 trillion in assets to manage, created a massive bubble in commodity futures prices.

Recent research on this issue has been extensive, and most of the studies use the publicly available CFTC data. Hamilton (2009) developed a formal model of price formation in the crude oil market that identifies a theoretical condition for price bubbles caused by speculative activity. Empirical evidence of the occurrence of price bubbles during the latest commodity boom is found by Gilbert (2010a). In his study Gilbert examines price changes for crude oil futures, three metals futures and three agricultural futures during 2006–2008. The results identify price bubbles for 7 out of 9 markets, but only for a very small percentage of the days investigated (e.g. 21 out of 753 days for crude oil futures). Gilbert and Morgan (2010) and Gilbert (2010b) find similar evidence, that is, that index futures investments had an impact on food prices during the 2006–2008 price spike. Tang and Xiong (2012) do not test for price bubbles, but find that the development of commodity index investments has led to an increased correlation between commodity futures prices and prices of other financial assets, pointing to a linkage between commodity futures price movements and investments in commodity indices. Singleton (2014) too finds that the recent flow of capital into index funds is positively correlated with changes in futures commodity prices.

However, a majority of economists expresses skepticism toward the argument that speculation caused price bubbles during the latest commodity boom (see e.g. Krugman, 2008; Pirrong, 2008). In fact, most of the empirical studies on this issue do not find that financial speculation has been important in driving commodity prices, see for example Alquist and Gervais (2013), Fattouh et al. (2013), Kilian and Lee (2014), Kilian and Murphy (2014) and Knittel and Pindyck (2016), who all investigate this issue on the oil market. Similar results, that is that speculative activity does not affect prices, is found for energy and agricultural markets by Brunetti et al. (2011), Hamilton and Wu (2015), Irwin and Sanders (2012) and Will et al. (2016). Brunetti et al. (2011) also find that market liquidity reduces the volatility and thus the risk in these markets. This is in line with the results in Deuskar and Johnson (2011). Irwin and Sanders (2011) present a thorough survey of the literature and conclude that a majority of the research does not support the view that speculation has had an impact on the commodity prices in the course of the twenty-first century. In a more recent survey Haase et al. (2016) review 100 empirical studies on the impact of speculation on commodity futures markets and come to a similar conclusion.

We argue, in line with the majority of the research findings quoted above, that speculators and other financial investors are not to blame for accentuated price volatility and bubbles in commodity prices. Revealingly, several commodities not traded on exchanges, and hence not subject to speculation, have exhibited equally strong upward price movements as those subject to exchange trade and speculation during the most recent boom. Most of the variation in prices appears to be due to fundamentals.

Other Impacts

Other impacts of commodity exchanges on commodity markets and commodity-producing industries have been suggested, although here too firm empirical evidence remains to be provided. For instance, it is plausible that producers will tend to adjust the quality of their output toward the standards adopted by the exchanges for the purpose of futures trading, even when the commodity is sold through other channels. This is because a correspondence with the exchange quality will normally make the commodity more widely marketable than it would be otherwise. In this way, the exchanges would tend to promote standardization and uniformity of quality.

Another plausible impact could be that by providing an assured outlet for physical trade, the existence of exchanges reduces the incentive for vertical upstream integration by commodity users. Such integration has been a common response to potential threats to raw materials supply, for instance because of producers' monopoly power. This line of reasoning suggests a lesser extent of vertical integration in industries that use commodities that are traded on exchanges. Here, too, one can argue the direction of causality: commodities will not be traded on the exchanges until there is a reasonable degree of competition among vertically unintegrated producers.

8 | Sustainability and the Threats of Resource Depletion

Fears of depletion of the physical resources upon which human societies and their cultures build are as old as humanity itself. Maurice and Smithson (1984) provide examples from antiquity to modern times, so Thomas Malthus (1798) was by no means the first to express concerns about the inadequacies of the physical resource endowment for human needs. Malthus, however, has had many followers. The dire predictions of the Club of Rome (Meadows et al., 1972) and of the Association for the Study of Peak Oil (Campbell, 1997) are but two of the more recent influential examples of this strand of thought. The messages of an impending depletion of this or the other component of essential physical resources in human use are usually accentuated and enjoy a wider hearing during periods of boom, when expansion in usage gathers pace and prices rise. Late in the twentieth century, concerns about the deterioration of the environment were added to the depletion fears. So far, however, the pessimistic messages have all proved wrong (Simon, 1996). Contrary to the depletion argument, the real prices of almost all resource products traded in competitive markets have experienced a long-run decline, or at most a very modest increase (see Chapter 5), while the conditions of the physical environment have tended to improve, not deteriorate, in consequence of economic growth (Lomborg, 2001; Radetzki, 2001).

This chapter treats a subset of the above concerns. It is devoted exclusively to exhaustible resources – comprising metals, minerals and fossil fuels. Outputs from agriculture, forestry and aquaculture, all being renewable, are not part of the deliberations. Furthermore, as appears from the chapter's title, we deal predominantly, though not exclusively, with depletion in an economic, not in a physical sense. There is no economic depletion, according to the definition of this concept, if inferior deposits that are used to replace rich and exhausted ones can provide output without an increase in cost. Our vista is broadened, however, by also considering sustainability, that is the social issues encountered by the extractive industries, which needs to be addressed for the long-run acceptance of these industries' activities. The significance of these issues has been greatly enhanced since the dawn of the twenty-first century.

The fear of depletion was strongly accentuated in the early twenty-first century with the emergence of a powerful commodity boom. The increase in demand for resources from emerging Asia spurred a forceful wave of investments in resource-rich countries to meet this booming demand. As a consequence, exploration and extraction increased in parallel. This, in turn, awakened a vivid concern about the short and long-term effects of nonrenewable natural resource extraction on the societies where production takes place. In extractive industries firms face a special need to consider the economic, environmental and social impacts of their activity to assure acceptance and hence survival of their operations in the long run. Our discussion in this chapter, though focusing on economic depletion as defined above, attempts to address these issues as well.

In the course of our studies of the economics of natural resources over four decades, we have not come across any clear-cut case of economic depletion of an exhaustible resource. But we can quote examples of formerly sought-after exhaustible resources whose production has declined, not due to depletion but because they have lost much of their value in consequence of new technology or a change in demand. Progress and innovation in the chemical industry suppressed the value of guano, a raw material for fertilizer collected from the islands off the west coast of South America, to the extent that its production ceased. Asbestos and mercury appear to be going the same way, in consequence of the discovery of their detrimental effects on health. And the instances of economic depletion that have actually occurred are found, ironically, among the renewable resources. Forests in ancient Rome were depleted by overuse, as was the case with fish stocks in the oceans during of the second half of the twentieth century, both of which resulted in substantial increases in price.

Depletion concerns an accentuated scarcity and it can be measured in different ways, four of which are popular with economists (Tilton, 2003):

• The trends in the adequacy of reserves from which the resource can be extracted provide an important physical insight into the seriousness of the depletion threat.

- The progress of real prices is seen by economists to reflect accent-uating or subsiding scarcity.
- The long-run change in the unit price in real terms of identified but unexploited resources still in the ground is an alternative measure of the extent of the depletion threat.
- Finally, the development of the long-run marginal cost of supply, equivalent to the total average cost in the marginal project, is yet another economic indicator of scarcity.

Since depletion is a slow, drawn-out process, long time series are needed to make measurement meaningful. For much of the rest of the chapter, we document and discuss the available data on each of the measures in turn.

The chapter ends with a discussion of sustainability in relation to the acceptance by society of the extraction of nonrenewable resources.

8.1 Availability of Reserves

A major concern of the Club of Rome in the early 1970s (Meadows et al., 1972) was the limited amount of world reserves of metals and fuels. Its publications asserted that, since the reserves of copper and other exhaustible resource products represented only some 30 years' current production, a growing world demand would be bumping against a binding resource ceiling by the end of the century, even when the prospects of additional finds were taken into account.

The authors of these gloomy forecasts apparently did not care to enrich their analysis by historical insights. In the 75-year period 1925–2000, world production of coal increased 2.7 times and that of iron ore 5.1 times; world output of copper expanded nine-fold and that of petroleum 24-fold. Natural gas and aluminum kept the record among major commodities; their output in 2000 was 68 and 133 times higher, respectively, than 75 years before (BP, annual; Darmstadter, 1971; Metallgesellschaft, annual). And yet, remarkably, reserves of each of these materials developed roughly in parallel, so as to assure a relatively stable reserves/production multiple (R/P), often at a level of about 30.

Growth of production accelerated after 2000. In the period 2000–2018, encompassing the strongest commodity boom since the Second World War, global coal output rose by 70%, iron ore and aluminum output increased 2.5 times, while output of copper rose by 59%. Increases in world production of petroleum and natural gas were somewhat more modest, 24% and 61%, respectively, in the 18-year period under consideration (BP, annual; USGS, annual). The fact that the R/P ratio for most commodities, including the ones enumerated above, has remained above 30 despite the explosive growth in extraction since 2000 is a forceful indicator that tendencies toward depletion have not been significant.

No miracle is involved in the stability of the R/P ratio noted above. Reserves are created through investments in exploration. A profit-maximizing firm will not invest in reserve creation beyond its perceived current needs for comfort and planning, just as it will avoid investing in plant and equipment beyond its planning horizon. With growing output, an R/P ratio of 30 is usually deemed comfortable since it will suffice for the next 15–20 years' production. This way of looking at reserves provides a convincing explanation of the amazingly stable R/P ratio observed over time. A quote by Adelman (2002), the grand old man among oil market analysts, reveals the stunning flexibility of the process:

In 1944 world proved reserves were 51 billion barrels. In 1945–1998, 605 billion barrels were removed, leaving 1035 billion ... As with any inventory, proved reserves increased not *despite* interim production but *because* of it.

Table 8.1 demonstrates that creation of reserves is continuing, and that the R/P ratios for the four minerals shown is comfortably above 30. We note especially that the R/P ratio for oil has increased substantially since 2005, mainly a result of the development of unconventional oil, discussed in Chapter 4. We note a decrease in the ratio for iron ore and nickel, but an increase for copper. It is important to stress that the absolute level of proved reserves for all of these minerals increased notably after 1995 and continued to do so also after 2005. Furthermore, even though the R/P ratio for iron ore decreased considerably after 1995, it is still the highest among the products shown.

Representatives of the Association for the Study of Peak Oil have expressed depletion concerns by pointing to the fact that oil production has exceeded "new discovery" since the 1980s (Bentley, 2006). This concern is fallacious because it does not take into account the very substantial appreciation of mineral and fuel deposits after discovery.

Table 8.1 *Proven reserves and R/P ratios for four minerals*

	Oil	Iron ore	Nickel	Copper
Proved reserves (million tons)				
1995	138 000	151 000	47	310
2005	164 000	160 000	62	470
2018	244 000	170 000	89	830
R/P ratio (years)				
1995	41.3	151	47	31
2005	40.6	105	41	32
2018	54.5	68	39	40

Source: BP (annual); USGS (annual).

For example, historical evidence from oil suggests that the ultimate extraction from a deposit represents a quantity about six times greater than the initially recorded discovery (IEA, 2005a). The sum total of global oil discovery and appreciation has progressed well above global oil production, explaining the continued growth of reserves. This is importantly the result of technical progress converting unconventional resources into economically viable reserves (see Chapter 4 for a more detailed discussion).

8.2 Evolution of Long-Run Prices

The early 1980s saw the triumph and perversion of the so-called Hotelling rule, derived from a now-classic paper in the exhaustible-resource literature (Hotelling, 1931). Subject to a set of restrictive assumptions, such as a known, finite resource and constant technology, this rule states that the unit price of the unexploited resource will rise over time at the real rate of interest. Enthusiastic, but not very thoughtful oil-market analysts and political decision makers perverted the rule into stating that the prices of exploited exhaustible resources must rise at the (real) rate of interest. Though no theoretical foundation nor empirical support was provided for this assertion, the perverted rule caught wide attention among investors, policy makers and other interested groups.

When applied to oil, the rule appeared to vindicate the idea that the price increases since the early 1970s were due to depletion and represented the beginning of a permanent upward trend. Forecasts of future oil prices were formulated in the early 1980s by reputable organizations, including Exxon and the World Bank, gloomily predicting perpetual real price increases from the then-elevated levels (Exxon, 1980; World Bank, annual a, 1981). Since these forecasts were widely believed, there followed monumental policy mistakes as the world tried to adjust to a continuously increasing oil price.

Increases in the long-run real price of exhaustible resources would indeed reflect depletion in most cases. After all, prices are the ultimate indicators of the total costs of marginal supply in an industry. And an increase in these costs mirrors accentuated scarcity, that is economic depletion. But when employing price series for measuring economic depletion, one has to carefully avoid periods when prices do not reflect cost conditions. This would be the case when there is monopolistic collusion (Herfindahl, 1959). Misinterpretation of the price impact of political crises in oil-producing countries as depletion, and use of the results for forward projections, was the major fallacy of the oil price analyses of the early 1980s. Other periods to be avoided when investigating depletion with the help of prices are temporary price spikes, usually caused by demand shocks, such as during the booms in 1973–1974 and in 2003–2015, as described in Chapter 6, for then the price tends to settle far above the total cost of marginal supply.

In Chapter 6, we presented some long-run trends of real prices, but these have to be reworked in the light of the above considerations to fit the needs of the present analysis. For metals and minerals, where market conditions remained reasonably competitive for most of the twentieth century, we link the Grilli and Yang (1988) 1900–1986 decline of 0.84% per year (see Chapter 5) with the 2.9% increase per year for 1986–2018 recorded in Figure 6.1, to obtain an average of +0.16% for the entire 118-year period.[1] It is worth noting that the increase in the real prices of minerals and metals occurs after 2003, as the period 1986–2003 does not indicate rising price levels. Thus, the increase in prices is importantly a result of the most recent commodity boom. A relevant long-run indicator for depletion should not be based on the inflated price levels due to a commodity boom. When

---

[1] One can argue that the shift between declining real prices until 1986 and the rising levels subsequently recorded is a harbinger of economic depletion.

performing the same calculation for the period 1900–2003, the real average prices decline by an annual average of 0.7%.

For oil, the relevance of prices as an indicator of depletion ends in 1972, as the price evolution in the period thereafter is importantly shaped by political upheavals in important producing nations that prevented the buildup and utilization of production capacity (Aguilera and Radetzki, 2016). In 1900–1972, the oil price fell by an average of 0.7% (Radetzki, 1990b), that is at the same rate as did the price for the metals and minerals group during the longer period quoted above. This price evidence from metals, minerals and oil does not support the view that economic depletion has occurred.[2] We would have liked to review long-run price series for hard coal and natural gas, but given the recent emergence of the international markets for these products, such series are not available (Radetzki, 2002).

8.3 Evolution of the Unit Price of Unexploited Resources

It needs to be remembered that the Hotelling rule, as originally stated, applies not to the prices of finished commodity products, but to the unit price of the resource still in the ground. Rising, real long-run prices of unexploited resources would indeed be an indicator of depletion. The rule that such prices must rise at the (real) rate of interest is unobjectionable within the confines of Hotelling's analysis, but it has little relevance in practice because the assumptions from which it is derived do not hold. The volume of ultimately exploitable resources is unknown, and what is known grows over time in consequence of exploration. Also, the progress of technology improves the efficiency and reduces the cost of exploiting a resource of a given quality. When these alternative assumptions are introduced in the Hotelling model, the rule of appreciating values of resources in the ground breaks down.

Records of unexploited resource prices are rare, but we have found a series of prices for oil deposits in the USA (Adelman and Watkins, 2005). This is displayed in Figure 8.1 below. It is not clear whether any conclusions about depletion can be drawn from the data. Indeed, the prices paid for the deposits do not show any upward trend during the

---

[2] In an intriguing analysis, Svedberg and Tilton (2006) assert that the deflators in common use to obtain real commodity prices exaggerate inflation, and that when this bias is rectified, the downward real price trend for many exhaustible resources may well turn around. They show that this is the case for copper.

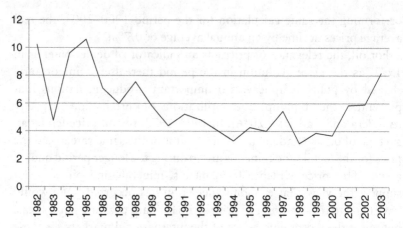

Figure 8.1 US oil reserve prices 1982–2003 (constant 2003 US$ per barrel)
Source: Adelman and Watkins (2005).

22-year period. Instead, they appear, unsurprisingly, to fluctuate with
the oil prices. But, like the oil prices during the period, the prices for oil
reserves do not reflect the costs for establishing reserves or for producing oil.

8.4 The Cost Evidence

The direct indicator of depletion tendencies is a rising cost of output,
including the cost of establishing or acquiring resources in the ground.
More precisely, what is needed is a time series of the total average cost
of an exhaustible resource from the marginal project taken into use at
different times. The reason why we devoted so much attention to price,
an indirect measure of depletion, is that the cost evidence, like that of
the price of unexploited resources, is extremely meager. Where it exists
at all, it commonly covers a limited period only, which makes it less
useful for the purpose at hand. Additionally, cost data are regularly
organized and presented in a different format than specified here, so it is
hard to interpret them unambiguously for the purpose of measuring
depletion.

The IMF (biannual, 2006) has compiled cost data for three metals for
the years 1985 and 2002, and these are elaborated in Table 8.2. The
data are subdivided into costs of "typical" and "least efficient" units in

Table 8.2 *Operating cash costs for three metals*

	1985		2002		2013	
	Typical[1]	Least efficient[2]	Typical[1]	Least efficient[2]	Typical[1]	Least efficient[2]
$/ton (nominal)						
Aluminum	1 000	1 200	1 000	1 200	n/a	n/a
Copper	1 000	1 400	1 000	1 600	3 600	5 300
Nickel	3 400	5 300	3 700	6 100	n/a	n/a
$/ton (deflated by UN's MUV index,[3] 2002 = 100)						
Aluminum	1 270	1 520	1 000	1 200	n/a	n/a
Copper	1 270	1 770	1 000	1 600	2 570	3 780
Nickel	4 310	6 720	3 700	6 100	n/a	n/a

[1] 50th percentile of the industry cost curve.
[2] 90th percentile of the industry cost curve.
[3] Unit value index of manufactures exports.
Source: IMF (biannual, 2006); UNCTAD (monthly).

the industry, the latter related to, though not identical with, the marginal projects of the respective industries. Quite significant reductions between 1972 and 2002 are recorded in the real costs of output in all cases. Similar data are difficult to find for more recent years. The only numbers we could obtain are for copper in 2013, but we assume that the development for the other metals has progressed in a similar way.

We expect that since 2002 the operating cash costs for many metals have increased considerably, as a result of the strong demand increase and accompanying rising price levels. Data for copper costs in 2013 reveal a strong increase of both the average and least efficient operating cash costs. This is not surprising, since with speedy demand growth and high prices cost controls are relaxed and more meager deposits are used, increasing the operating cash costs for the producing firms. Is this a sign of depletion? We argue that it is not: it is, rather, a result of high prices and a temporary investment frenzy triggered by booming demand levels.

Regarding energy, the IEA (2001) has compiled some striking data on declining oil costs until 1999. It finds that the global average total cost of new fields taken into production (i.e. precisely the measure needed to track economic depletion) was reduced from US$29 per barrel in 1981 to US$9 in 1999, and proportionately even more if the numbers had been expressed in constant money. This is not the consequence of a wholesale geographical shift of production toward OPEC's low-cost deposits, since OPEC's share of world output was virtually the same in the two years (BP, annual). Nevertheless, the decline exaggerates the long-run cost trends. Some of the reduction can be attributed to a one-time restoration of order in the late 1980s from the inflated cost levels caused by feverish investment activity in the late 1970s and early 1980s that was driven by a desire to benefit as quickly as possible from the high prices at the time. But a substantial part of the cost suppression is due to remarkable technological progress over the 18-year period (Bohi, 1999).

The cost data discussed above are strongly suggestive of a declining cost trend for exhaustible resource outputs until 2003, but there are clear indications of a sharp upward cost move in the 2004–2013 period. We argue that the increased costs are mainly due to the frenzied investment activity in the resource industries, sparked off by the commodity boom of the mid-2000s. Producers hurried to establish new capacity, and the prices of virtually all investment inputs exploded in consequence (IEA, 2006; IMF, biannual). We also assert that the investment-driven cost increase during the most recent commodity boom is temporary and has nothing to do with depletion. Costs will fall as the commodity boom ends and the investment activity subsides (as it did after 2011), much in the same way as occurred in the oil industry after the 1986 price collapse.

A hypothetical cost issue must be given consideration before this section is concluded. Economic logic posits that the most economical among known deposits will be exploited first, so over time there will be a tendency toward quality deterioration, even though new discovery could plausibly arrest or even reverse this tendency. The deterioration is behind the upward slope of the long-run supply schedule depicted in Figure 5.2. We noted when that curve was discussed that although it may be gently sloping upward, its level has historically tended to shift downward over time in consequence of cost-reducing technical progress, not least in transport, making distant resources economically accessible. The technological accomplishments in the extractive industries are thoroughly described in Simpson (1999). The downward shifts in the long-run supply schedule in turn explain the long-run decline in exhaustible resource prices discussed above.

However, as pointed out by Tilton and Skinner (1987), one cannot preclude a sharp upward jump in costs as cumulative output increases, if there is a discontinuity in the resource stock that forces the extractive industry to move to much leaner resources when the rich ones have been exhausted. Such discontinuities are indeed possible and the resulting higher costs and prices would be an expression of depletion. But the actual experience of two discontinuities suggests that their economic significance may not necessarily be grave, that in fact they could occur without leaving any economic mark at all.

The first discontinuity relates to copper and it took place early in the early twentieth century. It involved an extremely sharp decline in the grade of ores mined, as the limited availability of high grade ores became inadequate. In the USA, the average grade declined from almost 6% in 1890 to less than 2% in 1920. By 1960, the average grade had fallen further, to below 1% (Lowell, 1970). Worldwide data on grades are not available, but they undoubtedly followed those in the USA, with a lag. Yet, real prices of copper declined by almost 40% between the 1890s and the 1920s, as the industry adjusted and perfected its technology to the meager deposits in use (Radetzki, 1975).

The second discontinuity relates to oil and is currently occurring. It involves a shift from "conventional" oil deposits to "unconventional" ones, such as deep offshore, shale, arctic, bitumen and oil sands. Until recently, this was widely believed to involve a quantum jump in costs; but as production from unconventional deposits has grown it is increasingly evident that the shift is economically seamless, as is apparent from Figure 8.2. Unconventional resources are continuously reclassified into the conventional category as their exploitation expands, and the cost of their exploitation is falling.

Developments in the USA provide an illustrative example whose end has not yet been reached. Between 2008 and 2018 crude oil production in the USA increased by more than 125%, almost exclusively due to the extraction of shale oil (discussed more thoroughly in Chapter 4). Technological developments, in combination with high oil prices around mid-2000, had made it economically feasible to extract shale oil. Production of shale oil increased from 0.9 MBD in 2010 to 3.5 MBD in 2013 and reached 6.5 MBD in 2018 (61% of total US oil production), with expansion expected to continue (EIA, annual, 2019). The oil price collapse that occurred in 2014–2016 raised the question of how long shale oil production would still be economical. Continuous and very rapid efficiency gains in shale production

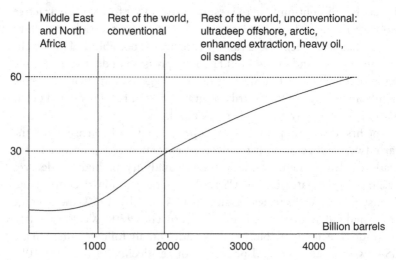

Figure 8.2 Oil resources and cost of exploitation, 2008 (US$ per barrel)
Source: Derived from IEA, annual, 2008.

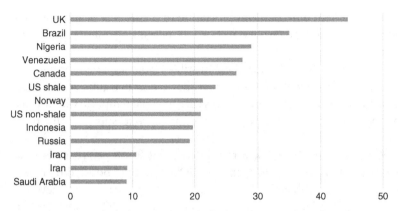

Figure 8.3 Cost of producing a barrel of oil in 2016 (US$ per barrel)
Source: WSJ (2016).

techniques have assured the resilience of this supply source (World Bank, 2018c).

Recent data on the total cost of oil extraction confirms this. Figure 8.3 presents the average total cost for producing a barrel of oil in 2016 (estimations made by Rystad Energy) for a number of countries, as well as for shale and non-shale in the USA (WSJ, 2016). Interestingly, we note that the average cost of US shale oil according to these estimations were almost equal to US non-shale oil. These numbers are almost hard to grasp, considering the relatively short time that shale techniques have been economically viable. Even though production costs and breakeven costs are often difficult to define and vary both over time and between different production facilities, many studies confirm a remarkable decline in US shale production costs (World Bank, 2018c). In sum, we conclude that the developments of shale oil fail to provide any evidence toward depletion.

8.5 Evidence of Depletion Summarized

Four types of evidence have been reviewed: reserves, real prices of exhaustible materials, prices of unexploited resources and costs of exploitation.

There is little sign of depletion in the reserve data. Reserve volumes are comfortably high and have grown in line with exploitation. A tendency for discovery to fall short of exploitation in some materials has been noted, but sizable appreciation of deposits in production has compensated for the discovery shortfall, permitting continued reserve expansion.

Increases in the real price of exhaustible resources would provide an indirect evidence of depletion in that they reflect marginal costs. Using prices to measure depletion requires care to avoid temporary high-price periods, because at the point prices can deviate substantially from costs.

Real prices for oil show a trend decline of 0.7% per year between 1900 and 1972. After 1972, they were "artificially" boosted by recurring political problems in many key producing countries, severely restraining the buildup of production capacity. In 2014, however, oil prices fell sharply, primarily under the influence of large-scale output additions of shale oil in the USA, effectively arresting the Peak Oil debate and other depletion fears. With the continued, successful shale revolution spreading from the USA across the world, oil prices in the longer run are likely to settle far below the levels attained in the past decades (Aguilera and Radetzki, 2016). Clearly, however, political and other "artificial" actions can lead to higher oil prices than what is motivated by capacity and costs. The September 2019 attack on Saudi production installations, temporarily reducing the country's output by half, is an illustrative example.

Metals and minerals prices fell in line with oil prices, by 0.7% per year between 1900 and 2003. From 1986 to 2003, however, the trend has been relatively flat. Developments after 2003 and until 2015 have been shaped by the commodity boom. The high price levels of that period were temporary. After 2011, as the boom ended, quotations were strongly reduced. The boom-period prices bear little relation to costs. Hence, they are not an indicator of accentuated depletion.

The price of resources in the ground could plausibly reflect changes in scarcity and thus depletion. Data on such prices are rare, but we presented in Figure 8.1 a series of price quotations for oil in the ground in the USA. The series appears to be synchronized with oil prices, and we deem it to have little significance as a measure of depletion.

A variety of real cost numbers were reviewed, not all of which were fully relevant for the purpose at hand. The thrust of these data sets is toward a decline over time, in line with the real prices. A sharp increase in costs was observed after 2002, but this is interpreted as a short-run phenomenon, caused by the investment frenzy that was triggered by the commodity boom of the following years.

Discontinuities involving sharp shifts to more meager deposits have occasionally occurred, and we briefly reviewed the cases of copper and oil in this respect. These two shifts have not left any perceptible mark on costs and prices, as technological progress compensated for the upward pressure on costs.

We conclude that the evidence of depletion is fuzzy and not very conclusive; but, if anything, it points to a relative relaxation of scarcity in the course of the twentieth century. Tendencies toward economic depletion have been compensated (or even overcompensated) for through cost-reducing technical progress in exploration, extraction, processing and transport of the exhaustible resource materials.

8.6 Sustainability: Satisfying Human Needs

In the twenty-first century concern about the short and long-term impacts on society of the extraction of nonrenewable resources has gained enhanced interest. The most recent commodity boom, with intensive investments and fast-rising production levels, has accentuated this interest. The concept of "sustainable development" has been the focus of ongoing discussions on the long-run role of extractive industries in society. Sustainable development is commonly defined as "development that meets the needs of the present without compromising the ability of future generations to meet their own needs" (WCED, 1987). However, sustainable development is not a clear-cut concept and we feel a need to begin this section by a discussion of sustainable development in relation to exhaustible resources.

It should first be noted that there is an inherent logical contradiction between sustainability and the extraction of exhaustible resources. The very term "exhaustible" implies that extraction cannot be sustainable – sooner or later the resource will be exhausted since it is finite, at least in a physical sense. A substantial literature on mining and sustainable development has taken this stand in exploring the constraints to sustainability imposed by the limited physical availability of minerals (see e.g. Gordon et al., 2006; Mudd, 2010; Poulton et al., 2013; UNEP, 2010). We take objection to this literature because in our perception the relevant discussion is *economic* not *physical* depletion, so the last source of a nonrenewable resource will in fact be too costly and will not be extracted.

We addressed the issue of economic depletion at some length in Section 8.4, and will now follow up by considering *how* the extraction of nonrenewable resources can be conducted in a sustainable way. In this more relaxed view of sustainability, extraction can, more precisely, be seen as sustainable if the benefit from the activity provides other forms of capital to society, which in turn yields future welfare that can fully compensate for losses due to depletion. The concept of sustainability is often divided into three "pillars": economic, environmental and social, all of which need to be addressed in order to achieve sustainability.

Economic Sustainability and the Extraction of Nonrenewable Resources

According to Tilton (1992) there are three factors that are important to consider when assessing *economic* sustainability in the extraction of nonrenewable resources. The first is the cost of actually developing the resource, since it will not yield any benefit in terms of growth and enhanced economic welfare if it is left in the ground. Second, it is important to ensure that at least part of the economic yield from the extraction is reinvested, to assure benefits accruing in some measure to future generations. The third factor is more directed to the national level: it deals with the avoidance of possible negative macroeconomic consequences related to resource extraction. Each of these factors will be discussed, following the deliberations in Eggert (2013).

The first factor is related to geological information and investments in exploration activities, since without geological knowledge it will not be known what deposits exist and what potential they hold. Furthermore, it is not until the resource is in fact exploited that it will add to economic growth and enhanced welfare in the country/region. Whether or not a resource will be developed depends on many factors, some difficult to influence (e.g. the characteristics of the deposit), others easier to address through policy (e.g. the institutional framework that governs the exploration and extraction of resources). As an example, many governments hold geological information that they often provide without charge to private investors. The expectation is that this information might plausibly lead to mineral extraction. The economic rationale behind this public policy is that the private sector often underinvests in the collection of geological information, which can plausibly reduce mineral exploration in a country and so reduce the potential future benefits from exploitation.

Whether or not a government is active in attracting foreign investors to exploit the country's mineral wealth depends largely on the mineral policies that are pursued. Mineral policies relate to the rules and legislation that govern the exploration for and exploitation of mineral resources. These policies address, among many other issues, land use and access to land; mineral royalties and taxation; as well as environmental protection (before, during and after the exploration and exploitation). These policies vary considerably across nations. It is common that more developed countries have stricter environmental regulations, while many developing countries often have higher mineral royalties that cut investor returns but benefit government budgets.

Second, in order to achieve economic sustainability it is vital that the rents from extraction are invested at least in part in a way that increases economic benefits in the future. Thus, it is important that the extracted nonrenewable resource is replaced by a sustainable asset that adds to future economic and social development in the country. These investments can take many different forms such as education, infrastructure, research and development or new types of businesses (Eggert, 2013).

In this way, natural resources, if managed properly, can be a great source of economic wealth for a country. If the rents from extraction are instead spent predominantly on current consumption, expatriated by foreign investors, invested unwisely or merely wasted, the extraction will not contribute to economic growth and enhancement of future welfare (Tilton, 1992). Achieving economic sustainability in this sense has proved quite difficult, especially in developing countries with immature social institutions. In the academic literature such inability is seen as an aspect of the "resource curse" (see Chapter 12 for a more thorough description).

The third factor relates to a plausibly negative effect on the domestic economy from a dominant extractive industry. This effect takes into account that other sectors in the economy can sometimes experience strains due to a large local/regional/national focus on mineral extraction. For example, a resource boom can lead to increases in the local/regional wage levels as the extraction industry expands and absorbs competent workers, who are in short supply. The increased wages offered by the extractive industry can be difficult for other sectors to match. Another effect often encountered is an appreciating currency that can develop into a survival threat for other tradable industries. Unstable mineral resource prices and excessive dependence on the production of a single resource are other problems often faced by national economies dominated by extractive activities. These are all manifestations of Dutch disease, a component of the broader resource curse, to be discussed in further detail in Chapter 12.

Environmental Sustainability and the Extraction of Nonrenewable Resources

The issue of environmental sustainability and mining takes two forms: the first has a focus on sustainable use of the stock of natural resources, while the second relates to the environmental impact from the extracting activity. The first was covered at some length earlier in this section, so the discussion here will deal with sustainability of environmental quality. Extraction of mineral resources is clearly associated with significant environmental impacts. The intervention in the physical landscape is often severe, especially in open-pit sites. Waste rock and tailings as a result of extraction provide serious environmental challenges. Preventing leakages into the nearby environment is an important environmental issue to tackle. Other hazardous substances, such as nitrogen, can discharge from the many explosives that are used. Frequently the infrastructure for the extraction site has significant environmental impacts as roads and railroads to the mine site are developed (though the positive impact of such infrastructure should not be ignored) (Widerlund et al., 2014).

Mineral extraction typically causes emissions of greenhouse gases, as well as of dust and aerosols. One of the most challenging environmental consequences from extraction of mineral resources is acid drainage. This is the discharge of acidic substances, which can have a strongly negative impact on local fauna and flora. The effects of acid drainage can be long lasting; in the worst case they can remain for thousands of years (Widerlund et al., 2014). Furthermore, it is clear that the nature of environmental challenges has been changing over time. New technological innovations can help in reducing the negative effects. However, other environmental challenges often arise, for example when lower-grade ores are extracted on a very large scale, or in the extraction of shale oil and gas.

It is clear from the above discussion that extraction of natural resources often has a profound impact on the adjacent natural environment. The impact starts at the exploration phase and it regularly becomes much more severe in the extraction phase. The environmental challenges often continue long after the extraction ends. Both short-run and long-run environmental aspects must be considered for the maintenance of environmental quality at an acceptable level. In the short run, the marginal cost of protective measures should be set equal to the environmental benefit obtained. Over time, the damage to the environment could plausibly subside as techniques that minimize environmental impacts are developed (Eggert, 2013).

Social Sustainability and the Extraction of Nonrenewable Resources

The social aspect of sustainability has so far received less attention than the economic and environmental aspects; however, recently this strand of research has increased sizably. For a general discussion of the concept of social sustainability see, for example, Dempsey et al., 2011, McKenzie, 2004, and Murphy, 2012; and for the mineral extraction industries in particular see, for example, Everingham, 2012, Hilson and Murck, 2000, MMSD, 2002, Solomon et al. 2008 and Suopajärvi et al. (2016). The extraction industries face a number of social challenges that are important to consider. For example, extraction is often located in sparsely populated and rural regions that are often heavily dependent on the income and employment created by the extractive industry. Tricky problems frequently arise because the extractive regions are commonly highly valued natural areas, and are often populated by indigenous people.

Dempsey et al. (2011) identify both physical and nonphysical factors that are important contributors to social sustainability. The physical factors are, for example, decent housing and an attractive public realm, while the nonphysical factors comprise education and training, social justice, participation and local democracy, as well as social inclusion, health, cultural traditions and general quality of life. By attending to these factors extractive industries can clearly contribute positively to the development of an attractive society, but they can also obstruct such positive developments. On the negative side, the literature on the subject points to situations where the extractive industries attract workers to the extent of interrupting social cohesion, creating scarcity in housing and causing pressures on the availability of other social goods, for example health facilities and schools (Greer et al., 2010).

Extraction of mineral resources often occurs in areas inhabited by indigenous people, and since such people regularly depend on traditional forms of livelihood based on the natural surroundings, the interests of the extractors on the one hand and the local community and its inhabitants on the other tend to collide. Research on this issue, especially concerning how companies in extractive industries can negotiate agreements with indigenous people, includes Fidler and Hitch, 2007, Heisler and Markey, 2013, O'Faircheallaigh, 2010, O'Faircheallaigh, 2013 and Parsons, 2008.

It has been shown that to achieve social sustainability it is vital for the extractive industry to gain acceptance by the local/regional community (Moffat and Zhang, 2014). Otherwise public opinion from different stakeholders can in fact hinder extraction of the resource. Thus, if the company addresses all relevant stakeholders and their needs, from the exploration phase to the closure phase, a socially sustainable development of the extraction is far more likely to occur. If the company fails in these efforts, it may well be forced into premature closure. This, then, is the link between attendance to the economic, environmental and social needs of society and sustainability of mineral extraction.

8.7 Conclusion

The weight of the evidence summarized in this chapter points to declining real prices of exhaustible resource products and suggests that the supply of such materials has become more ample in the past 100 years. We argue that this is the case despite the most recent commodity boom, with exploding demand and supply and prices for many primary commodities. We argue that, in line with previous commodity booms, we have witnessed a temporary, though violent, increase in real prices, which passed their peak a few years ago and have now reverted back to a much lower level with a resumption of the historical slowly declining trend. At the same time, it needs underlining that the historical evidence is incomplete and ambiguous, sometimes pointing in directions opposite to the main thrust. Furthermore, history is not necessarily a reliable guide to the future. Benign past trends could well be reversed due to an ever-increasing volume of exploitation and/or a serious slow-down of the cost-reducing technological progress in the exhaustible resource industries – a development that is conceivable, though not likely.

The possibility of such a somber future outlook must be put into a proper context, however. How serious would the problems be arising from a sharp reversal of the real price trend for a number of exhaustible resources of –0.7% per year over most of the twentieth century to, say, an annual +1.0% for several coming decades, due to depletion of the resource base? Not very serious, we would claim, and for several reasons. The following arguments posit that while a sharp slowdown in technological progress related to exhaustible resource outputs is unlikely but not implausible, it would require an unreasonable stretch of imagination to assert that the technological slowdown would simul-taneously apply to other economic sectors. And if it did not, then continued technical progress in all other areas of the economy clearly offers several avenues out of the depletion predicament.

First, while a 1% annual rise in the real price assumed above would certainly impose an economic burden on the exhaustible resource users, it would still involve a declining labor effort to earn a unit of the depleting resources,[3] given that hourly wages in real terms typically rise by more than 1%.

Substitution in favor of cheaper and more abundant resources offers a second means to ameliorate the emergent strains due to depletion. The substitution of glass fiber for copper in telecom wiring is a striking example of how a cheap and almost infinite resource (silicon) was substituted for a much dearer and potentially scarce one. The substan-tial increase in productivity that resulted from this substitution (glass fibers can carry much more data than copper wires) may be seen as a beneficial side effect. This substitution took place in the face of a long-run fall of the price of copper. The incentive to substitute would have been much more pronounced if copper prices had been rising.

Access to an advanced, broad-based technology platform facilitates the processes of substitution. Opportunities to resort to various types

---

[3] Barnett and Morse's (1963) seminal work attaches considerable attention to the use of wages as a deflator in deriving real commodity prices.

of substitution, related to both methods and materials, occur all the time and account for a significant proportion of economic growth in rich, diversified societies. The postindustrial era has been appropriately termed "the age of substitutability" (Goeller and Weinberger, 1976). Our societies' increased capacity for substitution greatly reduces the dependence on any individual, exhaustible resource material or group of such materials.

A third and related reason why depletion may be a burden but not a catastrophe is the gradual dematerialization of the advanced economies. This process was discussed at some length in Chapter 1, and Table 1.2 provides a stark illustration of the decline in the quantity of a resource needed to create a unit of economic value. Access to a minimum quantity of physical resource inputs is indeed necessary. Collapse would follow in the hard-to-imagine situation where the supply of such inputs was completely arrested. But the consequences would hardly be dire from an unlikely but conceivable process of depletion that raised the real prices of exhaustible resources by 1% per year.

The history of the price of light vindicates the above statement. It is available in two versions, which come to similar conclusions (Fouquet and Pearson, 2006; Nordhaus, 1997), and we choose the earlier and more straightforward one to make the case that the satisfaction of human needs is not particularly dependent on the real price movements of exhaustible resources, nor of finished goods, within a wide range. The central issue instead concerns the cost of satisfying human needs. This depends importantly on human resource inputs. Nordhaus' study tracks the real cost of light over a 110-year period. On the basis of price indices for the USA (1883 = 100), Nordhaus shows that the real prices of kerosene and electricity in 1993 had fallen by 25% and 97%, respectively. He also demonstrates that linked price indices for lighting devices, such as kerosene lamps and electrical bulbs of various types, do not indicate any significant real change. However the index of the real cost of a lumen, a unit quantity of light, had fallen from 100 in 1883 to only 0.1 in 1993, importantly because of the enhanced efficiency in transforming inputs such as kerosene and electricity into light. A given quantity of lighting in the latter year cost only one thousandth of what the same quantity of lighting had cost in 1883!

The figures forcefully demonstrate the power of technical progress to generate light with ever-decreasing inputs of exhaustible resources and finished goods. The real cost of light would not have been notably affected if the prices of fossil fuels had doubled or trebled, or even increased tenfold, during the period, owing to accentuated resource depletion. Human ingenuity, rather than the price of exhaustible resources has been the completely dominant factor underlying the ability to satisfy human needs in this particular case.

The relationships brought out by Nordhaus' study undoubtedly apply in many fields. For example, the resource use and cost of a telephone call or dispatch of a written message from Stockholm to Santiago, say, early in the twenty-first century is only a minuscule fraction of what it was 50 years earlier. Human welfare would not be compromised even if depletion led to substantial increases in exhaustible resource prices. Human inventiveness is a forceful and undepletable "ultimate resource" (Simon, 1996) to keep the threat of exhaustion at bay.

Despite our optimism, which is supported by evidence of technological advances and human inventions reducing the stress of depletion for many exhaustible resources, the role of sustainability in the extractive industries remains highly relevant. Sustainability of the extractive industries and depletion of the resources extracted are in fact closely related. To achieve *economic* sustainability it is important to explore and extract the resources and to invest the rents from this activity in goods that sustain the benefits to future generations. *Environmental* sustainability is met when the negative impact from extraction is carefully attended to and intervention is kept at a level where the benefits from protection equal its marginal cost. *Social* sustainability is achieved when the industry gains acceptance by the local/regional and national community. We have argued that the extractive industry will not be viable in the longer run unless it successfully attends to these issues. Extraction will cease either because the industry will fail in the requirements imposed on it by society, or because economically exploitable resources run out. This points to the relationship between sustainability and depletion.

9 | Fears of and Measures to Assure Supply Security

The discussions in Chapter 2 demonstrated how, in the course of the twentieth century, Japan, the United States and Western Europe, the world's industrial centers, have become increasingly dependent on imported commodity supply. Expanded needs due to industrialization and income growth, a relative depletion of the domestic resource base, and the secular decline in transport costs explain why it had become increasingly economical for advanced nations to replace the domestic production of a multitude of raw materials by imported supply. Primarily on account of differences in resource endowments, the dependence on imported primary commodities is most pronounced in Japan and least in the United States, with Western Europe in between.

The apparent indispensability of many commodities and the threat of international supply disruptions through wars and other disorders has long caused concern to importing nations. Influenced by the autarkic tendencies that evolved during the Great Depression, even Keynes (1933) deviated from the gospel of comparative advantage. He expressed the view that the leading economies' reliance on faraway sources of raw materials supply had become excessive, so a greater self-sufficiency might be warranted both on political and economic grounds, even when local production cost more than imports. Since the emergence of the latest commodity boom in 2005, the major industrialized countries have launched a variety of actions to overcome the perceived problems of commodity-imports insecurity.

We consciously employ the perceived concept, because the greater risks of relying on imported supply, as distinct from domestic supply, are not uniformly borne out by historical evidence. In fact, one can claim that the emergence of global markets, offering a wider potential diversity of import sources, may well make imports more secure than domestic supply. The breakdown of coal availability in the United Kingdom during the extended coal strike in 1984 would have been less accentuated with a greater role played by imports. Famines due to a crop failure are easier to avoid when consumption depends on geographically diversified imports.

Arguments for greater self-sufficiency of raw material supply have once again emerged on the political agenda, primarily stemming from the Trump administration and their ambition to promote national industries (see Chapter 3). The growing trade deficit recorded by the USA, especially toward China, is the main motivation for this policy shift and the imposed import tariffs are to encourage domestic supply. These actions have tended toward a sustained trade war between the USA and China, and have spread to all sort of goods (not only commodities) and also to other countries. The end of this protectionist wave is currently difficult to analyze, but imported supply security is at the heart of the situation.

The purpose of the present chapter is to explore the ramifications of the issue of imported-supply security and to scrutinize the alternative measures that have been used for overcoming the difficulties that an unreliable import supply of raw materials could cause. Domestic supply is conventionally assumed to remain secure and stable.

Even though the analyses should be of relevance to any country heavily dependent on commodity imports, the subject will be treated mainly with reference to the major industrialized nations. The focus is on supply disruptions which are unanticipated, occur suddenly and prevail only in the short-to-medium term. Monopolistic producer action, embargoes, wars, strikes and natural disasters are cases in point. No attention is given to the gradual supply changes that stretch over time periods long enough to permit full economic and technical adjustments. The disruptions under consideration involve sizable cuts in the quantity supplied, resulting in violently rising prices or physical shortages if the price is controlled.

The emphasis is on alleviating programs that are initiated or supported by the governments of the importing nations, although actions can of course also be taken by the commodity-using industries. Quite often the government actions are implemented in conjunction with the major importing firms.

In Section 9.1, we consider the circumstances under which supply disruptions become especially serious. Section 9.2 explores the nature of the difficulties likely to emerge. The menu of policies to overcome the problems is discussed in Section 9.3, while Section 9.4 summarizes the main findings.

9.1 When Are Supply Disruptions Particularly Serious for the Importing Economy?

The severity of a commodity supply crisis for an importing economy will depend on a number of factors. Some of these are due to conditions in the importing country, while others have to do with circumstances in the producing/exporting areas. We review these factors, starting out with the ones that originate in the importing country.

Import Dependence. Everything else being equal, the severity of the supply crisis in a given commodity will vary with the share of imports in total use in the importing country. An interruption to imported supply is unlikely to be serious if imports constitute a limited share of consumption, since in such a case the impact on total availability will be small and only the less important, marginal uses of the commodity will be affected.

Value of the Commodity Import in Relation to the Size of the Importing Country's Economy. Between two equally indispensable materials, a reduction in supply and an ensuing increase in price will be more painful if it involves the one representing the greater import value.

Substitutability of the Commodity. A supply crisis will have more severe consequences for materials with no close substitutes. Apart from the ease with which the functions of one material can be performed by another, substitutability has an economic and a time dimension. Easy substitution implies that the substitute material is available at a cost not much higher than the material in crisis. In this sense, palm oil is a good substitute for groundnut oil, since both have comparable costs and prices. In contrast, silver is not a good substitute for copper, for although silver has many of copper's desirable attributes its cost per unit of weight is about 70 times that of copper. If there is a supply crisis in copper, copper prices can rise a lot before it becomes economical to substitute silver on a large scale. Easy substitution also implies that the replacement can be introduced promptly. This may not be possible if there is capital equipment that is specific to the use of the original material, for then the need to rebuild that equipment will delay replacement.

Indispensability of the Final Product in Which the Commodity Is Used. A supply crisis will have more severe repercussions if the commodity is employed to make products that are vital to key functions in the importing nation. An import disturbance in nickel will raise greater complications than one involving imports of cocoa, because stainless steel, the finished product involving nickel use, is harder to forgo than chocolate.

The severity of a supply disruption will also be related to the circumstances characterizing the export sources.

Concentration of Export Supply. With geographically concentrated supply, the impact of natural or man-made disruptions, for example droughts, earthquakes, strikes, and political upheavals, will tend to be greater. Geographic proximity will also tend to facilitate the launch of supply-cutting cartels, especially when this proximity strengthens the political and economic affinity among the producers.

Difficulty in Substituting New Sources of International Supply for Current Ones. Disruption of supply from established import sources will be most severe when capacity utilization is high worldwide, leaving little prospect for switching to alternative sources. The severity of the disruption will also vary with the length of time it takes to develop new capacity and the differential between the cost levels of this new capacity and that of the established suppliers

Circumstances on the supply side also permit some judgment about the risk that a supply disruption will occur. Indications of political instability are taken as a sign of increased likelihood of a supply disruption. The history of earthquakes, violent weather or strikes in major supply centers can also help in assessing the risk.

This list of factors is helpful in singling out the commodities that may warrant special action to assure stable import flows. The degree of risk aversion among policy makers will determine how many commodities will be included in this group and how much will be done about them. Risk aversion appears to be greater in the United States than in Europe and Japan. Despite its much lower import dependence for most commodities, the United States has been by far the most energetic among the three in launching efforts to assure its imported commodity supply.

A group of "strategic" metals with exceedingly concentrated sources of global production probably come highest on the list of candidates for action to secure import supply.[1] In 2018, 88% of niobium (columbium in the United States) was produced in Brazil; 71% of rare earths and 82% of tungsten originated in China; South Africa accounted for 69% of world platinum output, and the share rises to 82% if Russia is added; in palladium the same two countries accounted for 73% of global output; while Russia and China together generated 80% of global vanadium supply. There is very little production of these "strategic" metals either in Japan, the United States or the European Union, so import dependence is almost complete. These materials are very hard to substitute in the short-to-medium term, and they all satisfy vital needs in the production of indispensable alloys and catalysts.

After the two oil crises of the 1970s, petroleum too has entered the list of products that warrant action to assure supply. In distinction from the strategic metals, whose trade values are quite small, petroleum trade weighs heavily in the importing countries' economies.

Other metals, for example copper, nickel, tin and uranium, have sometimes prompted action aimed at averting the risks of uncertain foreign availability. Iron ore and lead, in contrast, have attracted less attention in this respect, importantly because of a greater diversification of their sources of supply.

Among agricultural raw materials, natural rubber has been seen as a risk, on account of its importance for transport and other key industries and the heavy concentration of its supply in Southeast Asia. However, the availability of synthetic rubber, a good substitute for many purposes, has reduced the fear of supply cuts. Wool and cotton have prompted fewer disruption worries. Import dependence and supply concentration are very high in the case of tropical beverages, but supply disruptions have not been seen as a serious threat, probably because these products are not regarded as indispensable.

Base foods such as cereals, pulses, and meats have not been prominent among the materials causing worries about supply security, despite their nature as essential goods. The reason is a low degree of import dependence: in the USA a result of strong comparative advantage; in Western Europe and Japan due to long-lasting and far-reaching agricultural protection (see Chapter 3).

---

[1] Production data from USGS (annual, 2019).

9.2 The Nature and Severity of the Problems Caused by Disrupted Commodity Supply

A price rise is the first consequence of disrupted commodity supply. Given the low price elasticity of demand for indispensable raw materials, the price reaction can be quite violent. For strategic metals, this elasticity is (absolute) 0.1 or less in the short run, so the price could easily double in consequence of a 10% supply shortfall.

The price rise will impact immediately on the importing country's macroeconomy. The current account will deteriorate and inflationary pressures will be accentuated. For these effects to be perceptible, however, the imports and consumption of the commodity must represent a high value in relation to the importing nation's economy. This may be true of fossil fuels and possibly base metals, but hardly for any of the strategic metals.

The reduced supply will limit usage. Rationing of what is available can be done by price or by regulation. Price rationing is more efficient since it will favor discontinuation of the least economic uses. In both cases, some former users will have to do without the commodity and may be forced to close down their businesses. Unemployment could rise in consequence. Closures will also have dislocating effects further down the production chain. Such effects can be severe if the output of the commodity-using industry is essential to important sectors of the economy.

The commodity users who stay in business will make efforts to substitute in favor of other raw materials, or to invest in capital that saves on the disrupted commodity use. The cost of these adjustments will impact negatively on productivity, causing some slowdown in economic growth. These microeconomic dislocations will have a further negative effect on macroeconomic performance.

The consequence of a supply disruption to an importing country will be more severe if that country is hit in isolation, such as through a selective embargo, while other importers can obtain their requirements without problem, for then that country's international competitiveness will suffer. Political regulation is a prerequisite for embargos to have such effects, for without regulation market forces will assure a reallocation of supplies in favor of the embargoed nations.

The negative consequences will be strongest in the short run but will subside over time, even if the disruption continues. Economic forces will bring relief through substitution and savings in usage.

Attempts have been made to measure the economic costs of commodity supply disruptions on the basis of specific scenarios. The outcomes depend entirely on the assumptions underlying the scenario, namely how large and lasting will be the supply shortfall; how fast can alternative supply be mobilized; how and at what speed will the importing economy affected by the shortfall react?

The arbitrariness of the results emerges starkly from two old studies on chromium (US Bureaus of Mines, 1986). In the 1970s, analyses relating to (West) Germany concluded that the country's GDP would fall by about a third as a result of a complete unavailability of chromium supply. This drastic result must be due to an extreme assumption about supply, and equally extreme suppositions about inflexibilities in the German economic system. A study from the 1980s concerning the United States assumed a complete three-year loss of South Africa's chromium supply and a 90% loss of Zimbabwe's, concluding that these shortfalls would reduce US GDP by 0.2% in the first year, 0.1% in the second and about 0.05% in the third year.

Significant efforts have been devoted ever since the mid-1970s to determine the macroeconomic impacts of disrupted oil supply. IEA (2004) notes the wide array of quantitative results reached by its predecessors, importantly due to the differences in the models employed for the task. In retrospect, its own results are less than entirely persuasive. The study asserts that a sustained oil price rise of US$10 per barrel (from US$25 to US$35) will reduce the OECD's GDP growth by 0.4% in the same and the following year, and raise the rate of inflation by 0.5% in the same and the following five years. Given the dramatic and sustained oil price changes since early 2004, when the study was published, one would expect to be able to notice their impact simply by an ocular inspection of macroeconomic performance, even when there are other concurrent factors influencing GDP and inflation change. However, no such relationship can be detected from the numbers in Table 9.1. Catching the wider macroeconomic impact of commodity market disruptions is apparently a complicated task.

There are also important noneconomic aspects of commodity supply disruptions. For example, defense concerns underlie many of the efforts to assure strategic metal imports. When a military threat is serious, the

Table 9.1 *Oil prices and the macroeconomy*

Year	2002	2004	2006	2008	2010	2012	2014	2016	2018
Crude oil price (US$/bl)	25.0	38.3	65.1	97.3	79.5	111.7	99.0	43.7	71.3
Change from two years ago (US$/bl)	-3.5	13.3	26.8	32.2	-17.8	32.2	-12.7	-55.3	27.6
GDP growth (%)									
OECD	1.7	3.3	3.1	0.3	3.0	1.3	2.2	1.8	2.3[1]
China	9.1	10.1	12.7	9.6	10.6	7.7	7.3	6.7	6.6
India	4.6	8.1	9.7	3.9	10.3	5.1	7.3	8.2	7.1
Consumer prices (% change)									
OECD	2.7	2.4	2.6	3.7	1.9	2.3	1.7	1.1	2.6
China	-0.8	3.9	1.5	5.9	3.3	2.6	2.0	2.0	2.1
India	4.3	3.8	6.2	9.2	9.5	10.2	5.9	4.5	3.5

Source: BP (annual); IMF (biannual); OECD.stat, http://stats.oecd.org.
[1] Estimated value.

needs of the armaments industry will be satisfied on a high-priority basis, irrespective of the costs that are involved.

9.3 Measures to Alleviate the Consequences of Supply Disruption

Damaging disruptions of physical commodity supply in the international market are rare. Prices can vary a lot due to, for example, shifts in desired inventory levels, expectations about future events or outright speculation, but quantities are much more stable. Inspection of global agricultural-production data reveals no sharp, man-made disruptions. Relatively rare crop failures of up to 15% of global output from one year to the next have occurred in coffee and cocoa, whose production is geographically concentrated, while downward fluctuations have been much smaller for essential food products such as cereals and sugar, and for cotton.

From the minerals world we know of only four man-made disruptions of significant magnitude over the past 40 years.

The first relates to cobalt, an "indispensable alloy of strategic importance." In 1976, world production fell by almost 20%, in consequence of political upheavals in Zaire (now Congo Kinshasa) where more than half of world output was produced. The producer price reacted with a lag, from US$5.40/lb at the time the crisis broke out to US$25 later in the decade, and remained elevated for a four-year period. The substitution process triggered by the price change was painful and costly, but its force and speed proved that the metal was indeed dispensable. Demand in the USA fell by 53% between 1978 and 1982, and developments in other countries ran in parallel. By 1983, production had fully recovered, and the price had returned to its pre-crisis level (USGS, annual, 2002).

The second disruption occurred in the oil market in 1979–1980, initially in consequence of the Iranian religious revolution when the shah was deposed, followed very soon after by the Iran–Iraq War. Global oil output fell from 64.6 MBD in 1979 to 58.2 in 1981 (BP, annual), a 10% decline. The price more than doubled from December 1978 to May 1979, when it attained US$32 per barrel, and rose even further in the following two years (UNCTAD, monthly, 2000).

The third was the disruption of rare earth metals from China. Rare earth metals are used in devices that in the twenty-first century have become virtually indispensable in everyday life: mobile phones, computer memories, florescent light bulbs, wind turbines, hybrid vehicles, rechargeable batteries and many more. The high concentration of rare earth metals production and traded supply from China, in combination with a strong increase in demand for these materials since 2000, erupted in 2010 into a highly infected political issue. In 2010–2011, prices of rare earth metals exploded in consequence of repeated export quotas imposed by China. Between 2009 and 2010 rare earth exports from the country declined from about 50 000 tons to some 30 000 tons, a cut of 40% (Kingsnorth, 2010; Lynas Corporation, 2011). This obviously caused serious concerns in importing countries, which had become increasingly dependent on China's supply of these crucial materials. Additionally, in September 2010, due to a dispute over maritime boundaries, China completely stopped its export of rare earth metals to Japan (Areddy et al., 2010; Bradsher, 2010). In response the USA, EU and Japan launched a joint effort to put a halt to China's trade restrictions, widely considered as unfair and politically motivated. In 2014, the WTO in fact ruled in favor of the major importers, against China's claims that the restrictions were due to environmental and resource conservation concerns (USGS, annual, 2015).

The fourth disruption again occurred in the oil market: the September 14, 2019 drone attack on two of Saudi Arabia's largest production facilities. The estimated loss due to the attack was 5.7 MBD, which is more than half of Saudi Arabia's oil production and represents roughly 5% of global oil production. The production outage caused the largest daily price change in Brent crude oil price since 2010 (Hamilton et al., 2019). Even though the effects of the attack were exceedingly short-lived as full production recovery was attained by the end of the month, the attack illustrates the vulnerability of the oil market.

The fact that disruptions in the supply of essential commodities are rare does not necessarily alleviate fears of their occurrence, nor does it discourage action to overcome their undesirable consequences. But it is interesting to note that the intensity of such action tends to come in waves, with peaks after disturbing developments in commodity markets. One such peak occurred in the early 1970s and was related to the widespread belief in commodity power and the many cartel attempts launched at the time (see Chapter 10). After a long period of calm in the commodity markets, new concerns about supply disturbance and the need for measures to assure supply emerged in the 2000s with a focus on oil and gas, and in the 2010s focused on rare earth metals. The USA dominated the efforts of the 1970s, but in the 2000s the action had a more international character.

Two general remarks are pertinent before we discuss the security-of-supply arsenal in detail. First, when markets are truly global, a supply disruption is bound to be a global phenomenon too, warranting international action to come to grips with the problems. Actions by individual nations in isolation may be ineffectual and politically destabilizing, and the benefits, if any, may be appropriated by free riders (Griffin, 2009). Second, with the proliferation of commodity exchanges supply disruptions have lost some of their sting, since commodity users can insure themselves against price increases by hedging in futures markets. Of course, the users' gain must be juxtaposed against the losses incurred by the speculators who issue the insurance.

Many different measures can be employed to reduce the risk of disruption – and its consequences – to essential commodity imports. The menu can usefully be divided into: (a) measures intended to secure an uninterrupted import flow; and (b) those aimed at assuring a greater domestic availability that can be relied on in the event of an import breakdown. Our discussion follows this order.

Most of the measures to assure stable commodity imports relate to the choice of suppliers and the development of special relationships with them. There would be no need to be concerned about supplier choice if commodities were homogenous and markets operated under perfect competition, for then a supply disturbance would merely result in higher prices that rationed what was available among interested buyers. The realities of most commodity markets deviate significantly from this ideal. Problems could arise because some suppliers may be unable to offer the precise grades required. Furthermore, physical trade is typically conducted on the basis of standing relationships that take time to develop. Quite often, the price at which transactions are conducted reacts to shifts in supply with a lag. After a sudden reduction in supply, the buyers whose source had been knocked out would need time to establish new trading relations. In the meantime some of their demand would be unsatisfied, while price remained below market-clearing equilibrium. In such circumstances it becomes important to avoid the disadvantage suffered by the commodity user who is left out in the cold. There is a benefit in stable relations with reliable suppliers, even though, in the end, the supply disruption will result in higher prices for all buyers.

Choice of Suppliers

An obvious and straightforward measure in this regard is to diversify the importing country's sources of supply both on geographical and political criteria. The consequences of a breakdown of one source will seldom be critical if none of the suppliers accounts for a dominant share of the total.

The choice of suppliers should also favor ones deemed to be stable and secure. Three instances from the early 1970s point to the criteria of unreliability that continue to be valid in the twenty-first century, though they do not in all cases apply to the same countries. The embargo of 1974, imposed by the members of the Organization of Arab Petroleum Exporting Countries on oil sales to the USA and the Netherlands, made the members of the group appear unreliable. The short-lived embargo on soybean exports instituted by the US government in 1973 aimed at assuring domestic availability at a low price, but it reduced confidence in the United States as a reliable supplier and strengthened Brazil's position in the international soybean market. Canada's refusal to honor its uranium supply commitments to some European countries in the 1970s, also motivated by the priority of domestic needs, encouraged the development and expansion of alternative supply. Admittedly, the cases involving the USA and Canada are examples of government activism in primary resources that many years ago were replaced by policies favoring international collaboration and market solutions, but that recently have gained renewed relevance.

The efforts to assure stable imports through careful choice of suppliers do carry a cost. Diversification of import sources may reduce economies of scale. Geographical diversification can add to transport costs, especially for high-volume products such as oil, iron ore, bauxite and coal. A premium price can be commanded by suppliers with an established record of reliability. For this reason, the Netherlands and Norway have been able to charge a somewhat

higher price than Algeria and Russia over extended periods of time
for their sales of natural gas to Europe. Suppliers with an uncertainty
element, in contrast, have to accept a discount. This was long true
with coal and strategic metals from South Africa. Until apartheid was
disbanded, there was a risk that importing governments might
embargo South African exports.

Tighter Relations with Suppliers

In the 1950s and 1960s, direct foreign ownership was commonly
regarded by the multinational resource enterprises and their governments in the Anglo-Saxon world as the most effective means to assure
steady raw materials import flows. The profit motive was obviously
another reason for direct investments to exploit foreign natural
resources. Nevertheless, backward integration was seen as an important tool to assure not only against disruption of physical availability,
but also against destabilizing fluctuations of market prices. Irrespective
of what happened to prices, the owner could always count on the
output at the cost of production.

As events turned out, the backward integration proved to be of
doubtful value to the multinationals. Many of their direct foreign investments were nationalized in the 1960s and 1970s by the newly independent administrations in developing countries – at a substantial cost to the
investors, since compensation was meager when it was paid at all
(Chapter 11). More importantly, however, the nationalizations disintegrated the very foundations on which the policies of supply security had
been based. Even in cases where foreign ownership remained, its role for
supply security was diluted by the government activism in the host
countries that characterized the primary sector at the time.

In contrast to Anglo-Saxon practices, Japanese and to some extent
German supply security arrangements emphasized the establishment of
long-term supply contracts with independent raw materials producers.
Quite often, these contracts involved provision of long-term finance
with some concessional element, as an inducement to establish raw
material production (Radetzki and Zorn, 1979), along with technical
assistance in a variety of fields, for example exploration for minerals,
but they seldom included managerial control.

The long-term contractual supply arrangements entered into in the
1960s could stretch over anything from a year to more than a decade.

When long-term investment finance was provided, the supply obligations regularly lasted at least until the loans had been repaid. The standard contracts of the period specified both quantities and prices, the latter often with escalation clauses. Prices have come to play a reduced role in current long-term contracts. Such contracts, where they still exist, are basically agreements about quantities, while the prices are determined by commodity exchanges.

Long-term contracts do provide a shield against supply disruptions, so long as they last. The problem is that when they involve corporate parties in different countries, their enforcement is not easy. Hence, if changing circumstances create dissatisfaction with one of the parties, a renegotiation will be necessary for the contract to survive. The supply assurance at predetermined conditions, therefore, becomes quite limited.

The irony is that supply was forthcoming and disruptions had been rare irrespective of the mode chosen to assure supply. The Anglo-Saxon model was less successful, however, given the cost to the investors as their assets were nationalized. The Japanese–German mode, too, involved an added cost of supply, but it was not exposed to the detrimental effects of state takeover since there was nothing to nationalize.

A further irony is that the lessons about the outcome of the alternative modes to assure supply security seem to have been solidly forgotten, or maybe never learnt, by the new actors, often state owned, from China, India, Brazil, Malaysia and other developing countries. In the 2000s, these actors have gone on a somewhat indiscriminate buying spree to obtain foreign ownership positions, predominantly but not exclusively in fossil fuels field, in their efforts to assure their imports. The deals have comprised very substantial investments in countries presenting quite high political risk (IEA, 2007).

Tighter relationships with commodity suppliers also include treaties with political and/or economic content between the governments of the countries that trade. The importing government can offer political and military support, a foreign aid package, a generous bilateral trade deal or a long-term price guarantee, against a promise of first option on the raw material produced by the exporting country. The relationship between Saudi Arabia and the USA in the 1990s and 2000s has accommodated many of the elements listed here.

Other Measures to Assure Imported Supplies

Military power has long antecedents in its role as a guarantor of international commodity supplies. Both the Allied and the German and Japanese fleets provided protection to the commodity flows from overseas to Europe and Japan during the Second World War. Naval protection of petroleum shipping from the Persian Gulf has also come into use on and off during later decades, in times of political and military tension in the region.

Joint sharing arrangements among importers constitute yet another measure to alleviate the impact of supply shortfalls, especially when the buyers risk being unevenly hit. The petroleum-emergency policies under the auspices of the International Energy Agency (IEA, 2001), involving saving and sharing, put in place in response to the oil crisis of 1973–1974 are a case in point.

Barter-trading arrangements have sometimes been used to help in cementing bonds with foreign raw material suppliers. The commodity-importing country can become a priority buyer by offering the exporter some especially valuable goods (food, specialized manufactures) in return. Mutual priority barter arrangements prevailed for decades between Finland and the USSR, the former supplying high-tech manufactures in return for oil. The arrangements broke down with the collapse of communism in 1990.

Promotion of Domestic Output

With greater domestic output, the impact of an international supply disruption will be less severe. The measures to promote production within the country can be dealt with very briefly, since they were discussed in some detail in Chapter 3. Agriculture was the focus of that discussion, but the arguments and measures used have applicability to all commodity categories. As is apparent from that discussion, promotion of domestic output often has other, even stronger motivations, that is to maintain employment or to prevent capital destruction in the supported activities, irrespective of whether there is a threat to domestic supply.

Import restrictions commonly constitute a key element in the promotion of domestic output. These permit higher prices to be charged domestically than would be possible if there were a free import flow.

Subsidies to domestic production are often an element of protection. Public procurement is another tool to encourage domestic production. This measure, too, would ordinarily involve the payment of prices above the world market level to the domestic producers.

One recent example of import restrictions to promote domestic production is the import tariffs on steel imposed by the Trump administration in 2018 (see Chapter 3). The motivation for the tariffs is linked to import supply security as they were motivated by national security reasons. An investigation by the Department of Commerce found that the imported quantities of steel products were harming domestic producers, reducing US jobs and threatening national security in a broad sense (US Department of Commerce, 2018).

A grotesque historical example of the maintenance of domestic output using supply security as motivation relates to the production of hard coal in Germany and Spain with the help of huge subsidies. Stockpiling could accomplish the supply security objective at a fraction of the subsidy cost (Radetzki, 1995).

Stockpiling of Strategic Metals in the USA and Other Countries

Maintenance of commodity stocks is a classic measure for coming to grips with issues of supply security. Government efforts to establish and maintain stockpiles of strategically important imported commodities have been launched at different times in virtually all major industrialized countries that depend on imports (Vernon, 1983).

The efforts of the United States have been, without comparison, the largest and most persevering. Inventories of some 80 commodities (mainly but not exclusively metals) of importance for the country's defense efforts were built after the Second World War and expanded further in the early 1950s, in response to fears of shortage aroused by the Korean War. The US strategic stockpiles continued to grow until 1973, when their total value was assessed at some US$6.7 billion (around US$23 billion in 2014 money when using the MUV index). The stocks of many commodities represented very sizable proportions of total annual consumption in the USA. The situation was most extreme in tin, where the stock corresponded to a full year of *global* consumption (Cooper and Lawrence, 1975). By 1973/74, however, stockpiling had gone out of fashion. New directives were issued on the strategic needs, according to which some 90% of the stockpile was declared surplus and available for disposal (Mikesell, 1986). In 1992, the US Congress made a further downward adjustment of the strategic needs, and in 2010 the USA stored 28 commodities with a market value of US$1.4 billion.[2] Though the sales were gradual, they have at times had a depressing effect on the international markets. Fashions moved in parallel outside the USA. The governments of other countries also reduced or discontinued their strategic metals stock programs.

In line with the recent trade policy shift in the USA toward more protectionism, the stockpile program too has seen a bit of a revival, at least regarding the number of commodities involved. In 2018, the US administration stored 44 commodities in ten locations in the country, with a market value of US$1.2 billion. This is an increase of 16 commodities since 2015, when 28 commodities (valued at US$1.3 billion) were stored. Furthermore, a general strategy to ensure secure and reliable supplies of critical minerals was launched by the US government in December 2017. One of the main motivations behind this strategy is the US reliance on foreign supply for many commodities. In 2018 the USA was a 100% net importer of 18 nonfuel mineral commodities, of which 14 were identified as critical to the US economy. In total, 35 critical minerals, or mineral groups, were identified based on the criteria that the commodity is essential to economic and national security, that supply is vulnerable to disruptions and that the material has an essential function in the US manufacturing industry (USGS, annual).

The stockpiling programs of the United States reveal some of the problems surrounding this kind of policy. The US endeavors have historically had a strategic military objective. The determination of stockholding size then required a delineation of possible war scenarios, of the ensuing import shortfalls and their durations, and of the shares of these shortfalls that it was strategically important to satisfy from the government inventories. This proved fiendishly complicated, as the policy shifts described above demonstrate. When inventories are sizable, procurements and disposals due to a change in the perception of needs will destabilize markets and prices. Releases have been envisaged only in the event of scarcities caused by wars involving the United States itself. Shortages and ensuing price increases caused by other

---

[2] Home page of the DLA Strategic Materials, www.globalsecurity.org/military/a gency/dod/dnsc.htm.

circumstances normally did not warrant stockpile action, but sometimes nevertheless triggered a perverse political decision to *increase* inventory levels, so accentuating the upward price move. Complaints have been repeatedly voiced about the great inflexibility in the procedure for inventory releases. Much of the potential benefit would have been erased if these had prevailed and then there had been a sudden and acute war-related need.

The stockpile policies have involved a significant net cost. Apart from the storage cost and the interest on the capital that was tied up, one must reckon with a deterioration in quality due both to the passage of time and to the technical change that may have altered the needed specifications and made old stocks unsuitable for the most critical needs. Given that procurements would have tended to take place in tense situations when prices were high and disposals in relaxed market conditions with low prices, one would expect the transactions to yield losses on average. No assessment of the net cost to society from the stockholding programs has been undertaken.

The functioning of the US strategic minerals and metals stockpile has fortunately never had to be put to a fully fledged test during war or warlike emergencies. It is possible that its benefits would have proven well worth the cost incurred during peace.

The IEA Emergency Stockpile of Oil

In the 2000s, there has been a strong revival of supply security concerns, this time, however, with a heavy focus on oil. The revival has been triggered by greater OPEC activism, which along with the demand shock of 2004, importantly driven by China, led to an oil price explosion. Superimposed on these events have been political supply problems in Venezuela, Libya and Iran, along with actions by Russia to control oil and gas supply, purportedly for political ends. On the other hand, the concerns have been strongly relaxed by the spectacular rise of shale oil output in the USA during the 2010s.

The antecedents to an internationally managed emergency stock for oil stretch back to the first oil crisis of the early 1970s, when the IEA was established. The current membership of this organization overlaps, in the main, that of the OECD. Supply security measures have been one of IEA's major mandates. According to current rules (IEA, 2005b), the members that are net importers of oil have a legal obligation to hold emergency oil reserves equivalent to at least 90 days of the net oil imports of the preceding year. At the end of June 2019, stocks controlled by IEA members amounted to some 4.5 billion barrels, the equivalent of about 615 million tons and corresponding to 330 days of IEA's overall imports. The adequacy of this inventory can be gauged by comparing it with the largest supply disruption since 1973, that of the Iranian Revolution, which cut global supply by 5.6 MBD during six months, creating a shortfall of 1 billion barrels or 140 million tons.

Taking a clue from the criticism of the inflexibility of the US strategic stocks of metals, the IEA maintains an emergency response team to facilitate rapid and flexible action to emerging disruptions. For example, when Hurricane Katrina affected crude oil production in the US Gulf coast in August 2005, the collective decision to initiate emergency stocks was taken within ten hours (IEA, 2014c). The exact method of emergency stock releases does however differ between IEA member countries. To make the stock last longer, the maximum drawdowns are typically reduced during the following months of crisis, while at the same time other measures, for example surge production, redirection of imports and demand restraints, are introduced.

According to a study made by IEA, the global benefits of the member countries' ability to react to significant oil supply disruptions (based on the stockpiles) over 30 years was valued at an astounding US$3.9 trillion (IEA, 2018). The study uses an economic model to assess the effects of hypothetical oil supply disruptions on member countries' GDP, oil prices and net import costs with and without the emergency stockpiles. It is found that the main benefits of holding stocks are its limiting effect on supply losses, which implies avoidance of increased import costs and the resulting impact on the world economy.

No actions by the strategic inventory managed by the IEA were reported in response to the Iranian Revolution or the Iran–Iraq War of 1979–1980. But the inventory has played a role on three occasions since the creation of IEA. The first was during the Gulf War in January 1991, when 2.1 MBD were released. It was used again in September 2005, involving roughly the same quantities, to reduce the impact of Hurricane Katrina. The last time was in 2011, as a response to the prolonged supply disruptions due to the Libyan civil war. On all occasions, the stockpile interventions were far below the maximum potential, yet the added supply helped to calm the market in some measure.

9.4 Summary

While supply security is an issue that has emerged in response to an increasing dependence on imports of critically important commodities, it is important to remember that crises in supply are not limited to imported supply. In fact, a diversified network of imports may provide a better shield against disruption than a concentrated domestic supply subject to the vagaries of weather or strikes.

The rich industrialized world has long practiced deep agricultural protection, assuring high levels of self-sufficiency for indispensable food. For this reason, food is seldom in focus when measures to avert imported raw material supply crises are under consideration. Instead, the issue of supply security typically relates to metals, minerals and fuels, deemed to be essential and hard to replace.

A global supply crisis of significance is characterized not only by a substantial price increase; it must also involve a significant cut in supply. Such crises have been quite rare, and we have been able to identify only four (cobalt in 1978; oil twice, in 1980 and 2019; and rare earth metals in 2010) since the Second World War.

The implications for the importing economy will be felt in many dimensions. At the microeconomic level, the industries using the com-modity will suffer a cost increase and rationing will have to be employed when the price is regulated. Some firms will have to do without, and may face a survival threat in consequence. At the macro-economic level, the current account will deteriorate, inflation will gather pace and the growth rate may decline, but the commodity consumption and imports have to be very sizable for these effects to be perceptible.

Various measures have been tried to assure the stability of imports in the event of a supply crisis. Careful choice and diversification of supply sources, tighter relationships with suppliers, bilateral treaties and direct ownership positions in foreign production have been tried with varied success. Encouragement of domestic output or of domestic availability through strategic stockholding has also been common in the arsenal used to overcome supply crises. All these measures carry a cost and to be worthwhile, these costs have to be lower than the detriment from the crisis.

Supply disruptions occurring in truly global markets are best coun-tered by internationally coordinated measures. The emergency stockpile of oil under the direction of the IEA provides an illustrative example. The proliferation of commodity exchanges and futures markets has provided a means of price insurance to commodity users, thus reducing their pain and diminishing the need for public action.

Looked at in retrospect, the concerns and the costs incurred to overcome the vagaries of supply security may appear as somewhat exaggerated. The incidents of crisis have been rare, and the ability of the advanced economies to substitute out of the supply crises suggest that the cost of the measures used to assure stable supply must be quite small to make the efforts worthwhile. But then, history offers no firm insights about future events. If a supply crisis of huge dimensions and deep severity were to occur, then even the more costly among the measures considered in the present chapter might emerge as highly worthwhile.

10 | *Producer Cartels in International Commodity Markets*

Producer cartels are about monopolistic coordination aimed at raising the suppliers' revenues. Efforts to cartelize typically come in waves, and have occurred throughout the history of international commodity trade. This chapter focuses on the 1970s, when the most recent wave occurred. While it lasted, a number of academic efforts were launched to explain the functioning of commodity cartels in general and of OPEC in particular. Despite the theoretical developments and the many modeling exercises that were undertaken, many of the key issues concerning commodity cartelization remain to be fully understood. The remark from an influential survey of commodity cartelization from the mid-1980s (Gately, 1984) that "There are a large number of alternative theories, but a much smaller number of sensible applied models" retains its validity even more than 30 years after it was published.

The present chapter begins by studying the necessary minimum preconditions, in terms of elasticities and market shares, for successful cartel action. We then identify the markets where these preconditions appear to be fulfilled. There follows an account of the attempts by commodity producers to wield the market power to their own benefit, trying to answer questions such as: What were the triggers to the cartel action? How did it go? How did the buyers react? What prompted cartel disintegration? There is a heavy emphasis on oil, given the extraordinary price performance of this commodity since the early 1970 (Chapter 4), but we express skepticism about the role of OPEC in oil price evolution. The findings of our cartel analysis are not only of interest for the sake of history. They have a bearing on the future too.

10.1 Formal Preconditions for Successful Cartel Action

Successful cartelization measures involve either a restriction of supply or a rise in the price charged by the members of the collaborating group, leading to increased revenue for the group. With a given demand schedule there is a unique relationship between the quantity supplied and the price at which the market is cleared, so the two measures would have equivalent consequences. Where the institutional market arrangements involve producer-set prices, cartel action would ordinarily take the form of an increase in the producer quotations. Where primary commodity prices are set by exchanges, as is increasingly common, the colluding producers could achieve their aim by reducing supply until the desired price level is reached.

Under ideal conditions, producer collaboration should aim at maximizing the joint profits of its members. In terms of Figure 10.1, this would be achieved by reducing supply from Q_1, the competitive equilibrium, to Q_3, given by the intersection between the collaborating group's marginal cost and marginal revenue. Any output above this level would be unprofitable, because the marginal cost of that output exceeds the marginal revenue. This is the standard profit maximization rule applied by a perfect monopoly. The criterion for successful producer collaboration employed here involves the cruder rule of revenue maximization, which disregards the costs saved by production cuts. Under this criterion, output would be reduced from Q_1 to Q_2, the latter determined by the marginal revenue of the producer group being equal to zero. Revenue would then rise from P_1Q_1 to P_2Q_2. We have adopted this cruder rule for the purpose of the following discourse because we believe that this is about as much as a real world cartel could aim for.

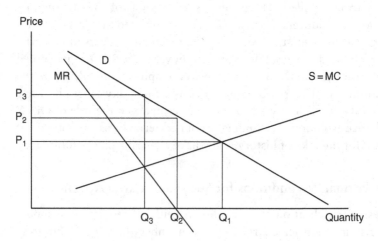

Figure 10.1 Maximization of profit and maximization of revenue

We know no cases of cartels that have defined their supply schedule with sufficient precision, and instituted income transfers between individual members, to make profit maximization a practicable policy.

The present analysis assumes that the participants in the cartel (here, leading producing or exporting nations) can reach full agreement on a marketing policy that aims at increasing their sales revenue and that they will adhere strictly to the policy rules. Even these more modest assumptions about the behavioral discipline within the group are somewhat heroic. The possibility of increasing the group's revenue over that reaped in the absence of joint action can be shown to be greater, first, the higher its share in global supply; second, the lower the (absolute) value of the price elasticity of global demand; and third, the lower the value of the price elasticity of outsiders' supply.

In formal terms, successful market intervention by the cartel requires that the (absolute) value of the price elasticity of demand for its output E_{DC} should be less than 1. If E_{DC} is greater than 1, the cartel's revenue will decline when the members jointly raise prices or cut supply. The value of E_{DC} is determined by the formula (Radetzki, 1976):

$$E_{DC} = (1/M)E_{DW} - (1/M)(1 - M)E_{SR};$$

where
M = the cartel's share of world supply;
E_{DW} = the price elasticity of world demand; and
E_{SR} = the price elasticity of supply outside the cartel.

An E_{DC} that is less than 1 implies that the marginal revenue from the cartel's aggregate supply is negative. Hence, the sales revenue will increase as supply is curtailed. A maximum will be reached when E_{DC} reaches a value of 1 and marginal revenue equals 0. This will happen when supply has been cut to Q_2 in Figure 10.1. The smaller the value of E_{DC}, the greater the potential for raising revenue through cartel action.

The success of the collaboration has an important time dimension. This is because the (absolute) price elasticities of world demand and of outsider supply (E_{DW} and E_{SR}) will tend to increase over time, as the end users and independent producers adjust to the conditions caused by the cartel's intervention. The higher prices resulting from cartel action can greatly increase the cartel members' revenue in year 1 over what they reaped in the competitive market that prevailed in year 0. If the higher price is maintained, their revenue in year 5 may prove substantially lower than in year 0, as a result of the gradual shrinkage of global demand and of the cartel's market share. Current value calculations of the revenue gains and losses over time will be needed to determine the benefit of such a course of events. But a cartel is unlikely to be judged a success unless it manages to keep the members' revenue above the competitive level for at least several years.

It may be something of a paradox that a cartel which commands no credibility in the outside world will have greater prospects of succeeding in its market actions than one which does. This is because if no one believes that the price-raising collaboration will survive, there will be no adjustment to the higher prices resulting from its actions. With no adjustments, the short-run values of E_{DW} and E_{SR} will persevere.

The above formula defining E_{DC} can be used to determine the limiting combinations of the price elasticity of world demand, E_{DW}, and the price elasticity of supply outside the cartel, E_{SR}, that have to hold for the price elasticity of demand faced by the cartel, E_{DC}, to be less than 1, and hence for cartel action to increase the collaborating group's revenue. Table 10.1 illustrates the limiting elasticity values for successful collaboration of a group whose share of world supply, M, equals 60%. It will be seen that the potential for revenue-raising action (numbers in italics) exists in all cases where the values of E_{DW} and E_{SR} are less than 0.4 (absolute values), but also for selected other elasticity-value combinations.

The value of E_{DC} is also related to the range of commodities under the cartel's control, but multi-commodity cartels will gain additional market power (a lower E_{DC}) from their wider coverage only if the commodities are each others' substitutes. No synergies will be obtained from launching a joint cartel by the coffee and copper producers. Since

Table 10.1 *Price elasticities of demand for output from a cartel* (E_{DC}) *that controls 60% of world supply* (M = 0.6)

E_{DW}/E_{SR}	0.1	0.2	0.4	0.7	1.0
−0.1	*−0.23*	*−0.30*	*−0.43*	*−0.63*	*−0.88*
−0.2	*−0.40*	*−0.47*	*−0.60*	*−0.80*	−1.00
−0.4	*−0.73*	*−0.80*	*−0.93*	−1.13	−1.33
−0.7	−1.23	−1.30	−1.43	−1.63	−1.83
−1.0	−1.73	−1.80	−1.93	−2.13	−2.33

there is little relationship between these two markets, price-raising supply restrictions in one will have no effect on the other. In contrast, the copper producers' market intervention will be reinforced by a simultaneous restriction in aluminum supply. When copper producers intervene in isolation, the higher copper price will induce substitution in favor of aluminum and the reduced copper demand will dilute the benefit from intervention. If the copper producers coordinate their action with the aluminum producers so that the prices of both products rise in parallel, no substitution from one to the other will be induced by the price change and the producers of both metals can reap higher earnings than if each group had acted separately.

The increased market power follows from the fact that the price elasticity of world demand, E_{DW}, is lower for copper-cum-aluminum than for each metal in isolation. The greater the substitutability between the products, the higher the benefit of joint cartel action for both and the smaller the possibility of establishing a successful cartel for each product in isolation. Attempts to launch a cartel by primary copper producers would be much stronger if they included a successful effort to get the suppliers of copper scrap on the bandwagon, given the substitutability between primary and secondary metal material.

However, market power is only one of several aspects that determine the prospects for launching successful cartels. Another is the ability to administer and coordinate the members' actions, so there is a trade-off between augmented market power and increased complexity in managing multi-commodity cartels.

10.2 Other Preconditions for Successful Cartel Action

The preceding section clarified why the control of a large share of total supply and low-price elasticities are necessary preconditions for successful cartel action. That discussion, however, is far from adequate for identifying the commodity markets in which cartelization is feasible.

A first ambiguity arises from the definition of total supply. One could look at the share of global output under the cartel's control or alternatively at the share of global exports accounted for by its members. The latter figure is usually higher, so it produces a more optimistic impression of the cartel's potential success, but it disregards the possible dilution of the collaborating producers' market power as independent supply switches between the domestic and export markets.

A second problem is due to the uncertainty and instability of the elasticity values. Price-elasticity estimates can vary greatly depending on precisely what is measured, the method used, the time period to which the estimate applies and the price level at the time of measurement. As noted, long-run price elasticities are usually substantially higher than short-run ones. In terms of Figure 10.1, the demand and supply schedules will be flatter if a longer time period is considered. Price elasticities can also vary with the absolute price levels. For instance, when the demand curve is a straight line, as in Figure 10.1, the price elasticity will rise as prices increase. Hence, measurements of elasticity made at a given time will not necessarily hold if a price change has subsequently occurred.

For these reasons, exercises such as that contained in Table 10.1 cannot bring out neat distinctions between commodities that are amenable to successful cartel action and those that are not. Clearly, considerable standard errors are attached to all elasticity estimates, and the best one could expect from such analyses is a first crude categorization of commodities according to the prospects for monopolistic manipulation.

A third problem concerns the practicalities of producer coordination that is intended to control commodity supply. Since cartel action is about cuts in supply the initial issue that needs to be resolved is the overall size of the cut. Well-established producers and producers with above-average cost levels are likely to be interested in greater cuts than new and low-cost producers who are keen to expand their output. The need to ensure full collaboration from producers who jointly account for a large proportion of the total will tend to result in agreements scaled down to suit the convenience of the parties that desire the lowest proportional output reduction.

Coincidental with determining the overall output reduction are decisions about its distribution among participating members. Optimally, only the high-cost output ought to be cut, but to be acceptable such a policy would require income transfers from lower-cost producers who are allowed to continue their operations to those who close down. This is rarely if ever practicable, so the sharing of cuts would typically be in proportion to output in the recent past, to actual capacity prior to the proposed action or to the capacity including expansions in the pipeline. These alternatives usually give rise to protracted quarrels as each cartel participant takes a position that will maximize their own yield.

After the joint supply cut has been implemented, each individual member will have a strong temptation to covertly increase their supply, and so benefit from the higher price while letting the others carry the burden of restriction. A close inspection of the participating members' adherence to the agreement will therefore be needed to prevent it from breaking apart.

A few important inferences for the practicability of international commodity cartels can be drawn from the above. The smaller the group of participating producing or exporting countries needed to attain the required share of world supply, the simpler it will be to reach and maintain a supply-restricting action. Agreement will be much easier to reach and administer in a group of four or five than in a group of 12 or more. Similarity among the participants will also facilitate monopolistic coordination. If they are of equal size, have matching cost structures and levels, pursue similar goals and operate in comparable social and political environments, an agreement will be easier to reach than when there are great differences within the group. The ease with which output can be cut and supply can be monitored will also affect cartel operation. The cohesion and trust within the collaborating group will benefit from transparency in the burden sharing.

Empirical studies of international cartel endeavors in commodity markets have often been simplified by regarding countries instead of producing corporations as participants. Individual producers are not always easy to identify and the volume of their exports may be hard to quantify. Identification and quantification are much easier to handle at the national level. There are also some more fundamental arguments in favor of treating national governments instead of corporations as cartel members. First, in many countries corporations are subject to antitrust legislation that makes their overt participation in cartel action difficult. Governments are not subject to such restrictions. Second, governments have and often do exercise sovereign powers to regulate exports as they deem fit. A third motivation for viewing governments rather than corporations as the key cartel players is that the 1970s, the decade when there were strong and widespread beliefs in "producer power" and numerous commodity cartels were launched, was just preceded by or coincidental with a great wave of nationalizations of resource industries, predominantly, but not exclusively, in developing countries (see Chapter 11). Efforts to intervene in commodity markets were often initiated by governments, with the newly nationalized corporations used as instruments for policy implementation.

The question of whether governments or producing corporations are the more efficient executors of cartel policy in international commodity markets has been discussed for decades, but still remains unsettled. Summarizing experiences from the interwar period, Rowe (1965) concludes that an effective international commodity-control scheme could be secured only with the active participation of governments. While the empirical evidence from petroleum, bauxite, phosphates and uranium in the 1970s (see Section 10.3) supports Rowe's conclusion, opposite views have been aired. For instance, Grilli and Yang (1988) assert that effective collusion is easier to achieve by a group of private profit-maximizing agents that can act in a covert manner than for governments with a variety of national goals, whose actions by necessity become a "semipublic international political affair." The dynamic of cartel launch sometimes follows a path where leading private corporations initiate the process and then approach the producing country's government to act as cartel fronts. This was the case in 1974 when Rio Tinto Zinc initiated discussions with the governments of Chile and Zambia about a copper-production cut, with the subsequent action handled by CIPEC, the Intergovernmental Council of Copper Exporting Countries.[1] A similar course of events took place somewhat later in the uranium market, where the leading private producers coordinated their marketing efforts using the Canadian government as their visible front (Radetzki, 1981).

The characteristics of commodity markets that are amenable to successful price-raising actions by producers can now be summarized, and the potential candidate commodities that meet the required criteria picked out. The method used will be that of successive elimination.

Reasonable prospects for cartelization require a low (absolute) price elasticity of demand. The commodities must not be easily replaceable by close substitutes. This excludes the group of edible oils and their raw materials, which are easily interchangeable and whose production is so dispersed that a joint-product cartel would hardly be feasible. The same is true for fruits such as bananas, apples and oranges.

Another precondition for successful cartel action is that the price elasticity of outside supply should be low, at least in a perspective of 3–5 years. This would exclude quite a number of commodities, for example the cereals group and sugar, whose production could be

---

[1] At the time Radetzki was working as chief economist of CIPEC.

speedily expanded in many places in response to higher prices that looked like persevering for couple of years. The same is true for products such as cotton, jute and possibly wool.

After these eliminations, we are left with rubber, the tropical beverages and most minerals, all characterized by limited substitutability and extended periods required to create new production capacity. One would now like to fine-tune the price elasticities of these commodities to get a better grasp of the prospects for market control, but given the sizable standard errors that surround existing measures of elasticity, we deem such an effort to be futile

The level of supply concentration might throw at least some additional light on the issue under scrutiny. With all else equal, a high level of concentration among producers (whether nations or corporations) should facilitate supply coordination. Tables 2.5 and 2.6 contain data from which information on concentration in global export flows can be distilled. Only some of the products listed pass the arbitrary criterion we have chosen: that the five most important countries should account for no less than 60% of global exports (in Table 10.1, M = 0.6 is used to distinguish commodities that might satisfy the preconditions for viable cartel endeavors). The products and their shares work out as follows: cotton 81%, coal 86%, iron ore 86%, rubber 85%, rice 67%, tin 61%, wheat 62% and wool 67%. We have used the same source as that employed for constructing Table 2.5 (http://comtrade.un.org) to add some further products with heavily concentrated exports in 2017, and find cocoa (66%), maize (76%), nickel (79%) and tea (63%) to pass the test. The cartel prospects for cotton, rice, maize, wheat and wool are unfavorable on account of their high short-run supply elasticities (see above), leaving a group of seven among the commodities investigated with some prospects for producer market-intervention criterion. We note with some surprise the low concentration for three products with cartel action history, namely copper 52%, oil 47% and coffee 40%.

Cartel prospects hinge not only on national supply concentration, but also on corporate concentration. Even though most competition authorities prohibit collaboration across corporations to raise prices, cartels still frequently occur both in national and international markets. Table 10.2 lists commodities where the five largest producers controlled more than 60% of global supply in 2012–2013. Intriguingly, they were all found in the mining industry.

Table 10.2 *Five leading corporations' share of global production*

	Year	Share of global tonnage (%)	Comments
Beryllium	2012	90	Largest company controls 87%
Diamond	2013	69	Based on value
Iron ore	2013	70	Based on seaborne trade
Niobium	2013	99	
Platinum	2013	80	
Zirconium	2012	63	

Source: Private communication with Magnus Ericsson, founder and former president of the Raw Materials Group.

Further insights into the role of concentration for cartel action would, however, require more profound analyses of the affinity of the producers, the structure of the export market and the industrial organization of the buyers of each commodity. Successful cartel action would be less likely where the buyers are few, financially powerful and able to retaliate.

10.3 Actual Experience of Commodity Cartels in the 1970s

The popularity of commodity cartels appears to occur in waves, usually triggered by one or several outside events, but the cartels that attempt to establish monopolistic prices are seldom long-lived and tend to disintegrate in consequence of stagnant demand and rising independent supply, both prompted by aggressive price policy.

In the 1930s, a number of price-raising international commodity cartels were established by producers in agricultural as well as in mineral commodity markets, somewhat counterintuitively, in response to the exceedingly low price levels that reigned during the great depression (Rowe, 1965). The monopolistic actions were widely viewed with sympathy and were overtly supported by the governments of the consuming countries, including the US government. Higher prices were seen as essential for the maintenance and expansion of commodity production, sometimes even for the survival of producers, and, at a wider level, for the restoration of world prosperity (Herfindahl, 1959). These cartel efforts were overtaken by events following the outbreak of the Second World War, with the ensuing scarcities and far-reaching government controls.

Another wave of commodity cartel action occurred during the 1970s, this time in response to the combination of widespread nationalizations of mineral resource industries following third-world independence from colonial bonds and a very strong boost in commodity demand in 1972–1974 that was triggered by the global macroeconomic boom in those years. A widespread perception of commodity power emerged among producers, especially in the developing world, and efforts were launched to establish producer associations, predominantly in the minerals field, with price raising as the primary goal. The most important and persistent was the oil cartel. The spectacular and lasting price increases in oil, reviewed in Chapter 4, have been commonly attributed to OPEC's market interventions, and so aroused a lot of enthusiasm among other commodity producers. Producer efforts to raise prices in non-oil markets were successful in some cases, though short-lived, and the failure was often due to shrinking demand for the cartel's output, as the longer-run price elasticity proved to be disappointingly high. In other cases, no visible price impact can be detected from the attempts at market intervention.

Bauxite

In the late 1960s, Jamaica began to urge the governments of bauxite-producing countries to form an association for the exchange of information, reduction of rivalries, establishment of a joint front to the multinational aluminum companies and coordinated increase of export taxes (Brown, 1980). Enthused by the apparently successful collaboration within OPEC, but also by booming demand for their product, the bauxite-producing countries founded the International Bauxite Association (IBA) early in 1974. By 1975, its members accounted for 85% of nonsocialist world (NSW) output. The production units were still largely owned by the vertically integrated aluminum companies, and there were not really any meaningful market quotations for the product. The cartel, therefore, largely operated through the increase of production and export taxes.

Jamaica's government was also the first to take action. At the time, the country was the world's second largest producer and, on account of transport distances, it enjoyed a considerable cost advantage in the US market. In 1974 and 1975 the government instituted a very sharp increase in its production levies and export taxes that went far beyond its locational monopoly. As a result, the import cost in constant money of Jamaican bauxite in the United States roughly doubled between 1973 and 1976 (Vedavalli, 1977) and continued to increase until 1980 (World Bank, 1994).

The Jamaican government apparently expected that the other members of IBA would follow suit, so eliminating the relative loss of Jamaica's competitiveness. To some extent, this occurred. Surinam instituted fiscal levies similar to Jamaica's. Guinea, too, raised its bauxite taxation, but by less than the two Caribbean countries. However, Australia, the world's largest producer and an IBA member, refused to join in these interventions.

Table 10.3 reveals an apparent depletion in the Caribbean producers' competitiveness over time, resulting in a substantial loss of their market share. The main gainers were Australia and Guinea, members of the IBA who were more concerned about their sales, and Brazil, which never joined the association.

The falling market shares of Jamaica and Surinam would have been easier to handle in an expanding market. In fact, the NSW demand for bauxite fell by 6.5% between 1974 and 1982, importantly due to the extended recession in the wake of the 1973–1974 oil crisis. This speeded up the erosion of the cartel.

The frequent alterations of Jamaican taxes and levies in the 1970s and 1980s, along with other concurrent changes implemented in its

Table 10.3 *Bauxite output among leading producers in the NSW*

	1974	1982	1990
NSW total (m tons)	71.3	66.7	99.9
Jamaica (%)	22	12	11
Surinam (%)	10	5	3
Guinea (%)	11	18	16
Australia (%)	28	35	41
Brazil (%)	1	6	10

Source: Metallgesellschaft (annual).

bauxite/alumina industry (e.g. production controls, nationalizations) make it difficult to isolate the impact on the government's revenue from the bauxite levies. Nevertheless, the price-raising interventions must be deemed a failure. The country's share of the NSW market declined from 22% in 1974 to 12% in 1982, with no subsequent recovery. The Caribbean policies clearly favored Australia and Brazil, which declined participation in the market management. Jamaica, the original founder of IBA, formally withdrew its membership in 1994 and the association collapsed soon after (Crowson, 2006).

In terms of the formal analysis (Section 10.1), the cartel's lack of success was caused by E_{DC} being too high in the medium term. The very low value of E_{DW} was overwhelmed by a low M (the initial market share of the Caribbean producers) and a high E_{SR}. The advantage of the Caribbean nations' resource endowment was not pronounced enough to give them a durable market power.

As an afterthought and to reflect on the remarkable long-run flexibility of (even exhaustible) raw materials supply, consider for a moment the evolution of events from the early 1990s, when IBA collapsed, until the 2010s. In 1990, NSW bauxite output amounted to 100 million tons and the four IBA members listed in Table 10.1 still supplied 71% of that total. By 2013, the market had expanded to 230 million tons but the share of the four had shrunk to 34%, while formerly insignificant suppliers had grown to dominate the market. In that year, Indonesia supplied 24% of the total, China 19% and India almost 9% (WBMS, 2014).

Phosphate Rock

Booming demand and the apparent success of OPEC led to a decision by the state-owned Moroccan phosphate rock producer, Office Chérifien des Phosphates, to raise its producer price from US$14 to US$42 per ton in January 1974, and then again to US$63 in July of that year (UNCTAD, monthly). In the short run, this intervention was highly effective because the state-owned phosphate enterprises of Algeria, Togo and Tunisia and the mixed-owned producer in Senegal, along with the members of the US export cartel,[2] Phosrock, raised their

---

[2] US legislation does permit export-oriented cartel measures, so long as there is no impact on the country's domestic market.

list prices in close concert with the Moroccan action. The entire group accounted for more than 70% of global phosphate rock exports at the time, almost half of which were from Morocco (UNCTAD, 1981).

The price-raising scheme proved short-lived. In 1974 itself exports from all the participants in the scheme increased significantly, so the price gain was exacerbated by gains in volume. In 1975, however, a severe world recession reduced demand. The higher prices also resulted in deferred farmer demand and substitution in favor of other fertilizer raw materials. E_{DW} proved to be quite high and the cartel was unable to withstand the strains that emerged, despite its high market share. The Moroccan phosphate rock price was reduced to US$49 in 1976 and to US$38 in 1977 (UNCTAD, monthly). In constant dollar terms, the 1977 price was on a par with pre-cartel levels.

Uranium[3]

The international uranium-mining industry entered the 1970s in a state of profound depression. It had been built to satisfy the huge military demand during the 1960s. With the military needs fully satisfied by the end of the decade, the existing uranium capacity was far in excess of nuclear-reactor needs for many years into the future. The low prices did not provide full cost coverage for a large segment of the industry, so many producers left the business.

The depressed market was the trigger that brought producers together in an effort to safeguard their survival. A series of meetings initiated by the government of Canada took place in 1971. The governments of France and South Africa were represented and leading private producing companies from a number of countries took part. The meetings were intended to "put some order into the international uranium market ... to coordinate uranium production and marketing policies" (Nucleonics Week, 1971).

This embryo to the uranium cartel was quite frail while the market remained weak. The most it could do was to reduce rivalry among members and issue directives aimed at preventing further price falls. At the end of 1973, however, a number of unrelated but coincidental factors completely reversed the market situation. The most important of these was a decision by the US uranium enrichment agency (at the

[3] This draws on Radetzki (1981).

time state-owned, with a virtual world monopoly) to change the rules under which it marketed its services. According to the new rules, enrichment had to be commissioned decades in advance of actual needs and there were high penalties for cancellation. Owners of existing and planned nuclear reactors signed up to excessive enrichment contracts and then went on a buying spree to secure their future uranium requirements.

Having institutionalized their collaboration in the preceding years, the uranium producers responded by temporarily withdrawing from the market, so the prices exploded. The spot quotation went up from less than US$7/lb U_3O_8 in late 1973 to more than US$40 by mid-1976, in spite of a NSW output increase of 15% between the two years. Prices in long-run contracts signed in this period followed suit. The producers reentered the market only after prices had reached the US$40 level. The cartel worked under very favorable conditions. The private producers were actively supported by the governments of the major exporting countries. The group accounted for a high proportion of the NSW supply, but the precise level of M is hard to establish given the covert nature of much of the cartel's operations. It faced a price elasticity of demand (E_{DW}) that was close to zero. New capacity to produce uranium would take a long time to establish, and in the meantime E_{SR} remained quite low. So, the prices stayed very high through most of the 1970s.

The subsequent decline was caused by an increasing realization among the nuclear utilities that they had greatly overcommitted themselves to uranium purchases, given the shrinking plans to expand nuclear capacity. Demand for newly mined uranium was sharply reduced, as the excessive inventories held by the nuclear power generators were scaled down. New production came on stream by the end of the decade, and discoveries of large and very rich uranium deposits in Canada and Australia altered earlier perceptions of impending scarcity. After five years of exceedingly high profitability for the industry, the prices in constant money were back to the levels that had prevailed before the cartel burst to life.

Copper and Iron Ore

Two further attempts at establishing commodity cartels in metal mineral markets need to be mentioned, but they can be treated quite briefly, since they both failed to institute effective price raising measures (Crowson, 2006).

CIPEC was formed in 1967 by the governments of Chile, Peru, Zaire (later renamed Congo Kinshasa) and Zambia for the purpose of raising prices through collective interventions in the copper market. Yugoslavia and Indonesia joined later, while Australia and Papua New Guinea became associates. Like the bauxite and phosphate exporters, the governments of the main copper exporting countries were enthused by OPEC's apparent success and CIPEC tried in 1974–1976 to raise prices with the help of production cuts, but the efforts failed due to mistrust among members and because the eight members controlled too small a share (37% in 1975) of global mine supply. Additionally, there was a large scale supply of copper scrap over which the primary producers had no control. CIPEC subsequently dwindled in importance with the collapse of production in Zaire and Zambia, and the withdrawal of several members. It was formally dissolved in 1988 and its remaining functions were taken over by the International Copper Study Group, formed in 1993.

The Association of Iron Ore Exporting Countries (APEF) attempted in 1975 to set export prices. The effort was unsuccessful, first, because two important members, Australia and Sweden, were unwilling to go along; and, second, because Brazil and Canada, both sizable export suppliers, refused even to join. APEF reduced its role to collecting statistics on market trends, until its demise in 1989.

In 2014–2015, a few years after the end of the commodity boom and in the face of a large increase in iron ore production, accompanied by dwindling iron ore prices, the possibility of an iron ore cartel has been voiced. The current fourth-largest iron ore producer, Fortescue, has argued for a "managed cartel," where the export of Australian iron ore producers would be "predetermined" (Hurst, 2015). This would be an attempt to control supply from the Australian export market. As indicated in Table 10.2, the conditions to form a cartel in the iron ore market are favorable as producer concentration is relatively high. The three largest producers, Rio Tinto, BHP Billiton and Vale, currently control 58.3% of seaborne traded iron ore. Furthermore, these three companies have almost equal shares of this market. However, despite these conditions, there is so far little evidence that a cartel will be formed. Our doubt rests on the fact that the three largest producers are also the players with the lowest production costs, thus it is not they but the smaller producers that suffer most as prices decline.

OPEC

OPEC was brought into existence in 1960.[4] Its major purpose was to form a united front in an attempt to arrest the fall in the member governments' revenue per barrel (Griffin and Steele, 1986). Until the early 1970s, the organization led a dormant life in a market situation characterized by excess supply.

By the early 1970s, the market had strengthened substantially due to the very fast growth of world oil consumption (8.3% compound annual growth between 1960 and 1972).[5] The world macroeconomic boom of 1972–1974, during which all primary commodity prices exploded, permitted the OPEC governments to find acceptance among the multinational oil firms that exploited their oil to very large posted price rises, hugely increasing their fiscal revenues, while the oil companies passed the increase on to the final consumers. With the very low short-run price elasticity of demand for oil, there was little need for downward supply adjustments in response to the higher price. Given the speedy demand growth, one might well argue that the market would have accepted the price rises and maintained them in the short to medium term even in the absence of OPEC and without coordination among the oil multinationals.

The instrument used by the OPEC group during most of its life to restrain output and strengthen prices has been a formal production quota system, instituted in 1983 and maintained ever since. Quotas could certainly strengthen prices, at least while they lasted. However, besides typically having a short duration, the quota system was highly disjointed. The price goals and the timing of quota application have shifted in an erratic manner. A variety of rules governed the establishment of quotas for each member – for example historical output, production capacity, reserves, production costs or population – and

---

[4] The original members – Iran, Iraq, Kuwait, Saudi Arabia and Venezuela – were later joined by Qatar, Indonesia, Libya, the United Arab Emirates, Algeria, Nigeria, Ecuador, Gabon, Angola, Guinea and Congo, but Indonesia and Qatar subsequently rescinded their membership. In 2019, OPEC had 14 members.

[5] All production, consumption and proved reserve figures in this section are from BP (annual).

these rules changed over time. Variously motivated exceptions from quotas have also been common, where individual members were permitted to produce without restrictions. Additionally, the shallow nature of the production restraints and constant cheating by most OPEC members made a significant price impact of OPEC's actions unlikely. A comparison of actual OPEC output with the quota ceilings between 1983 and 2001 (Molchanov, 2003) reveals that production exceeded the ceiling by 6.9% on average, with numerous occasions when the excess ran up to 15% or more. Production in excess of permitted quotas has continued after 2001 (Laherrere, 2011). Ironically, full compliance has been achieved only during episodes (such as 2005–2006) when the production ceiling itself tested the limits of each member's available production capacity, such that cheating by excess output was not feasible. In fact, data over the past decades (IEA, monthly) reveal that, excepting Saudi Arabia (the dominant OPEC producer), Kuwait and UAE, virtually full technical capacity utilization has been the rule among the group's members.

With about one third of OPEC output and a production policy often independent of the rest of the cartel Saudi Arabia's actions have on several occasions had a strong price impact, but the objectives have varied over time in a somewhat incoherent manner (Aguilera and Radetzki, 2016). One instance occurred early in 1979, when the Iranian Revolution had pushed up prices strongly and the Saudis implemented a sizable (though short run) output reduction, resulting in a further price explosion to levels in real terms not seen since the 1860s. Another took place in late 1985, after a five-year period during which the Saudis virtually on their own defended an excessive price that severely depleted their market share. A sizable output increase led to a price collapse early in 1986, and an eventual recovery in the demand for the country's oil. A third instance relates to the Saudis' attempt to arrest the price rise following from the production loss due to the war between Iraq and Kuwait in the early 1990s and the simultaneous Russian oil industry malaise after the USSR breakdown. Between 1989 and 1992, the Saudis increased their output from 5.6 to 9.1 MBD, thereby greatly reducing the price boost from Iraqi, Kuwaiti and Russian production declines. It should be added that between 1988 and 2010, Saudi production persistently exceeded the quota it had agreed to (Laherrere, 2011). A fourth instance occurred in late 2014, when the global oil market was characterized by oversupply and poorer OPEC members appealed for production cuts to boost prices. These appeals were blocked by Saudi Arabia, with the argument that the market should be left to balance itself at lower price levels. This strategy, it was hoped, would rebuild OPEC's market share by driving high-cost US shale producers off the market (Reuters, 2014). Yes, prices have been influenced, sometimes strongly, by Saudi Arabia's interventions, but not uniformly upward, and certainly not by the cartel's collective action.

The turbulent developments in the oil market between 2014 and 2019 have triggered a variety of OPEC actions. In 2014 and 2015, OPEC members exceeded their agreed production quotas on a regular basis. At the same time, Chinese economic growth slowed down, so reducing oil demand, while US shale oil output exploded, making the country by far the world's largest producer. These developments in combination led to the drastic price decline at the end of 2014, as is evident from Figure 4.1. OPEC first accepted the low prices and maintained its high output for 1.5 years in the hope of bankrupting the US shale producers. In fact, US shale production continued to expand despite the much lower price levels (Financial Times, 2015).

However, by late 2016 shrinking financial reserves prompted OPEC members to cut production (for the first time since 2008) by about 1 MBD. This agreement was set for the first six months of 2017 and was accompanied by reductions from Russia and ten other nonmembers. The new strategic partnership, that is OPEC and 11 nonmembers with Russia at the lead, has been called OPEC+ and has contributed to a stabilization of oil prices. The new production levels were at first extended through March 2018, and in December 2017 Russia and OPEC even agreed to increase the production cut to 1.8 MBD until the end of 2018. By mid-2019, the OPEC+ oil-output restriction was renewed, with the agreement to decrease production by 1.2 MBD until March 2020 (Reuters, 2019).

Market conditions were completely overwhelmed in early 2020, as this manuscript goes into production, by the Corona crisis. Demand for oil from the transport sector collapsed, as numerous countries locked themselves up to limit the virus spread, reducing global oil usage in April by some 30 MBD (out of a total of about 100 MBD) and prices fell to even lower levels, since it was clear that decisions to cut output within and outside OPEC were completely insufficient to restore market balance.

For a credible, long-run impact on prices, the market interventions of a colluding producer group would have to include constraints on investment, capacity expansion or a widening of the colluding producer group. Restrictions on capacity expansion have never been applied collectively by OPEC. As discussed in Chapter 4, two circumstances with no relationship to the cartel's market management have in fact brought about a general constraint on capacity growth in OPEC members, with some even experiencing sizable capacity shrinkage.

The nationalization of large parts of the oil industry in most OPEC countries in the 1970s resulted in a very severe loss of efficiency and an enduring inability of the young, state-owned firms to undertake complex investments (Radetzki, 1985). Furthermore, the ensuing greedy extraction of most of the profits earned by these firms, for the benefit of government budgets, left inadequate funding for investments (Aguilera and Radetzki, 2016). This added to the difficulties in raising production. The inability to expand capacity had a far more potent influence on market prices than the cartel's production quotas.

Table 10.4 depicts the lagging performance of OPEC as a whole in the world oil industry. The group's share of global output in 1973, a not very impressive 51.6%, declined to only 41.5% 45 years later. Its contribution of a quarter to global output growth is remarkably low, given that almost three quarters of global reserves are located in OPEC countries and that they comprise the huge and economically exceptional ones of the Middle East.

A more focused and even more dramatic evolution in production capacity due to the debilitating effects of the resource curse in selected OPEC countries is presented in Table 4.3 and the surrounding text of Chapter 4, to which the reader is directed.

We assert that state ownership, government greed and the resource curse, in combination, adequately explain the exceptional performance

Table 10.4 *OPEC and world oil output (MBD)*

	1973	2018	Change
OPEC	30.2	39.3	+9.1
World	58.5	94.7	+36.2
OPEC share (%)	51.6	41.5	−25.0

Source: BP (annual).

of oil prices since the early 1970s, and that OPEC's collective internal actions have not yielded any significant price impact.

Is our vision of OPEC's impotence credible, given the predominant popular view of the oil cartel as outstandingly successful, even forming a precedent for other commodity groups? As a matter of fact, a number of serious studies, undertaken at different points in time, appear to share our vision. Thus, MacAvoy (1982) argued that the observed trend of oil prices could be adequately explained by a competitive model. In the same vein, Alhajji and Huettner (2000) contended that statistical tests fail to support a cartel model of OPEC behavior, while Smith (2005) found the "evidence" of OPEC behaving as a price-raising cartel inconclusive. The study by Bina and Vo (2007) is more assertive and assures us that OPEC is neither a cartel nor exhibits any sign of market domination, market control or monopoly. Finally, adopting a 50-year perspective, Gately (2011) concludes that ever since the early 1970s, OPEC has not exploited its market power to raise prices, although its capacity stagnation has certainly had long-term effects on world oil prices. OPEC's limited ambitions in market and price management could be the explanation for the group's long survival.

We do note, however, that since early 2018 OPEC has become more active in external actions; the creation of OPEC+ being the most noteworthy example of efforts to impact global oil prices. It remains to be seen how long this partnership will last, especially considering the history of Russia's relation with Iran, Saudi Arabia's regional rival.

10.4 Conclusions

Not many commodity markets are amenable to successful monopolistic collusion. The necessary but not always sufficient formal conditions are low price elasticities of demand and of outside supply. Even when these conditions are fulfilled, concentration among suppliers and a considerable degree of cohesion is essential for success.

The urge to launch cartels comes in waves and different circumstance can trigger their establishment. During the 1930s, depressed prices prompted cartel action by bringing together producers that faced a survival threat. The attainment of independence by developing countries in the 1960s and the subsequent nationalization of resource industries established a firm belief in "producer power" that resulted in concerted monopolistic interventions in many commodity markets in the 1970s. Experiences from these periods reveal that price-raising cartels normally have a short life. Government participation appears essential for launching and maintaining price-raising intervention. Even then, cartels tend to disintegrate after some years, as the critical elasticity values increase over time.

OPEC is exceptional in that it came into being and still exists at an age of over 50 years. But then, we have argued, convincingly we hope, that its survival is due to its impotence as a market mover. Concurrent developments in world oil markets have activated OPEC, most recently through the formation of strategic alliances with nonmember countries. The long-run results of these actions remain to be analyzed.

11 | *Public Ownership of Commodity Production*

11.1 Introduction

Why is it important to devote special attention to the issue of public ownership in a book that deals with international commodity markets? The answer is straightforward. As will be shown, state-owned enterprises have for several decades accounted for sizable shares of global supply in many commodities. There is a common belief that these enterprises behave differently from privately owned supply agents. This claim must be investigated. For if it is true, then analyses of how international commodity markets function that are based solely on the private enterprise paradigm could plausibly go seriously astray.

There is another reason – very important though not equally central to the themes of the present book – to study state enterprises in commodity production and trade. Such enterprises are particularly dominant in the developing world. A majority of them were established through nationalizations in the 1960s and 1970s because it was believed that public ownership would speed up the economic development process in the newly independent nations. It is essential to verify whether the purported benign effects of nationalization have in fact occurred, especially since these beliefs have recently gained renewed popularity as state-owned enterprises, predominantly from emerging Asia, increasingly compete with private firms for acquisitions in the global market.[1]

There are two important limitations to the subject treatment in the present chapter. First, it deals only marginally with the former socialist

[1] One important difference with the increase of state involvement in 2020,
  compared to the situation in the 1960s and 1970s, is that it is not the result of
  a wave of nationalizations of previously private companies. Rather it is
  a situation where nations, with a strong state involvement, become increasingly
  important in global markets.

countries, where prior to 1990 virtually all production was in public hands as a matter of course. Until that time, therefore, there was hardly any private entrepreneurship to provide a rod of comparison with state-owned enterprise.

Second, the subject is limited, by and large, to the mineral and energy industries. Many countries, especially developing ones, have a large proportion of their mineral and energy sector activities operated by state-owned corporations. In agricultural production, in contrast, public enterprises are regularly of minor importance. In both developing countries and rich, industrialized ones, the limited government presence as agricultural producer mainly reflects the dominance of small-scale operations that have always remained in the hands of the local private farmer. A World Bank study from the mid-1980s notes that state ownership in agriculture seldom exceeded 5% of the sector's output, while in mining 75% or more was common (World Bank, annual a, 1983).

Despite the virtual absence of state-owned production in agriculture, governments have exerted a major influence over the agricultural sector. This has been done in many countries through ownership of agro-based industries, such as sugar refining, or by the maintenance of fiscal monopolies, as for beverages and tobacco. Sometimes public involvement has taken the form of development of corporations that provide finance and other services to agriculture. In many cases, public marketing boards have held a monopoly as suppliers of agricultural inputs and a monopsony as buyers of agricultural produce. These boards have ensured stable prices to farmers, but often at a level to yield ample profits to the government owner when the goods were sold in international markets (Floyd et al., 1984). The twenty-first century has witnessed a growing interest for foreign investments in all kinds of agribusiness by state-owned enterprises, mainly from China, to assure the domestic supply to the investor nation of high-quality agricultural products. As discussed at length in Chapter 3, international trade policies, too, have had a very profound influence on agriculture, both in industrialized and developing countries. But state-owned enterprises for the production of agricultural commodities have not been common.

This contrasts starkly with the conditions in the minerals and energy sectors, where state ownership is pervasive. But it is important to note that the entry of the state on a large scale in these sectors is a relatively recent phenomenon, emerging soon after the crumbling of the colonial empires. Observing the case of copper, Sir Ronald Prain (1975) concluded that production in which the government held any sort of interest in the early 1960s was a mere 2.5% of the nonsocialist world total. By 1970 the share had risen to more than 40%. Broadly the same picture emerges for the metal mineral industries in general. In the mid-1950s, state involvement in the world outside the socialist countries was insignificant. At that time the metal mineral industries of Africa, Asia and Latin America were completely dominated by privately owned multinationals from the leading industrialized market economies. In the early 1980s, when state ownership of metals and minerals stood at its peak, it accounted for something like one third of overall capacity in the world outside the socialist countries. The emergent state-enterprise phenomenon was heavily concentrated in the developing countries, where it accounted for about one half of total capacity. In the industrialized market economies the share was limited to about 10% (Radetzki, 1985).

In petroleum, the emergence of important state-ownership positions is even more recent. As late as 1966, the share of state-owned production in the world outside the socialist countries was negligible, and consisted in the main of the Mexican, Iranian and Iraqi production facilities, nationalized in 1938, 1951 and 1963, respectively (Marcel, 2006). Many more nationalizations occurred during the 1970s (Algeria, Libya, Kuwait and Saudi Arabia, among others), importantly inspired by OPEC's aggressive interventions of the early–mid-1970s, so that by 1979 the state-owned share had risen to 55% (Vernon, 1983). The trend of increased nationalizations has continued. Figure 11.1 demonstrates that by 2010 the private multinational oil corporations have been completely marginalized in terms of ownership of proved oil reserves, and this picture is corroborated by a more recent assertion that, by 2013, over 90% of reserves were under the control of national oil companies (*Economist*, 2013, August 3). Despite our failure to find more recent data, we have little reason to believe that a significant change has since occurred.

The recent, very fast economic expansion of many developing countries with a strong history of state-owned enterprises, such as China, India and Malaysia, has increased concerns about the influence of these growing, state-owned players on the global markets (see e.g. *Economist*, 2012, January 21). This concern is further accentuated as many state-owned firms are shifting their earlier main focus on

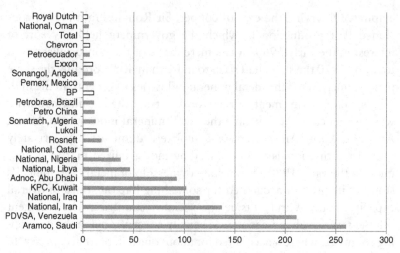

Figure 11.1 Proved oil reserves by company, 2010, billion barrels
Note: State-controlled companies in grey.
Source: Oil & Gas Journal (2011).

domestic markets, thereby becoming some of the world's largest and fastest-growing multinational companies that compete with private players for resources and business also in international markets. We argue that this trend is spreading beyond emerging Asia. For example, the Brazilian government, which supported privatizations in the 1990s, is now increasingly concerned with the maintenance of state control over giant natural resource businesses such as Vale and Petrobras in which it has maintained part ownership. The government of South Africa, too, appears to be increasing its involvement in its natural resource industries (Kahn, 2013). Hence, the need to elucidate the role of public ownership is clearly of high relevance.

This chapter continues by clarifying a few methodological issues. How precisely is state enterprise defined? And what do the percentage shares quoted above represent (Section 11.2)? We subsequently explore the motivations for establishing public ownership in the mineral and energy sectors, in industrialized as well as developing countries (Section 11.3). Then, after pointing to the features that characterize state-owned mineral firms (Section 11.4), we analyze the likely impact of state ownership in minerals and energy on the domestic economy (Section 11.5), providing in the process the rationales for the wave of privatizations in metals and minerals and the shrinkage of state-owned enterprise in these industries after 1980. The chapter ends (Section 11.6) by discussing the impact of state ownership on the international markets for minerals and oil.

11.2 How to Define and Quantify the State-Enterprise Sector

We noted above that concerns about publicly owned firms are based on the belief that these enterprises behave differently in some way from private corporations. If differential behavior is the focus of interest, then the state-enterprise sector should be defined not by equity ownership but by the extent of government control, since control, rather than equity holdings, will determine behavior. In practice, the state-owned sector is almost always measured by the state equity holding, because this is most easy to observe. The underlying presumption is that publicly held equity and control go hand in hand. This is by no means invariably true. The practice of using equity ownership as a differentiating rod between the private and state sectors is also due to the impracticability of establishing and measuring the degree of government control in a uniform way.

Even when equity ownership is employed, some ambiguities remain to be resolved. Many analysts include within the state-owned universe all enterprises in which the public equity holding is 5% or more, on the presumption that the government is a particularly influential owner and that even a significant minority holding constitutes a kind of "golden share," providing this holder with substantial ability to exert their influence. Others include in the state-owned group only the firms that are majority owned by governments. The two measures will obviously yield very different quantitative results. Yet a third approach is to assume state-owned capacity to be proportional to the government's equity holding in each firm. Though this approach avoids the arbitrary borderlines of the first and second methods identified above, a distinct disadvantage is that the measure does not permit a clear-cut identification of individual enterprises as either state or private.

The proportional rod was applied in deriving the state-owned shares in metal and mineral industries that are listed in Section 11.1. The sources for the petroleum industry figures quoted do not state the method used for quantifying the public enterprise share. Vernon's assessments appear to be based on individual country submissions, so in all likelihood a variety of methods were used.

RMG Consulting, a Swedish consultancy in global mineral economics, has developed a more sophisticated definition of state control, that is *either* majority share ownership *or* a minority ownership with no other dominant owners. Table 11.1 assesses the size of state ownership using this definition for a group of major metal minerals. It presents state ownership in mining as a share of world production, both in centrally planned economies, and in market economies of the western world. Prior to 1990, all production in the socialist block was state owned. Since 2000, China has completely dominated the share of state-controlled production for all minerals presented, except nickel (where China's share of the centrally planned economies' production is about 50%).

The time series in the table show a clear peak for state ownership in the 1980s, followed by a sharp shrinkage due to the wave of privatizations that were concentrated in the 1990s. Thus, at the beginning of the twenty-first century the share of mineral production from state-controlled corporations was at its lowest point for many minerals. The increase of China's state-controlled mining after 2000 marks an end to the declining trend seen since the 1980s. Even though the share of state-controlled mining in the western world continues to decrease, there is a rise in the global share of state-controlled mining due to the increase in Chinese mineral production.

11.3 Motivations for Public Ownership in Mineral Industries

The metal minerals and fossil fuels industries throughout the world have been a favorite area for government intervention in a variety of forms, including the taking up of direct equity positions. The authorities' desire to be involved and have control has had a variety of explanations. First, the widespread perception of mineral wealth as a national patrimony has often been used as a motive to sanction public participation, for instance to prevent the appropriation of this patrimony by private, and especially foreign, interests.[2] A second and related argument for intervention has seen the extraction and processing of minerals as strategically important, either because such activities have ensured critical supplies of key inputs into domestic manufacturing, including the defense industries, or due to the very

---

[2] Wenar (2008) goes even further in that he discusses natural resource ownership as an element of human rights.

Table 11.1 State-controlled share in mining (% of world production)

	1975	1984	1989	2000	2005	2009
Bauxite total	**31.7**	**37.9**	**38.3**	**24.5**	**24.4**	**29.9***
ME	17.4	24.8	26.7	18.7	13.5	13.1
CPE	14.3	13.1	11.6	5.8	10.9	16.8
Coal total	na	**64.1**	**62.9**	**42.2**	**51.5**	**52.5***
ME		8.7	8.7	13.1	13.0	10.8
CPE		55.4	54.2	29.1	38.5	41.7
Copper total	**48.7**	**58.7**	**52.5**	**27.7**	**25.5**	**25.0**
ME	26.7	35.2	30.6	22.4	20.3	18.2
CPE	22.0	23.5	21.9	5.3	5.2	6.8
Gold total	**22.2**	**28.5**	**21.3**	**13.2**	**15.0**	**17.6**
ME	2.3	3.4	2.3	6.2	4.7	4.1
CPE	19.9	25.1	19.0	7.0	10.3	13.5
Iron ore total	**53.4**	**67.5**	**64.9**	**38.0**	**29.7**	**31.8**
ME	19.5	23.0	22.5	27.1	14.7	11.4
CPE	33.9	44.5	42.4	10.9	15.0	20.4
Lead total	**38.5**	**44.0**	**40.8**	**26.4**	**36.2**	**45.9**
ME	8.6	12.7	8.2	4.1	2.4	2.5
CPE	29.9	31.3	32.6	22.3	33.8	43.4

Table 11.1 (cont.)

	1975	1984	1989	2000	2005	2009
Manganese total	**64.7**	**68.2**	**62.1**	**32.0**	**33.5**	**34.2**[1]
ME	22.8	13.1	13.4	14.1	9.4	8.5
CPE	41.9	55.1	48.7	17.9	24.1	25.6
Nickel total	**26.2**	**45.3**	**45.0**	**19.7**	**18.8**	**21.5**
ME	2.8	14.2	12.2	9.6	8.9	10.7
CPE	23.4	31.1	32.8	10.1	9.9	10.8
Tin total	**38.7**	**42.9**	**37.7**	**57.9**	**51.5**	**54.3**
ME	22.1	24.0	15.7	17.4	15.7	16.1
CPE	16.6	18.9	22.0	40.5	35.8	38.2
Zinc total	**38.0**	**39.9**	**40.9**	**30.4**	**29.8**	**32.1**
ME	10.6	14.0	11.7	9.5	3.9	4.1
CPE	27.4	25.9	29.2	20.9	25.9	32.1

Note: (a) Controlled share is defined as capacity with majority state ownership or capacity with dominant state-ownership position with no other dominant owners; (b) ME = market economies, CPE = centrally planned economies; (c) Between 1975 and 1989 countries included in the CPE are Albania, Bulgaria, Cambodia, China, Soviet Union, Cuba, Czechoslovakia, Germany, Hungary, Mongolia, Democratic People's Republic of Korea, Poland, Romania and Vietnam. Between 2000 and 2005 CPE countries are China, Cuba, Democratic People's Republic of Korea, Laos, Mongolia and Vietnam. In 2009, the same countries as in 2000–2005, with the exception of Mongolia, are represented in CPE.
[1] Presents shares in 2008. *Source:* World Bank (2011).

large size of many mineral ventures. Third, the immobility of mineral deposits has facilitated far-reaching public intervention without any risk that the activity might escape beyond the government's reach. And fourth, the recurrent generation of high rents in mineral and fossil fuels endeavors, coupled with the difficulty of appropriating such rents through fiscal measures, has aroused strong temptations for public ownership. Motivations such as the ones enumerated here explain many of the public-ownership positions in mineral industries in the industrialized market economies. It helped that the period between 1945 and 1975, when most were established, was one of marked socialist leanings and strong worldwide beliefs in collective action.

The more prominent examples of state ownership in minerals in rich industrialized economies included all stages of aluminum production in France; aluminum smelting in Germany, Italy, Norway and Spain; copper mining through refining in Finland; iron ore production in France and Sweden; coal mining in Germany and the United Kingdom; parts of the petroleum industry in Norway and the United Kingdom; all stages of the natural gas industry in France; steel production in several Western European countries; and uranium mining and uranium enrichment in France and other countries, notably including the USA. The modes for establishing these ownership positions have varied. In a few cases, they resulted from confiscation of enemy property at the end of the Second World War (aluminum smelting in Norway). In some instances, the state acquired its ownership stake by bailing out bankrupt private enterprise. In others, the government purchased the equity at a price agreed through negotiations (Swedish iron ore) or determined unilaterally through government decree (French aluminum). In yet other cases, the operations arose out of government initiatives from scratch (petroleum in Norway).

However, as noted, a major proportion of the state-owned mineral and oil enterprises outside the socialist economies were established in the developing countries. Although the arguments and motivations enumerated here are certainly valid in explaining the existence of state ownership in the developing country group too, an additional perspective is required for a fuller understanding of the emergence and growth as well as of the performance of the publicly owned mineral and energy sectors in developing countries.

As was argued briefly in Chapter 1, the 1960s and 1970s involved a historically unique economic emancipation process for a majority of the developing countries, following the severance of formal or informal colonial bonds. With gradually improving administrative, technical and managerial capabilities in the postcolonial period, the ambitions and abilities of the authorities to promote development through control and direction of the national economy were expanded. The implications were general and far-reaching, and the takeover of foreign production assets was an important part of the process. Williams (1975) estimates that between 1956 and 1974, around one quarter of overall foreign direct investments in the developing countries was nationalized, some 60% of it without compensation. Metal minerals and oil constitute a large proportion of the foreign-owned property taken over by governments.

The great national importance of the mineral and oil sectors, in many cases its predominantly foreign ownership and secluded enclave character vis-à-vis the rest of the national economy, made them major targets for public policy initiatives. The wish to implement radical change was enhanced by a feeling that the mining and oil multinationals in charge of operations were arrogant, unwilling to give local talent a chance to participate and to develop managerial skills, and generally insensitive to national needs.

The initiatives to control and direct the mineral sector took a variety of forms. The ultimate and most far-reaching measure in the developing countries that were heavily dependent on mineral exports was to nationalize the industry, in part or completely. The motivation to nationalize was usually based on the view that other intervention measures – such as taxation or specific regulation pertaining to, for example, investment, employment or exports – were inadequate and that only direct ownership could provide the means for extracting a major proportion of the mineral rent and for establishing effective control over these key industry branches. The practice of compensation payments to previous owners varied from none at all to sums that might appear as adequate to impartial observers. However, the former owners invariably complained about the compensation received.

11.4 Distinguishing Characteristics of State-Owned Mineral Firms and the Environments in which They Operate

In principle, ownership per se should have no impact on behavior. All corporations, both private and state owned, are supposed to be subject to the same existing legal and institutional regime. The difference in behavior arises for two reasons. First, when the government is both owner and regulator of industrial firms it is likely to bend the rules in favor of the companies it owns. Regulation in the field of, for example, environment or labor conditions will tend to be applied in a more relaxed manner on the state-owned firms, with obvious consequences for corporate behavior. A second difference arises because in state enterprises the owners exert influences, distribute favors and erect operational constraints, all with the purpose of affecting corporate behavior for *political ends*. The goal of profit maximization is typically subordinated to the pursuit of a broader set of social goals or specific agendas that politicians in a position of influence choose to pursue.

Ideally, one would have liked to establish a clear-cut distinction between the private, profit-seeking mineral firms, on the one hand, and the state-owned mineral enterprises, characterized by their broader social pursuits, on the other. In the real world, the distinction between the two types of enterprise is hazy. Private firms usually approximate, but seldom conform fully to the pure microeconomic paradigm. In recent decades, the privately owned resource enterprises in many countries have been increasingly conditioned, by law or convention, to assume many functions other than profit maximization. "Social responsibility" has since the 1990s become a vaguely defined mantra that the private profit maximizers have been forced to adopt to avoid being attacked by a plethora of NGOs with distinct and incompletely overlapping agendas. The state-owned enterprises come in many different shapes. Their characteristics range between those indistinguishable from private corporations at one extreme, and to those where a variety of social and political considerations predominate over concerns for return on capital, at the other. But although the line is blurred, there does appear to be a significant difference in goals, characteristics and behavioral patterns between the average private and state-owned mineral firm.

The emphasis in the following characterization is on state-owned resource firms in developing countries. After all, this group has experienced the fastest growth, and it currently accounts for a dominant share of the total state-owned universe in the mineral and energy industries worldwide. We begin by considering the state-owned firms' distinctive behavior in current operations, discuss briefly their financial environment and continue by scrutinizing how investment behavior may differ between the public and private entities.

Operations

In a performance review of state-owned firms in the minerals industries in developing countries, a crucial distinction needs to be made between newly established, inexperienced and hence inefficient corporations, on the one hand, and mature ones that have been there for some time and have acquired the necessary expertise to run their operations with reasonable proficiency, on the other. The relevance of this distinction is predicated on the fact that a large part of the existing state-owned universe was set up through successive waves of nationalizations of foreign-owned positions, which were concentrated in the 1960s and 1970s. Since gaining experience and improving performance efficiency is a time-consuming process, it follows that a review covering the past several decades will encounter a significant proportion of cases characterized by low efficiency due to inadequate experience and not to state ownership per se.

Nationalizations frequently involved extended and heavy set-up costs. The state-owned firms established to manage the operations that were taken over from the foreigners usually had a difficult start. The old owners, dissatisfied with the compensation offered, were often unwilling to provide assistance. The new managers regularly lacked the appropriate experience, but were compelled to take on wide-ranging responsibilities long before they had a chance to acquire the necessary skills. For this reason, the result was almost invariably chaos and confusion that disrupted operations. The disruptions regularly reached a maximum soon after takeover, and then gradually subsided over a long period of time. Initially, the inexperienced management was often unable even to maintain production at full capacity levels, and the cost of output tended to rise.

Available evidence suggests a wide variation in the time needed for overcoming the disruptions and inefficiencies due to managerial inexperience after nationalization. The speed of improvement in this respect appears to be related to the level of economic development of the country, the extent of earlier exposure of the national managers to the problems of the industry, and the ability to make constructive arrangements with outside specialists for managerial support and training. Overcoming the loss of efficiency due to inexperience at the time of nationalization took no more than five years in the case of Venezuela's iron ore operations. In Indonesia's tin industry, more than 20 years were needed to develop a national management cadre of international quality standard after it was taken over from the Dutch owners in the 1950s. In Zambia, where the government took a majority holding of the copper industry in 1970, the process was never completed (Radetzki, 1985) and the neverending inefficiencies provided a strong rationale for the decision to privatize the industry in the 1990s. The speed of improvement has also been related to the mode for selecting top management. It was fastest where appointments were made on the basis of managerial skills and least impressive where selection was guided by a desire to disseminate political favors.

The inefficiency due to inexperience that has characterized a substantial part of the state-owned-enterprise group through the past decades is, with few exceptions, a transient feature. Since the late 1970s, after the waves of nationalization subsided, the state-owned universe has become increasingly proficient and mature.

But while the deficiencies due to a difficult start have by and large been overcome with time, it is evident that state-owned resource-extracting firms, in both developing and industrialized countries, also suffer from systemic and permanent weaknesses. These enterprises are often forced by their owners to pursue a more complex and diversified goal structure than privately owned firms. In addition to the generation of a return on the capital put at their disposal, the state-owned units are regularly required to attend to a profound "social responsibility" agenda, comprising employment, skill creation and technological progress at the national level; regional development; and foreign exchange generation – even when pursuit of these goals compromises their profitability and long-term financial health. In Auty's (2003) terse terms, the executives are "sidetracked into performing political favors" as their enterprises "become providers of political patronage."

Even where the nonprofit objectives provide bona fide contributions to social development, their addition to the goals of the state-owned firm are bound to involve a cost, and so to result in higher costs of production. The requirement that the activity should yield not only mineral output, but also the output of one or other social good is akin to the requirement that byproducts be extracted from the ore, along with the main product. There is a cost in obtaining the byproducts, whether mineral or social. But while the resource byproducts typically enhance profitability to the firm by the revenue they generate the social byproducts do not, with the result that profits are suppressed. If society attributes sufficient value to the social byproducts, the outcome may nevertheless be desirable and need not involve any inefficiency from society's point of view.

There is another reason, however, why the subordination of the profit motive to a set of social goals will often result in unequivocal inefficiency and will tend to increase the firm's production costs even further. Multiple goals make it harder to measure managerial performance and so are likely to lessen the pressure to minimize costs. Where several goals are pursued at the same time, high-cost levels will be easier to justify by the pursuit of some or other social objective than it would be in a firm where profit maximization is the sole yardstick for measuring the quality of management.

The three arguments just spelled out, namely (a) a transient inefficiency due to inexperience; (b) the costs involved in pursuing social goals; and (c) a permanent inefficiency due to lesser pressure to minimize costs, should lead, on average, to higher costs of resource production in state-owned enterprises than in private firms exploiting mineral or fossil fuel deposits of a corresponding quality.

Financial Environment and Investment Behavior

The financial environments under which state-owned mineral firms operate differ a lot depending on country, government and industry. Gillis (1980) asserts that state-owned firms lived under particularly lax financial conditions in the 1970s. The owner governments often endowed them with an implicit guarantee for financial survival. They were hardly ever allowed to go bankrupt. Undercapitalization resulting from unprofitable operations was remedied through new financial infusions. Through their owners, such firms had better access to subsidized capital, from the government budget or from international development agencies, than did private mineral corporations.

The impact of such financial guarantees and implicit subsidies, where they occurred, for the state-owned firms' relative competitiveness should not be overemphasized. The benefits could be regarded as compensation for the costly social obligations that these firms were forced to assume. Clearly, the governments of countries heavily dependent on the mineral industry could not possibly find the means to provide subsidies to that industry over the long run. Furthermore, there should be no need for subsidies after the initial period of inefficiency that was due to inexperience. A majority of the large state mineral firms exploit superior resource deposits, so except during periods of severe price depression or when recklessly robbed by their owners, they should reap significant Ricardian rents to assure reasonable corporate financial comfort even after their social obligations have been paid for.

Moreover, while Gillis' (1980) observations were shared by many analysts at the time, they are clearly less than general. They may reflect a fortunate subgroup of firms or, more importantly, the positive government attitudes of the 1970s when many of the state-owned positions had been recently established and hopes about their long-run contributions to national development were high. Finally, one cannot preclude the possibility that the perception of lax financial conditions applying to state-owned firms was a myth actively fostered at the time by private producers.

Two decades later, the financial circumstances of the state-owned mineral firms were definitely not superior to those in the private sector. The firms' access to capital from international development agencies had become strictly controlled by finance ministries, who worried about budget deficits. The flow of funds was clearly from corporate profits to government budget, often to the extent that reinvestment and capacity expansion were impaired. The survival guarantee remained, but nonperforming managements saw privatization as a clear threat. The somewhat romantic view of state ownership as a tool for automatic national progress, which needed to be nurtured, had been replaced by a more realistic and much tougher attitude.

Pinpointing systematic differences in investment behavior between state-owned firms and private multinational corporations in the mineral and oil industries may be as difficult as the identification of dissimilarities of the respective financial environments in which they operate. The difficulty arises mainly from the diversity of investment objectives imposed by the owners of the state mineral enterprises. Several such objectives can be stated: The simplest rule could be to encourage investments which look profitable, whenever adequate funding is available. This is no different from the guiding rod employed by private enterprise. If the country is richly endowed with natural resources, the policy may be to afford preferential treatment to the state-owned enterprises in the development of this wealth, and so to ensure a predominantly national character to the mineral industry. Yet a third rule may be for the government to induce or require state-enterprise investments in uncommercial ventures, for example to promote regional development or to use the output to satisfy national strategic needs. The last rule will reduce profitability. It is akin to the requirement that the firm pursue some social goals in its operations.

Three important constraints on the investment activities of the state-owned mineral enterprises should be noted. First is the government's need to appropriate operational surpluses to balance its budget. This has sometimes left the state firm with inadequate funding for its investment plans. Second and related to the first is the execution of government control through excessive bureaucratic meddling, which tends to paralyze investment decisions and their execution. Examples from the oil industry of how indecisive and overactive bureaucrats effectively arrest the process of investment decisions are amply described by IEA (2014b). The third constraint has to do with the transitional inefficiencies discussed above. Investment in new capacity is undoubtedly the most complex activity in the natural resource sector, and one that takes much longer to master than the operational problems. Such inefficiencies add to costs and deter investment.

Empirical observations confirm the vast differences in investment behavior within the state-owned group. On one extreme, some state enterprises were simply robbed by their government owners, who extracted available cash flow to the extent that the firms were decapitalized. There were no means for investment and little for reinvestment. In some cases, resources were not available even for proper maintenance and the companies were forced to cannibalize equipment and spares to maintain any operations. One of the worst examples is Gecamines, the state-owned copper producer in the Democratic Republic of Congo (Bomsel, 1994), whose mine output went down from 500 kt in 1975 to only 35 kt 20 years later. ZCCM in Zambia represents another sad copper story: its output fell by half in the corresponding 20-year period – but the industry has recorded an impressive recovery after it was privatized around the turn of century. Other examples of non-investment and shrinkage due to government greed comprise Comibol (Bolivia), Centromin and Petroperu, the latter both in Peru. Petroperu had been reduced by 1989 to little more than a conduit for channeling oil revenues to the government, even at the expense of maintaining exploration and field development (Auty, 2003).[3]

The nationalized oil producers in OPEC countries represent another case of very weak investment in capacity expansion, a theme discussed in more detail in Chapter 4. In short, the members of the cartel control 72% of the world's proved oil reserves (estimated in 2018), including huge deposits in the Middle East that are extremely cheap to exploit. Yet, between 1979 and 2018 the share of global output from the OPEC group declined from 46.2% to 41.4% (BP, annual). More than three quarters of global oil production expansion during the period was generated by non-OPEC countries, despite their much inferior resource wealth. We argue that the bleak performance of OPEC countries had a number of causes of which cartel policy, that is holding back production to reap rents, is not a significant one (Chapter 10). More important factors behind OPEC's relative decline were the general weaknesses of state enterprise, elucidated above, and the serious disturbances caused by the resource curse (Chapter 12), supplemented in some cases by inadequate financial resource availability, both preventing the establishment of new production capacity, in some cases even preventing the maintenance of existing capacity.

The above experiences of OPEC contrast sharply with state-owned enterprises that built managerial competences speedily and whose owners encouraged expansion and left the firms with sufficient resources to implement the necessary investments. Vale, previously CVRD, of Brazil is one example. It impressively expanded its iron ore production and sales, and at the same time it ventured into other minerals, notably bauxite. At the time of its privatization in the 1990s, it was the world's largest iron ore producer and held important positions in several other metal minerals. The record of Codelco of Chile, which continues to be fully state owned, varied over time. Mined copper output rose by no more than 8% in the ten-year period 1985–1995, but subsequently increased by almost 50% in the following decade. However, the output of other Chilean copper mines, predominantly privately owned, expanded by 370% and 180%, respectively in the corresponding periods (COCHILCO, 2005).

---

[3] It should be mentioned, however, that the privatization wave in both Peru and Zambia has involved other state-owned companies (mainly Chinese) taking over previously nationally owned mines.

The nationalizations of the 1960s and 1970s frequently involved ruptures of the international vertical integration chains that were maintained by private multinationals. The downstream processing facilities located in the mineral importing countries were out of reach for the nationalization efforts. The ruptures remained in the metal mineral industries in the decades that followed, since the state-owned mineral firms were particularly unwilling to launch investments outside their home territory. The investments of Chilean Codelco and Zambian ZCCM in European downstream processing of copper were clear exceptions from the common practice (Radetzki, 1990a).

The metal mineral experience of forward integration contrasts with that in petroleum and natural gas. After a period of hesitation some of the state-owned oil enterprises, notably from Norway, Kuwait and Venezuela, undertook energetic efforts in the 1980s and 1990s to integrate forward by buying up refineries, distribution chains and other downstream facilities in the industrialized importing nations. The intention, presumably, was to secure outlets for the crude oil they produced.

The appetite for foreign investment has grown tremendously among another selected group of state-owned oil firms after 2000, but the character of these investments has been dramatically different from the post-nationalization forward-integration efforts. A perception in mid-2000 of oil depletion, and thus forthcoming scarcities, sent many state enterprises in China, India, Brazil and other developing countries with fast oil-consumption growth on a worldwide hunt to acquire reserves or developed production facilities, to assure domestic needs for oil and gas. The government owners of these companies have been strongly supportive of this new trend. Even Petronas, the state-owned corporation of oil-exporting Malaysia, has joined the bandwagon. Intriguingly, these companies have been prepared to assume political risks in their engagements in, for example, Chad, Sudan or Venezuela that were considered unacceptably high by many private multinationals (Aguilera and Radetzki, 2016; IEA, 2006).

This quest for investments abroad by state-owned corporations has by no means been limited to the oil industry. Similar tendencies have been noted in metal minerals, and lately also in agricultural production. It is mainly the state-owned enterprises in emerging Asia that have been on a widespread spending spree abroad in the 2010s, primarily motivated by a desire to assure domestic consumption needs. In an interesting study,

Gallagher and Irwin (2014) analyze outward foreign direct investments (OFDI) promotion by Chinese state-development banks, and compare this development to similar behavior of banking predecessors in Japan and South Korea. The government of China created China Development Bank and China Export-Import Bank in 1993, as a means to fulfill the country's "go global" policy and also to have governmental control over investments abroad. From 2002 to 2012, the total value of government financing for state-owned companies to invest abroad was estimated at US$140 billion, and most of the lending was directed toward natural resource acquisition. It was in fact an outspoken goal set by Jiang Zemin (president of China 1993 to 2003) that China should take advantage of investments in natural resources in resource-rich countries, mainly in Africa, Latin America and South Asia. According to the findings in Gallagher and Irwin (2014), the mining and oil sectors also received some 80% of overall Chinese OFDI loans between 2002 and 2012.

It is clear that until 2012 the main motive behind China's OFDI was to secure the country's supply of minerals and fossil fuels. Since then, however, there have been signs that foreign investments from China are becoming more diverse, and in particular there has been an increased focus on the agriculture sector. In a report from the US Department of Agricultural, the understanding and motivations of the increased investments in foreign agricultural and food assets from China are analyzed (Gooch and Gale, 2018). It is noted that in 2016 over 1300 Chinese firms invested abroad in agriculture, forestry and fisheries, at a value of US$26 billion. In 2014, the state-owned China National Cereals, Oils and Foodstuffs Corporation invested US$1.5 billion for a stake in Noble's agribusiness (Asia's largest commodity trader) and US$1.29 billion in Nidera (a global commodity service and solutions provider for agricultural markets) with its head office in the Netherlands, two of the largest investments in agribusiness that have ever occurred (EY, 2015). Investment in these sectors increased by 500% between 2010 and 2016. The main motivations for these investments are an increased reliance of food import, concerns related to national food security, as well as rising foreign reserves (Gooch and Gale, 2018).

11.5 Impact of State Ownership on the National Economy

This section briefly reviews how the establishment and operations of state-owned mineral enterprises have impacted on the national economies of their home countries. In turn, we will assess whether the public takeovers have really contributed to improved government control, greater national revenue and other goal fulfillments. After illuminating the disappointments about public ownership that emerged widely during the 1980s, the section discusses the subsequent worldwide wave of privatizations in metal minerals, but not so far in oil, as well as recording some revival of resource nationalism prompted by the resource boom of 2004–2014. It ends by addressing state-owned companies in China.

Control

As noted, many of the publicly owned units in the mineral industry were taken over from foreign owners and an important motivation for the state action was that foreign control over these important industries compromised national sovereignty. State ownership, it was felt, would provide the government with a crucial tool for directing national development. This objective was not satisfactorily achieved. At least two problems were involved. Both have to do with the unclear relationship between the management and their owners, typical of state enterprises (Aharoni, 1982).

The first problem, involving too much and poorly coordinated owner intervention, tends to make successful control and direction hard to attain (Dobozi, 1987; Wälde, 1984). In many cases, the owners cannot be clearly identified, and they certainly do not speak with one voice. The state commonly exerts its ownership rights through a variety of individuals and institutions. There is bound to be a tendency for the political-owner representatives who happen to have the greatest influence at a particular time to extract short-term economic or political benefit for themselves or their constituency, without considering the longer term, when they will no longer be in charge, or the nationwide implications.

The second problem is that the blurred nature of the principal–agent relationship has sometimes allowed state mineral enterprises to grow into powerful political and economic empires, unrestrained by government control and public accountability. Influential politicians were often put in charge as CEOs of the large state-owned corporate structures. Their political clout permitted the bosses to act with a much greater independence from, say, the ministry of finance, than would have been possible for a foreign owner, who could always be threatened with nationalization. The specialized ministry often became the spokesman of the state firm, rather than an instrument for government control.

Pertamina, the Indonesian state petroleum company, provides perhaps the most striking case of lost government control. Its management implemented unwieldy diversification into transport and tourism with borrowed money, all on its own initiative. The government regained control only after it had to rescue this corporation from impending bankruptcy in the early 1980s. In Latin America, a large proportion of the foreign borrowing during the 1970s, which eventually resulted in a widespread debt crisis, was incurred by the state-owned enterprises, without proper monitoring by the governments. Quite contrary to the original intentions, the nationalizations in many cases led to a reduction, rather than an increase, of effective government control.

Mineral Rent

Another very important motivation for nationalization has been the governments' desire to reap the entire mineral rent. Under foreign ownership, a substantial part of that rent was dissipated abroad. The share of rent accruing to the nation did indeed increase strongly when firms were taken over from foreigners. Some dissipation continued because the newly established units often had to rely on costly foreign management contracts and consulting services. More important, however, was the fact that mismanagement reduced the total amount of rent in many cases, shrinking the public revenue in absolute terms.

World price developments for metals and minerals provided an additional cause of disappointment, but this was obviously not a result of nationalizations. The 1975–1990 UNCTAD metal and mineral price index in constant money turned 22% below its value in 1960–1974. This decline reduced the mineral rents even more.

Zambia provides a drastic example of reduced public revenue due to a combination of emerging but persevering inefficiency and declining price after the nationalization of its copper industry. In 1965–1970, a period of private ownership, the average copper price was US$1.92/lb and the annual government revenue from the copper industry amounted to US$758 million on average (all money is expressed in constant 1980 dollars). In 1971–1974, after the government had taken

Table 11.2 *Zambian copper industry performance*

	Output (kt)	Global share (%)	Cost (US $/lb)[1]	Profit before tax (US$m)	Tax paid (US$m)
1974	710	9.3	0.63	775	477
1982	530	6.5	0.77	-186	3

[1] Constant 1981 dollars.
Source: Radetzki (1985).

over as the majority owner, the copper price settled at US$1.49/lb, but the public revenue declined to US$438 million per year. Between 1975 and 1980 copper prices averaged US$0.90/lb, while the annual government income fell to US$30 million, less than 4% of the revenues prior to nationalization (Zambia Mining Yearbook, various issues; World Bank, annual b, 1986; IMF, 1982). Underinvestment and persistent shortcomings in the nationalized firms resulted in falling production and rising costs in the 1980s. This further accentuated the suppression of government income. Table 11.2 provides additional detail. The disillusion with state ownership and desire to privatize that emerged in the 1980s should not surprise.

In at least one crucial respect, petroleum differed from metals and minerals. A variety of events assured oil prices in 1975–1990 that were more than 200% higher than in the preceding 15 years (Aguilera and Radetzki, 2016; Radetzki, 2006). Reasonable profitability could therefore be maintained despite the shortcomings of state ownership, and so the pressures to privatize remained weak.

Other National Goals

How have nationalizations contributed to the noncommercial goals that the public enterprises were asked to pursue? The evidence as well as the measure of comparison are quite opaque on this count. Nationalization of most of the managerial functions after takeover must have speeded up skill creation within the country by providing a broader exposure to managerial responsibilities. This benefit has to be set against the cost of temporary inefficiency due to inexperience, but also, more importantly, due to the many managerial appointments based on political favoritism and not on merit.

The state-owned mineral enterprises have clearly also pursued a variety of social goals more energetically than could be expected from private multinationals. Given the cost incurred by the firms in the pursuit of the noncommercial objectives, the net benefit to society of these endeavors is somewhat uncertain. Employment creation and regional development are certainly worthy social pursuits, but the capital intensive, commercially oriented state mineral enterprises appear to be highly unsuitable tools for the purpose. The social welfare effects would no doubt improve if the firms were simply required to maximize profits and if the government established more appropriate institutions for achieving social goals.

Before ending this somewhat disillusioned assessment of the impact of state-owned mineral enterprises on the national economy, it is worth repeating that these firms come in many different shapes and that some have been highly successful. For instance, Codelco, the Chilean state-owned copper corporation, has been given a clear-cut mandate by the government to maximize profits and to leave the pursuit of social goals to others. It has maintained a high international reputation for cost suppression, rising productivity and expansion through efficient execution of investments. That is fine. But even in this case, an outside observer may be perplexed by the company's inability to close units generating perennial losses and wonder about the purpose of arrangements, in force many years after democracy was restored, whereby a sizable royalty is paid by this state-owned corporation directly to Chile's military establishment or the regular habit of incoming national presidents to appoint a new CEO, irrespective of the performance record of the preceding one.

Disillusion and Privatization

In the 1980s and 1990s, a worldwide wave of privatizations led to a sizable abdication by the governments from their positions as owners and managers of industry. The shift in metal minerals is starkly apparent from Table 11.1. Several factors explain why this happened. The ideological revolution prompted in the 1980s by Margaret Thatcher and Ronald Reagan played an important role in bringing about the turnaround. It strengthened the belief in the ability of unregulated markets as instruments for solving social and economic problems, while casting serious doubts on the abilities of government as entrepreneur. It pointed to *political failure* as a much more serious and more frequent problem than *market failure*. In the metal mineral industries, the postcolonial push for economic emancipation had become a spent force, while the glaring deficiencies of state ownership described above became increasingly apparent. Borcherding et al. (1982) and Megginson and Netter (2001) present interindustry surveys of the weak efficiency levels of state-owned enterprises, though they do not appear to have taken the temporary nature of part of the inefficiencies into account. One study of Brazilian iron ore (Schmitz, 2004) even contends that privatization of state-owned units improved productivity in the private industry too. Historically low metal prices in the 1980s reduced the mineral rents, shrinking the hypothetical gains of national ownership. In numerous cases, the mining multinationals were being welcomed back, in recognition of the value and uniqueness of the inputs that they could provide when they took over state-owned property. Constructive collaboration replaced political demagoguery between the parties, and amicable arrangements for the development of new projects, with management responsibilities entrusted to the private partner, become common.

The wave of privatizations in metal minerals appears to have come to an end. This is apparent from the number of privatization deals and the amounts involved in the transactions. In 1997, 20 deals were recorded for a total of US$5 billion. By 2000, the numbers were down to four deals and US$0.3 billion (private communication with Magnus Ericsson, then with Raw Materials Group). Ironically, the buildup of the state-owned universe occurred in a period of high prices and elevated mineral rents, while its dismantling took place in years of depressed mineral markets. This must obviously have reflected negatively on the expenditures of state takeover and the receipts of sales in the privatization process.

Our general observations of the disappointing performance of the state-owned resource sector are further corroborated in some measure by a recent study of the Indian mining industry. This study undertook empirical tests of the efficiency of private versus publicly owned firms in the resource extraction industry (Das, 2012). By assessing the total factor productivity for both private and public mining firms in India between 1988 and 2006, the study reveals that the efficiency of privately owned firms is almost double that of public firms in the non-metallic sector, and somewhat less (1.5 times) in metallic and coal mining firms. For the Indian petroleum industry, the study's surprising conclusion is that, since the mid-1990s, public and private firms have been equally efficient, suggesting but not explaining a sharp productivity improvement of public oil companies in the 1990s.

Privatizations played a much lesser role in the oil industry. Those that occurred took place predominantly in Western Europe, with British Petroleum PLC being the most notable example. In developing countries, state ownership remained virtually intact, and not only in OPECs' member nations. In 2019, the major oil companies in Brazil, Malaysia and Mexico, for example, were still predominantly in state hands. A reasonable explanation for this lack of privatization is that the perseverance of elevated oil prices and profits has resulted in a more forgiving attitude toward state ownership by helping to disguise its inherent inefficiencies. High prices have also discouraged privatization because of fears that it might direct part of the high rents away from the governments. A recent development toward privatization in the oil industry requires mention. Saudi Arabia, in an attempt to generate resources for the diversification of its economy, is planning to sell about 5% of shares in Aramco, the giant state-owned oil company (*Economist*, 2019, November 2). Interesting implications, not least for OPEC policy, may follow once the deal has been completed.

Mineral and oil prices experienced an exceptional and durable price boom between 2004 and 2014 (as discussed in Chapter 6). The high prices, in turn, prompted a selective revival of resource nationalism. Many exporting countries raised taxation in efforts to increase the government's share of the rent. One example of this phenomenon was in Australia, which on July 1, 2012 implemented a minerals resource rent tax on profits generated from mining. The tax was formulated so that 30% of the rents from large firms in the iron ore and coal industries should be retained by the Australian state and expended on pensions, tax cuts for small business and infrastructure projects in the regions mostly affected by mining. However, this tax can be seen as a failure for at least two reasons. First, the actual revenue from the tax was not even close to what was initially expected. Second, the tax turned out to be very complex and expensive to operate. For these reasons, the tax was repealed on September 2, 2014.

In a similar endeavor, several African governments have taken joint actions to gain increased control over their mining industries as a means to ensure that a larger share of the resource rent is directed toward national social and development processes (African Union, 2009). This was a natural response for mineral-exporting countries while prices and rents remained high. Against the negative historical experiences of state ownership, one may express doubts about the resolve of recent resource nationalism now that the boom has ended and prices declined.

China and State-Owned Enterprises

About 40 years have passed since China introduced the economic reforms that successfully transformed the country from a closed agrarian economy to an industrial global-market player. The reforms have allowed markets to play an important role in resource allocation in the country, however, state ownership still remains the dominant ownership form in the economy as a whole. Even though the state sector has declined, state-owned firms still account for about 30% of total GDP, far more than countries in the OECD. Furthermore, on the Fortune Global 500 list as many as 109 corporations are based in China and of these, 85% are characterized by state ownership (Guluzade, 2019).

It would appear that the main strategy of the Chinese government is to continue to support state-owned companies, and so to make them bigger and more efficient. This is achieved by the State Owned Asset Supervision and Administration Commission, established in 2003 with its main aim to supervise and restructure state-owned firms to become modern profit-oriented companies (Guluzade, 2019). In sum this implies that the Chinese government allows markets to be a resource allocator, while at the same time maintaining control over the final decision-making in these firms.

Indeed, state-owned firms are often utilized by the government to implement policies that will stabilize the economy and promote infrastructure developments. For example, it is estimated that centrally administered state-owned companies accounted for more than 70% of the value of infrastructure projects under the Belt and Road Initiative (Stratfor, 2018). Furthermore, after the global financial crisis in 2008 it was realized that state ownership can play a critical role in sustaining growth in an economic crisis, thus weakening the incentives to restructure ownership.

The impact of Chinese state ownership on global commodity markets is that many of the firms in commodity-related markets are so big as to significantly impact on commodity prices and trade flows. This Chinese influence is one of the motivations behind the trade disputes between China and the USA that emerged after Donald Trump assumed the US presidency. The argument that these firms exert unfair competition, as they are claimed to be heavily subsidized, has been emphasized by the Trump administration on many occasions. The true market impact of the Chinese state-owned firms might well be exaggerated given their inherent inefficiencies. Nevertheless, a strong push has emerged to reduce existing subsidies, but so far to little effect. If anything, the US pressures have strengthened support for state ownership rather than weakening it (Guluzade, 2019).

11.6 Implications for International Mineral Markets

The explosive growth of the state enterprise universe in the mineral industries during the 1960s and 1970s, and the trauma through which many of the state-owned firms came into being, gave rise to widespread concerns and a variety of claims and exhortations about their likely impact on the international mineral markets.

One important worry has been that the widespread nationalizations in developing countries will result in inadequate mineral supply, with harmful consequences for user industries in importing countries. The underlying argument was that state-owned firms are so inefficient and so heavily taxed that the cash flow remaining at their disposal would be insufficient for adequate capacity expansion, or even for capacity maintenance (Giraud, 1983; Mikesell, 1979). This worry clearly had little foundation, given the lax supply conditions and the low prices for most minerals (in some measure including oil after 1985) during the 1980s and 1990s. Interestingly, Mikesell's and Giraud's argument that state ownership causes serious supply constraints has resurfaced as a part-explanation to the exceptional oil price performance after 2005 (Aguilera and Radetzki, 2016; IEA, 2006).

An opposite concern has been that excessive investments due to a lax financial regime, and an inflexible response to price changes due to the suppression of profit maximization in favor of social goals, both characteristics of state mineral enterprises, will result in lower average prices and greater price fluctuations, with severely detrimental consequences to the privately owned mineral industries (Metallgesellschaft, 1984; Mining Journal, 1983).

At a more general level, and not limited to the resource industries, a concern primarily voiced by the developed economies has been evolving in the course of the twenty-first century. This is that expanding state ownership in industry and trade will have a distorting effect on global commerce and on competition in international markets. This would follow from the especially favorable treatment of the state-owned units by their owners and the multiplicity of objectives pursued by these units, with a general disregard for profit maximization as the ultimate goal. An OECD report by Kowalski et al. (2013) reviews these issues. Since it relates to industry in general and not specifically to natural resource extraction, this concern is only of indirect interest for our deliberations. Furthermore, there is little to go on in terms empirical investigations to determine the seriousness of this concern.

To return to state ownership in the minerals and oil industries, the lead theme of this chapter's investigations, we note that no convincing empirical support has been provided to back up the claims that the dissemination of state ownership has compromised supply or that it has suppressed prices. And a detailed econometric analysis of the copper industry failed to confirm a lesser price sensitivity of supply in state-owned than in privately owned firms, though it indicated that such sensitivity was lower in poor countries and especially in countries heavily dependent on copper exports (Markowski and Radetzki, 1987).

There are in fact not many convincing claims that can be made about the impact of the establishment and operations of the state-owned enterprise universe on the mineral markets. The temporary as well as the permanent, systemic inefficiencies of state-owned enterprises resulted in higher production costs but seldom in higher prices, because these firms regularly exploited attractive intra-marginal deposits. Nationalizations often involved ruptures of the vertical integration built by the mining multinationals. While this does not appear to have reduced the reliability of supply, it did introduce a greater openness and more competition in the markets for raw materials such as bauxite and iron ore. The more competitive conditions under which the raw materials have been increasingly traded in the twenty-first century (Radetzki, 2013a) might conceivably have lowered their prices.

In a 2018 report, commissioned by the Extractive Industries Transparency Initiative, that analyzes the governance of state ownership in upstream oil, natural gas and mining, large diversities in performance and operations are emphasized. On the positive side, it is found that some state-owned firms in the extractive industries have indeed generated more revenues for their government, improved local technologies and skills, and addressed local market failures to an extent that private companies would be hesitant to undertake. However, it is also noted that many state-owned enterprises face challenges, such as weak financial performance and inefficient project developments, which lead to considerable misallocation of resources. The report further notes that state-owned oil, gas and mining firms in the OECD countries were characterized by high rates of corruption and a general lack of transparency (Bauer, 2018).

The absence of striking conclusions follows from the finding that state-owned enterprises show a great diversity, so a uniform impact of their establishment and operations is hard to identify.

12 | The Monoeconomies: Issues Raised by Heavy Dependence on Commodity Production and Exports

This chapter is devoted to the special problems encountered by nations that are heavily dependent on a small group of commodities, or, in an extreme case, reliant on a single commodity (monoeconomies). We begin by discussing the measures of commodity dependence and define mono-economy in the process. We then turn to exploring the problems of export instability, fiscal extraction and exchange rate policies, which often arise in commodity-dependent countries. We finally deal with *Dutch disease* and the *resource curse*, two ailments of particular significance to monoeconomies.

12.1 Measurement of Commodity Dependence

The degree of national dependence on primary commodities can be measured in a variety of ways. One can try to establish the share of the commodity sector in either GDP or in investments, employment, government income or exports. The nature of the production and consumption of a specific commodity composition will influence the level of the alternative measures. Among commodities accounting for an equal share of GDP, one that is capital intensive (petroleum extraction) will normally account for a higher share of investments and a lower share of employment than another that is labor intensive (coffee). All else alike, the share of government revenue will vary with the generation of rent in the production of a specific commodity. Even when dependence as measured by the share of GDP or employment is high, the export dependence could be limited if most of the commodity is consumed at home (rice in Bangladesh).

The difficulties in defining commodities in a uniform way, discussed in Chapter 2, tend to blur the assessments of commodity dependence. Such dependence is sometimes measured by considering the raw material extraction exclusively. This is the practice when the share of agriculture or minerals in GDP is measured (United Nations, annual a). In other cases the processing activity is also included. The export share measurements usually consider processed commodities, such as metals or butter and flour, along with their raw materials (WTO, annual). The inclusion of processed products will obviously increase the dependence figures. These ambiguities notwithstanding, it is usually not difficult to point out the countries that are heavily dependent on commodities.

Through most of the twentieth century, the division of work in the world economy was such that the industrialized market economies dominated manufactures production and raw materials imports, so heavy commodity dependence typically occurred in developing nations. The latter then provided the industrialized world's import needs. This is no longer so. Taking nonfuel commodities as the measuring rod, recent statistics (UNCTAD, annual b, 2018) reveal that this commodity group accounts for 15.6% of the developed countries' total goods exports in 2017, which is about 3.6 percentage points more than the corresponding figure for developing countries in aggregate. The picture changes if fuels are included, for then the commodity share of developed countries' exports rises to 25.4%, while that of developing countries increases to 32.8%. Nonfuel commodities currently account for only 4.8% of China's goods exports, manufactures for 93%, a significantly higher share than recorded by the developed nations (75%). These Chinese figures are nontypical for developing countries. They are the result of China's extraordinarily fast growth and industrialization since the 1990s.

Reliable and systematic intercountry comparisons of dependence on an individual commodity are hard to come by, except in the case of export shares – and even these figures can be misleading where re-exports (sometimes after slight processing) are significant. Export shares is the measure applied in Table 12.1. The table lists all the countries where the leading nonfuel commodity exceeded 40% of total exports in 2013–2017.[1] This is the definition we employ for monoeconomies.

Several reflections come to mind when the contents of Table 12.1 are reviewed. First, all the 17 countries are poor and very small economies. This is not surprising. Figure 1.1 demonstrated clearly that poor

---

[1] The six countries that are completely reliant on exporting fish and fish products (almost exclusively small islands) have been excluded.

Table 12.1 *The monoeconomies: leading nonfuel commodity accounted for 40% or more of total exports in 2013–2017*

Country	Commodity (SITC rev. 3)	Share of total exports 2013–2017 (%)
Botswana	Precious stones (667)	85
Burkina Faso	Gold (971)	61
Burundi	Gold (971)	44
Comoros	Spices (075)	66
Congo	Copper (682)	42
Guinea Bissau	Fruit/nut (057)	88
Guyana	Gold (971)	45
Jamaica	Aluminum ores (285)	46
Kyrgyzstan	Gold (971)	40
Malawi	Tobacco (121)	48
Mali	Gold (971)	68
Nauru	Crude fertilizer (272)	64
Sao Tome and Principe	Cocoa (072)	67
Sierra Leone	Iron ore (281)	44
Somalia	Live animal (001)	71
Suriname	Gold (971)	47
Zambia	Copper (682)	67

Source: UNCTAD (2019).

countries tend to be heavily dependent on the primary sector. More developed, larger or geographically more extended economies are usually more diversified, so a single commodity will seldom dominate any important aspect of the national economy. Second, many commodities of significance in international trade, such as wheat, sugar or maize, do not dominate the exports of individual countries. Third, the nonfuel monoeconomy phenomenon varies in significance over time. A table similar to Table 12.1 but related to exports in 1982–1983 contained 19 nations, of which 14 exhibited over 60% dependence (Radetzki, 1990a). Similar data for 2013–2014 reveal that only 14 countries were defined as monoeconomies, of which seven had dependence over 60%. During 2013–2017 the phenomenon of export dependence increased again, as 17 countries were defined as monoeconomies, and nine of these exhibited over 60% dependence. Fourth, nations seldom stay as monoeconomies for a very long time. In 2002–2003, 15 countries were defined as monoeconomies in a similar manner (Radetzki, 2008), but only seven of these have stayed as such (Burkina Faso, Jamaica, Kyrgyzstan, Malawi, Mali, Suriname and Zambia).

Oil is exceptional among commodities. In 2016–2018, the average annual value of crude oil and oil-products exports was US$1134 billion (see Table 2.2). No other commodity comes anywhere near this level. Even if we aggregate the value of all the following commodities ranked by export value in the table, we would still only reach about US$1217 billion. Commodities such as copper (global export proceeds US$60 billion), precious stones (105), iron ore (43), wheat (42) and coffee (39) appear as dwarfs in comparison to oil.

Given the exceptional size of the oil market, a number of the exporters of this commodity are monoeconomies par excellence. Table 12.2 lists the eight countries whose oil exports exceeded 80% of overall goods exports. The countries whose exports are dominated by oil are more diverse than the nonfuel monoeconomies. There are some that are of considerable geographical size, for example Angola and Libya, and there are some (Kuwait) that have been made quite prosperous by their

Table 12.2 *The oil monoeconomies: oil and oil products accounted for more than 80% total exports in 2013–2017*

Country	Oil and oil products share of total exports 2013–2017 (%)
Angola	96
Azerbaijan	89
Chad	85
Iraq	97
Kuwait	82
Libya	80
Nigeria	81
Venezuela	90

Source: UNCTAD (2019).

oil resource wealth. In addition to the countries listed in Table 12.2, there are 17 more nations where oil and oil products account for at least 40% of overall exports, the guiding rod in constructing Table 12.1. The number of oil monoeconomies has varied since 2000, primarily due to the large fluctuation of oil prices.

In monoeconomies, the leading commodity will not only dominate exports but will also play other important roles. Thus, its share of GDP or employment will often exceed 10% and it will easily account for 25% or more of government revenue. A heavy dependence on commodities creates special complications – sometimes also opportunities – for national development. Resolving these complications will require special policy actions that avoid the potential pitfalls of relying on a single commodity, but that also help to realize the opportunities inherent in rewarding commodity production and trade.

12.2 Export Instability

We noted in the discussion on price formation in Chapter 5 that primary commodity prices tend to fluctuate much more than the prices of manufactures or services. Unless there are compensating variations in the quantities traded, one must expect a greater variation in the export revenues of countries with a heavy commodity component in their exports, and for monoeconomies in particular.

This deduction is indeed corroborated by empirical evidence, at least at a high level of aggregation. Analyzing exports for the 1950s, 1960s and 1970s for different country groups, MacBean and Nguyen (1987) conclude that instability, measured as the mean absolute deviation from the trend value of export revenue, was much lower in the 19 industrialized countries than in the 89 developing countries included in their sample, both for the period as a whole and for each decade separately. They also notice a persistently higher instability among poorer countries with a heavy commodity dependence, when the developing country sample is divided into two subgroups. More to the point, Ghosh and Ostry (1994) note a steady increase in the volatility of commodity prices from the early 1970s to the early 1990s, with an ensuing destabilization of the export earnings and the macroeconomy in commodity-dependent nations. However, commodity price instability was somewhat reduced in the 15 years to 2005, mainly on account of greater geographic diversification of agricultural production (IMF, biannual, 2006).

IMF's finding is supported by a more recent study (UNCTAD, 2012b), which examines volatility of commodity exports between 1960 and 2010, based on monthly prices of 48 commodities (covering 75% of the world's and 85% of developing countries' commodity exports). It is found that, overall, commodity price volatility has increased over the last 50 years, with some variations during the period. For example, between 1991 and 2002 price volatility was at its lowest, and it was at its highest between 2003 and 2010. Unsurprisingly, the UNCTAD study notes that export volatility varies considerably depending on the basket of commodities on which a nation relies. The study also discusses the risks and difficult adjustment problems faced by monoeconomies after the collapse of prices at the end of commodity booms. The above nuances and reservations notwithstanding, it is a safe conclusion that price volatility is greater for commodities than for other product groups and export income volatility is more marked for countries heavily dependent on commodities compared with other countries.

To get a feel for the national significance of the instability in export revenue that can occur in monoeconomies, consider a case where the leading commodity accounts for 60% of exports and where total exports correspond to 25% of GDP. Then, if the price of the leading export doubles from one year to another, a not-exceptional development in commodity markets, the increase in export revenue will correspond to 15% of GDP. If price then falls again to the old level, the decline in the export revenue will correspond to 13% of GDP, on the assumption that the entire initial increase in export revenue was added to GDP, and more, if the assumption does not hold. The impact will be even greater if export supply responds to the price changes.

Even for countries that are not monoeconomies on the definition adopted above, the export revenue changes due to commodity dependence can be quite important in relation to the national economy. These changes, caused predominantly by international price variations, are unpredictable and, in the main, outside the control of the exporting countries. A study by UNCTAD (1987), quite relevant despite its age, assessed the difference between actual nonfuel commodity export revenue in 1980–1984 and projections of that revenue, based on an extension of the actual 1970–1980 trend. The average annual shortfalls in the five-year period of depressed commodity prices corresponded to 2.6% of GDP in Chile, 5.8% in Costa Rica, 7.3% in Ghana, 8.4% in Guyana, 7.0% in Honduras, 8.9% in Ivory Coast, 4.2% in Jamaica, 10.1% in Liberia, 10.6% in Niger, 9.9% in Papua New Guinea and 2.7% in Thailand. The shortfalls in individual years would of course be substantially higher.

Are these numbers big or small? An impression of their significance is obtained by comparing them with the rise of the OECD countries' aggregate import bill in consequence of the oil price increases in 1973 and 1979. On each occasion, this rise corresponded to between 2% and 3% of the area's GDP and it was followed by drawn-out macroeconomic pains for the region, though of course the numbers were higher for individual OECD nations. From this perspective, the export instability experienced by many commodity-dependent countries and the ensuing economic vagaries are extremely high.

A priori, there are a number of strong grounds for the belief that instability retards growth. Most of these were spelled out succinctly in a famous memorandum written in 1942 by J M Keynes (1974). When producer incomes vary in an irregular and unpredictable way, they will hamper a rational investment pattern in the commodity-producing industry. What may seem a very good investment opportunity while prices are high can turn out to be a loss-making venture when the price level drops. Such experiences will tend to discourage total investments. Export instability can also be expected to have a negative impact on the macroeconomy, through such variables as imports, savings, employment and government revenue. A number of studies confirm empirically a negative relationship between export volatility and growth. Blattman et al. (2007) study the impact of terms of trade volatility (arising from volatile commodity prices) on commodity-dependent nations' economic growth performance, using a panel of 35 countries for the period between 1870 and 1939. The study confirms that countries which depend on exports of commodities with volatile prices grow more slowly compared to other countries. On a similar note van der Ploeg and Poelhekke (2009; 2010) provide evidence of a negative relation between volatility and growth. Since countries with a high share of natural resource exports (of GDP) are much more volatile, the authors conclude that volatility is the "quintessential feature" of the resource curse (not resource abundance).

Some other studies on this issue could not confirm a negative relationship between export instability and growth (Behrman, 1987; MacBean, 1966; Sachs and Warner, 1999). This could be because the research approaches used were not perceptive enough to reveal the relationship, or, as Behrman suggests, because the problems in empirical estimates have obscured the negative effects. But it might also follow from the existence of a positive relationship between export instability and the macroeconomy. Such a counterintuitive result could follow from the observed asymmetry, with short commodity booms followed by extended periods of subdued prices. The price spike would then be merely a windfall, too brief to influence the longer-run policy stance, which would instead be determined by the subdued market conditions. In this way, instability could plausibly yield temporary benefits without destabilizing the macroeconomy (private communication with Graham Davis, Colorado School of Mines).

Despite the inconclusive analytical results, export instability was a very important policy issue to the international community for several decades after the Second World War. The merits of intergovernmental policy intervention through international commodity agreements and compensatory finance schemes in fact dominated the international commodity debate in the 1970s and 1980s. These policy measures can be regarded as elements of the government activism that characterized the period between the 1930s and 1980s (see Chapter 1). Both efforts had serious inherent contradictions, which explains why they were, for all practical purposes, dismantled long before the turn of the century.

Stabilization of prices over the business or harvest cycle has been the proclaimed objective of commodity agreements. Buffer stocks along with export restrictions have been the main tools employed. Where prices fluctuate due to regular changes in demand, as is the case for metals, stabilization of price will even out exporters' income, but often at a cost of lower average revenue over the cycle. This is apparent from the simplified diagrammatic representation in Figure 12.1. A stabilized price, P_2, will yield an average revenue equal to P_2Q_2, which is clearly less than the average of P_1Q_1 and P_3Q_3, which would be earned with fluctuating prices. If changes in supply due to varying agricultural harvest conditions cause the prices to fluctuate, stabilization of price may well destabilize export revenues. Figure 12.2 shows that with

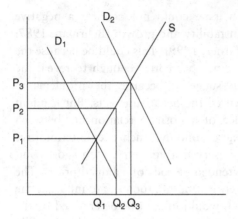

Figure 12.1 Price stabilization with variable demand

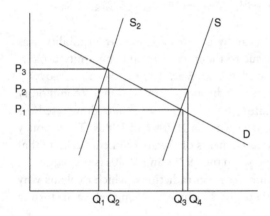

Figure 12.2 Price stabilization with variable supply

a meager harvest, a higher price, P_3, will compensate for the limited quantity supplied, Q_2, so that revenue will not be much different from P_1Q_3, earned with a lower price in a good harvest year. Stabilization of price at P_2 destabilizes income to P_2Q_1 and P_2Q_4 between good and bad harvest years. These perverse effects of price stabilization obviously reduced the developing exporting countries' incentives for launching and operating commodity agreements.

An even more important fallacy of the commodity agreements has been the inability to correctly determine the equilibrium around which prices would be stabilized over the cycle. In practice, operations often came to aim at defending a price level above equilibrium, requiring ever greater funding, and collapse often followed, given the importers' unwillingness to support and fund this more ambitious goal. The International Tin Agreement broke down in the mid-1980s for precisely this reason. The failure of the economic provisions of the coffee and cocoa agreements in 1988 and 1989 shook fundamentally the belief of governments and development economists in commodity agreements. Over the following years, the agreements have been transformed, and their ambitions and goals have dramatically shrunk. In the early 2000s, none of the seven commodity agreements existing at the time (cocoa, coffee, cotton, grains, olive oil, sugar and tropical timber) contained any economic provisions that attempted to regulate markets by supply or price management. They had all developed into administrative fora for producer–consumer consultations, market transparency and sources of statistics.

The results of a study by Gilbert (2011), covering the entire period since the Second World War, reinforce the doubts and reservations expressed above. Gilbert analyzed the tools (e.g. price bands and stockholding or supply-control obligations) of different international commodity agreements whose stated objective was to stabilize commodity prices. The study covered six international commodity agreements with sharp economic (interventionist) clauses (cocoa, coffee, natural rubber, sugar, tin and wheat). The main conclusion was that, in general, these agreements have not been successful in reducing volatility, which may explain why none of them is any longer in force. The sugar and cocoa agreements failed due to administrative inefficiencies, the tin agreement broke down because of managerial hubris, the coffee agreement lost support from both consumers and producers, and the natural rubber agreement failed as prices were difficult to revise downwards.

In contrast to commodity agreements, the international compensatory finance schemes established in the 1960s and 1970s were to respond much more pointedly to the problem of export revenue instability. Their aim was precisely to compensate for shortfalls in the export revenues of individual countries, with contributions from the schemes during export shortfall periods and repayment when export revenues had recovered. But they had one serious shortcoming in common with commodity agreements. Stabilization requires that an equilibrium level (of export income in this case) be determined. This problem was never resolved, so contrary to the schemes' aims the contributions and repayments often resulted in destabilization of the foreign exchange flows.

The Compensatory Financing Facility (CFF) of the IMF was established in 1963 but its activities became quantitatively important only after 1975. In 1980–1986, the heyday period, 69 countries borrowed a total of about US$10 billion under this facility. Of these countries, 52 had a nonfuel commodities share in total exports of 50% or more (UNCTAD, 1987). By the new century, the facility went into hibernation and was finally abandoned, some time after its last review (in 2004), when it was concluded that it had not been used since its last revision in 2000. The Exogenous Shocks Facility and the Trade Integration Mechanism, both programs within the Poverty Reduction and Growth Facility Trust of the IMF, followed the CFF. The Exogenous Shocks Facility was in 2010 replaced by the Standby Credit Facility as part of a reform to be more flexible to the needs of low-income countries (IMF, 2019). These new programs are not compensatory finance schemes like the ones introduced in the 1960s and 1970s, rather they represent IMF lending facilities that contain a few of the characteristics of the former compensatory schemes.

Another scheme for stabilization of export earnings, STABEX, was established in the mid-1970s by the European Economic Community (EEC). It was much smaller than the IMF scheme and its geographical reach was limited to 60 developing countries associated with the EEC under the Lomé conventions, nearly all former colonies of some EEC countries. The amounts set aside for STABEX payments in the 1980–1984 period amounted to less than US$1 billion and actual payments exhausted all the available resources (UNCTAD, 1987). STABEX continued through the 1990s in reduced form and was ultimately abandoned in 2003 as it was considered too unwieldy to operate successfully (private communication with Gino Debo at the European Commission, September 2006).

Disappointment with intergovernmental commodity stabilization arrangements has prompted a number of commodity-dependent economies to establish financial buffer institutions of various kinds. State marketing boards were set up long ago in many developing countries with the objective of protecting domestic producers of agricultural commodities from excessive price fluctuations in the international markets. Many of these agencies became statutory national monopsonies and developed into fiscal instruments to extract public revenue from the agricultural sector (see Section 12.3), with stabilization evolving into an unimportant side objective. Since the 1980s, however, there has been a marked policy shift in many of the boards back to the original goal of stabilizing the prices paid to farmers.

Other domestic measures that have been adopted by a growing number of countries have had the purpose of stabilizing government revenue from commodity production. These measures have usually involved the investment of strongly fluctuating fiscal revenues from the commodity sector into a stabilization fund, with annual withdrawals into the government budget at levels that were considered sustainable in the long run. Canada, Chile, Ghana, Norway, Papua New Guinea, Venezuela and Zambia, among others, have at times tried to improve the stability of their government budgets in this way (Davis and Tilton, 2005). At the subnational level, Alberta and Alaska in Canada and the USA have done likewise. Since the 1990s, some of these efforts have contained elements of private, market-oriented efforts. The stabilization schemes have met with reasonable success, at least in richer economies.

Sugawara (2014) examined the effect of stabilization funds on the volatility of government expenditure in resource-rich countries. By using a panel data set of 68 countries (of which 32 used stabilization funds) over 25 years (1988–2012) he found that the existence of stabilization funds contributed positively to smoothing government expenditure. It was further revealed that the success of stabilization funds is related to the institutional framework in the economies and in particular to the avoidance of political meddling in the funds' affairs. Similar conclusions are found in, for example, Davis et al. (2001) and Bagattini (2011), while other studies fail to confirm desired relationship, for example, Crain and Devlin (2003) and Ossowski et al. (2008). Thus, the analytical conclusions on the effects of stabilization funds on fiscal outcomes are mixed.

The marketing boards and stabilization funds are of course confronted with the same difficulties that the international measures had to face: The measures require the establishment of an equilibrium level of price or revenue, around which stabilization can be centered. If that level is wrongly set, the measures will not be sustainable and may cause serious dislocation when they break down. It could be that national decision makers, being closer to the issue, have a better feel for the equilibrium than international bureaucrats. Also, one may presume that national policies in this field exhibit greater flexibility and faster reaction patterns than international measures.

A simple and straightforward price stabilization measure that has been used much more widely since the 1990s is hedging with the help of futures on the commodity exchanges. Two developments have promoted the use of this stabilization tool. The first and most important is the proliferation of commodity exchanges and, by extension, rising liquidity and falling cost of futures trading (see Chapter 7). When considering this stabilization tool, one should nevertheless recognize that there is a cost involved, since futures prices always include a reward to the market maker for offsetting risk. The second development that has promoted hedging is the wide-ranging privatization that occurred in many resource industries in the 1980s and 1990s (see Chapter 11). Private profit-maximizing firms have exhibited a greater readiness than government bureaucrats to use the exchanges for securing future prices.

Finally, there is evidence that developing countries have significantly increased their savings in response to export instability. Between 1974 and 1994, the external current account balances rose by 3.5% of average imports in nonfuel primary commodity exporting countries, and by even more among fuel exporters (Ghosh and Ostry, 1994). These are quite significant amounts. Current account surpluses and growing exchange reserves were even more fashionable in developing countries, including the monoeconomies, in the decade after 1995. The developing world in aggregate improved its current account position from –2.2% of GDP in 1995 to 1.4% in 2000 and 4.1% in 2005. Shifts from sizable deficits to large surpluses occurred in all major developing regions (IMF, biannual, 2006). Growing foreign exchange reserves afford substantial protection against export instability, even though one may claim that, in the absence of instability, the resources could have been immediately employed for valuable development purposes. In the decade following 2005, the strong improvement in the current account balances in the developing world has not continued. The current account balances in these countries, in aggregate, fell from 4.1% in 2005 to 1.2% in 2010, and are expected to become slightly negative at –0.2% in 2019 (IMF biannual, 2019). The decline in current account balances for countries dependent on commodity exports is not surprising in a situation of declining commodity prices since the end of the commodity boom in 2014.

The key problems of instability caused by high commodity dependence are as old as Joseph's advice to the Pharaohs and simple to summarize: when harvests fluctuate, set aside from fat years for consumption in meager years. High reliance on commodities with unstable supply, demand and price can seriously destabilize the national economy. Efforts to even out prices and revenues may therefore often be appropriate and worthwhile. Stabilization involves a significant cost and if the actions are to gain credibility, considerable resources have to be set aside for the purpose. Furthermore, the averages and trends of the series to be stabilized are extremely hard to determine. Actions that ex ante may appear as purposeful for the attainment of stabilization can easily turn out to have effects quite opposite to their intentions. The costs and the disappointing results explain the limited enthusiasm in recent times for grandiose international measures to stabilize commodity markets and commodity revenues. Down-to-earth national efforts on a more modest scale may have a greater prospect of achieving the desired ends.

12.3 Extraction of Fiscal Revenue

An economy which is heavily dependent on the production and trade of a particular commodity will ordinarily have to rely on that commodity for a large part of its fiscal revenue. That heavy reliance calls for fiscal caution to avoid damage to the sector where the commodity is produced. The two issues that have to be resolved are (a) how much revenue can be obtained, and (b) what should be the form of fiscal extraction, in order not to kill nor weaken the milking cow. When considering these issues, it may be instructive to keep two general rules applying to all fiscal systems in mind. The first is that the tougher the fiscal regime, the more likely it is to damage the activity to which it is applied, especially where the tax income is employed to lure capital to other sectors via tax holidays or subsidies (Davis, 1994). A fiscal system that leaves little surplus to the owner will certainly discourage investments in expansion and, in the extreme case, even in capacity maintenance. The second rule is that stable fiscal conditions with predictable outcomes are of great importance to those considering involvement.

With a given level of fiscal toughness, investors will be discouraged from involvements by fiscal instability.

The public-sector share of GDP in most developing countries, including the major commodity producers, was quite low in the early 1960s. It experienced a very substantial expansion during the following decades, as the increasingly emancipated government administrations of these countries enhanced their ambitions to establish physical and social infrastructure facilities, promote national entrepreneurship and contribute to development in other ways. The expansion of public expenditure had to be financed by increased revenues. Where the commodity sector dominated the economy, it was seen as an obvious source for a large part of the growing revenue needs. For lack of experience or due to insufficient foresight, or simply because of short-run greed, the overall fiscal impositions became so onerous in many countries that they led to a stagnation or decline of commodity production and trade, in absolute or relative terms. The extractable fiscal revenue ceased to grow or contracted in consequence.

The maximum fiscal extraction policy compatible with unchanged output is one where all revenue above the variable cost of production is creamed away, leaving no return at all to the invested capital. So long as the variable costs are covered, it will be economical to maintain production in existing facilities. This policy is feasible only in the short run, however. Its consequence would be a complete cessation of capacity expansion and capacity maintenance, and so output would soon start to contract.

In the long run, the resource rent is an important determinant for how much revenue the tax collector can take from the commodity sector without harming their tax base. The resource rent is the part of the profit that is attributable to the superior quality of the land, climate or mineral deposit, over the marginal quality of these resources used in the global production of a commodity. Superior resource bases, consisting of conveniently located fertile soils that enjoy a favorable climate or rich mineral deposits, have provided a strong comparative advantage to a number of countries in the production of commodities. The resource rents generated by these activities have made them by far the most important sources for tax in many nations.

In principle, the entire resource rent can be taxed away without impairing the long-run viability of commodity production. When the relatively high-cost Canadian Tar Sand and Brazilian deep offshore oil deposits represent marginal oil production, then any cost advantage due to the superior deposits in, say, Saudi Arabia or Nigeria, could be taxed away, leaving the investors in these countries with no more than the normal return on capital investments, that is about the same as that obtained by investors in the marginal resources. A moral argument in favor of fiscal appropriation of the entire resource rent has often been forwarded (Wenar, 2008): The resource rent represents the superior natural endowment of the nation, a kind of patrimony. The state, as the representative of the nation, should therefore have a first right to this rent.

In practice, the determination and extraction of resource rents raises many difficulties. For instance, a reduction in global demand or technical progress, which result in price declines, will normally lead to closure of the highest-cost units, and so diminish the size of rent throughout the industry. The existence of resource rents provides a strong attraction to private investors and a policy of complete government appropriation will reduce their interest, with long-run consequences for the sector's growth. Furthermore, low costs and high profitability could be due not to a superior resource base, but to the monopolistic supply of superior management or technology which may cease to be available unless it is allowed to keep its returns. Partial extraction of the rent is therefore the most that can be accomplished, if one wants to avoid causing long-run harm to the industry.

The fiscal regimes applicable to commodities in monoeconomies and other commodity-dependent countries tend to give an impression of complex and confusing structures that are difficult to disentangle and hard to compare. On closer scrutiny, however, most of the fiscal provisions can be categorized as variations of three alternative measures used by governments to obtain revenue from the commodity sectors (Kumar and Radetzki, 1987).

A first measure, the *royalty*, extracts the fiscal dues on the basis of the volume of production or the value of sales or exports. Royalties come in many different forms. They can be shaped as a levy per ton produced or per dollar sold. Especially for agricultural products, they have often been imposed by state marketing boards to which the farmers were compelled to sell at prices below those quoted in international markets. In the case of minerals, royalties often have the more straightforward form of export taxes.

Royalties are very widely used and are regularly regarded as the prime tool for extracting the resource rent. Appropriation of resource rents with the help of royalties requires a differentiation of royalty rates between products and production units, depending on the quality of the resources that are being exploited. A "just" differentiation to reflect the superiority of the natural endowment in each case is complex and time consuming. Royalties are therefore often applied at fixed rates, for example 5% on all copper sold and 10% on gold and cocoa. Such generalities create injustice for those who exploit inferior endowments.

Royalties have the important advantage of easy assessment and application. They also afford the government a relatively stable revenue, since production and sales ordinarily vary much less than profits. This advantage must be weighed against the harmful consequences of this fiscal tool. To producers, royalties basically constitute additions to cost, which have to be paid irrespective of profit levels. A high royalty can easily wipe out the entire profit, or even impose losses, when pretax profits are low. Producers will therefore avoid ventures with less than exceptional profits prospects or with cyclical price and profit patterns, since the viability of such projects will be continuously or recurrently impaired by high royalties. The less outstanding resource endowments that could support commodity production with only normal profitability will not be developed at all when royalties are high.

Although we deal here with the imposition of royalties by individual countries on their own, it is important to note that royalties have been used on several occasions to implement international monopolistic coordination, most notably in the case of OPEC. Prior to the nationalization of the oil-producing installations, sales taxes were predominantly used by the OPEC countries to raise export prices. The same was true of the monopolistic effort by the Caribbean countries to raise bauxite prices in the mid-1970s.

The second measure, the *profits tax*, extracts the fiscal dues on the basis of profits, that is on the income that remains after deducting all costs of production. Withholding taxes (e.g. on dividends or on professional fees paid abroad) are usually regarded as part of the profits tax system. A major variation among profits taxes concerns the specification of allowable costs. Another variation is between proportional and progressive profits taxes. One approach in designing a progressive profits tax is through an "additional profits tax." By creaming off a substantial proportion of profits that are considered "above normal," the additional profits tax can be employed as a substitute to royalties for extracting resource rents. A variety of additional profits taxes have come in to use in the United Kingdom and Russia, among others, to appropriate part of the very high profits earned by oil companies after the sharp oil price increases during the 2000 decade (IEA, monthly). The commodity boom that evolved after 2004 again sparked discussion on introducing excess profit taxes for mineral commodities in a number of commodity-producing countries. As was mentioned in the previous chapter, Australia in fact imposed an additional profits tax on the extraction of coal and iron ore in July 2012, but due to a number of difficulties, including ensuing price falls, it was abolished in 2014. This illustrates the inherent difficulty in designing taxes. A tax structure that may seem quite constructive when price levels are soaring could become the opposite when they fall to depressed levels.

While avoiding some of the problems with royalties, notably that no tax is imposed when there is no profit, profits taxes are much more difficult to assess and impose – especially when producers are many and small, as is frequently the case in agriculture. The necessary estimation of profits requires accepted accounting standards, which often do not exist in poor countries. Since profits fluctuate much more than volume of output or sales, it follows that profits taxes yield a far greater variation in public revenue than royalties, a clear disadvantage to the public authorities. This variation will be particularly strong when an additional profits tax forms part of the fiscal structure.

The third measure for fiscal extraction is through provisions affording *public ownership* positions in the production activity, for free or on concessional terms. Public ownership for fiscal extraction is often employed when it is felt that neither royalties nor profits taxes provide adequate tools for capturing the resource rent.

The extent of fiscal extraction through public ownership depends entirely on the degree of concessionality through which that ownership is acquired. Confiscation of private property carries no direct cost to the public authorities, even though the indirect costs of the ensuing mistrust felt by the former owners may be considerable. If the government pays for what it acquires, the extent of fiscal extraction will be inversely related to the price. No extraction will occur if a full market price is paid for the acquisition. A common government practice has been to demand a minority equity share for free at the time of the original investment decision, as compensation for the resource rent inherent in the assets to be exploited. This practice has similarities with a royalty. In other respects, ownership participation resembles the profits tax in that it assures the government of a share of the profit, so long as a profit is earned. Ownership, however, is not always easy to transform into a fiscal income flow. A detriment is that it may expose the government to the costs involved in reinvestments and expansions.

Although public ownership may be desired on other grounds it is an opaque tool for fiscal extraction, both due to uncertainties about the right commercial price for the acquisition and because of the painful legal or moral obligations that may arise with an ownership role. Furthermore, as noted in the preceding chapter, because of the inefficiencies characteristic of many state enterprises, the involvement of government as owner often leads to a reduction in the size of the overall resource rent.

Private investors have had varying attitudes to public ownership acquisitions on concessional terms. In the 1950s and 1960s, when the mining multinationals still reigned supreme, they regularly regarded such government involvement as undesirable in principle because of the perceived dilution of managerial control. After the hugely painful nationalizations of the 1960s and 1970s, many investors became more favorably inclined to a degree of government participation because they saw such partnership as an assurance of fair treatment to themselves.

Parenthetically, it may be noted that the production-sharing agreements practiced by Indonesia, some of the republics of the former Soviet Union and many other host countries in their relations with multinational corporations in the extractive sectors are akin to concessionally acquired ownership positions. Under these, the government remains the sole owner, while foreigners finance the investment and run the operations in return for a share of the output.

Where commodity production is dependent on massive imported inputs, as is often the case in minerals, import duties may offer an additional and straightforward tool for fiscal extraction.

The producers face a tradeoff between the size and form of the fiscal burden. While they may prefer one fiscal tool to another, a fiscal package using unpopular tools might nevertheless appear preferable if it involves a lesser overall tax burden.

Royalties, frequently imposed in the form of price controls through which state marketing boards purchase crops or overvalued exchange rates, have dominated the taxation of agricultural commodities. The primary reason is the administrative difficulties in imposing profits taxes on large groups of small-scale agricultural producers. The small-scale and predominantly national ownership also explains why public ownership in agricultural production has been quite limited.

In many cases, the government impositions on agricultural commodity production have been excessive and have resulted in a shrinkage in the relative or even absolute levels of output. Many African governments overtaxed their agricultural producers in the 1960s and 1970s, and this led to a shrinking market share as production relocated, mainly to South East Asia and Brazil; but some African countries also did quite well in the ongoing change. The trends have not been equally clear between 1985 and 2000 (UNCTAD, annual b, 2005).

From the early 1960s to the early 1980s, Ghana's share of the world cocoa market shrank from 40% to 14%, that of Nigeria from 18% to 11%, as a result of heavy export taxes. At the same time, Ivory Coast, with much more favorable fiscal treatment of its cocoa producers, expanded its share from 9% to 26%. Admittedly, part of this increase was accomplished through exports of cocoa that had been smuggled out of Ghana, but this too was an effect of excessive taxation. In the 1990s, Africa as a whole lost further cocoa market shares to Asia, but Ivory Coast continued to consolidate its market position. Mainly for fiscal reasons, the share of Nigeria and the Democratic Republic of Congo in the world palm oil market shrank from 48% to virtually zero in the 20 years to the early 1980s, while that of Malaysia expanded from 18% to 71%. In the following two decades, the Asian share of the market continued to expand as Indonesia increased its share of exports (in 2014 the country accounted for over 50% of global palm-oil exports). Overtaxing lost Egypt half its international market share in cotton in the two decades to 1985. Sri Lanka's tea exports dwindled from one third to one fifth of global exports, while Kenya, which treated its tea producers more fairly, saw its share triple to 9% during the 20 years to 1985, and further expanding to become the world's largest exporter of black tea in 2014 (UNCTAD, annual d, 2015; World Bank, annual a, 1986). The declines in fiscal bases came as surprising disappointments to the governments of the high-tax countries.

In the case of minerals, the fiscal menu has been much more varied but, for historical or other reasons, the emphasis on the respective tools has varied considerably among countries (Faber, 1982). Royalties have been applied in some measure by most mineral-exporting countries. Public ownership positions acquired on concessional terms have been quite common, though the reasons for these acquisitions have usually gone beyond fiscal concerns (see Chapter 11). In contrast to the farmers, mineral enterprises possessed a degree of administrative sophistication that made the application of profits taxes practical.

Excessive fiscal ambitions slowed or arrested the expansion of the mineral industries in some countries. This was true, for instance, of Zambia and Peru, though, as discussed in Chapter 11, intriguingly the overtaxation often also applied to fully state-owned entities. An extreme case in this respect is provided by Peru's overtaxed oil sector (Aguilera and Radetzki, 2016). Very high royalty impositions by some Canadian provinces in the early 1970s virtually arrested all mineral exploration efforts, but there was no visible impact on mineral output because the royalties were soon withdrawn. The internationally coordinated efforts of some bauxite producers to increase prices through export taxes substantially reduced the demand for their output, with a lag (Chapter 10). In the weak mineral markets of the 1980s, there was a reversal of earlier fiscal trends in selected cases. Some leading mineral-exporting countries have attempted to attract foreign investments by offering internationally more competitive fiscal arrangements. Chile has been extremely successful in this respect and has seen its share of world copper mining rise from 11.3% in 1975 to 31.0% in 2014 (Metallgesellschaft, annual; USGS, annual, 2015).

These experiences reveal that monoeconomies have to tread a difficult balance in designing their fiscal systems. On the one hand, the governments need fiscal revenue to cover public expenditures and the commodity sector is their major revenue source. Lax taxation of oil in the Middle East and bauxite in the Caribbean in the 1960s resulted in very meager national benefit to the countries producing these commodities. On the other hand, they have to be cautious in the determination of the overall fiscal burden and in the selection of fiscal instruments. The instances of agricultural shrinkage, listed above, point to the potential dangers. Wrong decisions have proved counterproductive in many cases.

Most of the instances of overtaxed and shrinking commodity production quoted above were the result of misconceived expectations about the primary sector's ability to generate public revenue.

However, there may be cases where excessive fiscal burdens are imposed precisely for the purpose of diminishing what is considered an excessive commodity dependence of the national economy. The market instability of the dominant commodity may be considered to be overly onerous. The country's competitive advantage in the commodity may have contracted or the commodity market may be in a structural depression, so that there is little likelihood for large and sustainable private or public revenue generation. In such circumstances, the fiscal policy could have the explicit purpose of speeding up a contraction of the sector through fiscal squeeze and of encouraging diversification by an expenditure policy that promotes, say, manufacturing or other commodities with more dynamic market prospects.

Intriguingly, fiscal squeeze aimed at reducing commodity dominance and promoting diversification is sometimes urged for precisely the opposite reason, that is when the commodity sector has an outstanding ability to generate resource rent and fiscal revenue. This is the subject of the next section.

12.4 Dutch Disease and the Resource Curse

Two evils that are said to afflict economies heavily dependent on commodities will be dealt with. The first, Dutch disease, arises from an export-oriented resource bonanza that can give rise to far-reaching macroeconomic reorientation, with ensuing sectoral adjustment. The second, the resource curse, is the purported tendency for nations heavily dependent on minerals and fuels to record slower economic growth than other countries at a corresponding stage of development.

Dutch Disease

The term Dutch disease was coined in the late 1970s to describe the economic change to which the Netherlands was subjected, in particular the stagnation and shrinkage of manufacturing, in consequence of the country's highly profitable exploitation of natural gas through the 1970s. For several reasons, the concept is a misnomer. First, the syndrome is not particularly Dutch. Other countries have experienced much more accentuated impacts of resource bonanzas, some of them long before the Dutch natural gas discovery. More than a hundred years ago, the booms in gold mining in Australia, in guano exploitation in Chile and Peru, and in sugar exports from Cuba led to far-reaching and sometimes quite painful structural change in these economies. More recent instances comprise the cases of Zambia (copper 1965–1974), Niger (uranium 1975–1981), Colombia (coffee 1976–1986) and Nigeria, Saudi Arabia and Norway (oil after 1974). Second, there is reason to question the term "disease." The additional export income from the bonanza provides a potential for increased national welfare. It can also be used for overcoming the pain of dislocation caused by the commodity boom. It would be hard to justify a policy recommendation that the country forgo the extra income so as to avoid the need for adjustment and change.

To explore the macroeconomics of Dutch disease, it is instructive to subdivide the national economy into three sectors, namely (a) the booming commodity sector; (b) the sector where other tradables are produced, whether for export markets or as substitutes for imports; and (c) the sector for non-tradables, goods and services that do not enter international trade (Corden, 1984).

The earnings from the commodity boom invariably result in a substantial increase in the demand for tradable as well as non-tradable goods and services. The price of tradables is determined outside the country and so is not affected by the commodity boom. Increases in demand will be satisfied by expanded imports, which are perfectly price elastic (the booming country is assumed to account for a small share of world imports). By contrast, the supply of non-tradables is limited by domestic production capacity, so their price will tend to rise as domestic demand expands. The shift in relative prices between tradables and non-tradables makes domestic production of tradables less attractive. Hence, their output stagnates and a greater proportion of domestic demand is satisfied through imports.

The difficulties of the tradable sector are accentuated as the booming commodity activity attracts labor and other inputs by bidding up their price. The high profits in the booming commodity production make it easy to absorb the higher costs. The tradable sector, in contrast, has no excess profits, so its international competitiveness is weakened as the input costs increase. In the absence of the booming commodity, increasing costs throughout the economy would weaken the current account and force through a devaluation. This would restore the international competitiveness of the tradable sector. With the commodity bonanza, exports and the current account develop strongly, with no need to devalue.

The ultimate effects of the resource bonanza are quite similar to those that follow from lavish receipts of foreign aid. An accentuated overvaluation of the domestic currency perseveres. A withering of domestic tradable activities ensues, along with an increasing dependence on imports and the booming commodity. If it was not one before, the nation subject to Dutch disease becomes a true monoeconomy. The problems with that will be quite bearable if the bonanza persists. In practice it regularly does not, and often it ends with a bang.

Nigeria provides an interesting and painful case study. Before the oil price increases of the 1970s, the country was self-sufficient in food and a sizable exporter of agricultural commodities. The high oil prices and export incomes in the late 1970s and early 1980s led to an inflationary boom that resulted in an increasing overvaluation of the country's currency. The agricultural sector could not compete internationally, so agricultural exports dwindled, while food imports substituted for shrinking domestic food production. There was no pressure to restore competitiveness of the declining sectors through devaluation because the booming petroleum revenue assured a positive current account. Neither was there any urgency to arrest the Dutch disease. Oil prices were believed to follow a permanent upward path and the petroleum industry was seen as a lasting generator of high and rising income for Nigerian society. There was little anticipation of the oil price collapses in 1986 and again in 2014 and the ensuing painful adjustments that were forced on the country.

The bonanza can end for a variety of reasons. In the case of oil, the price collapses were due to the Saudi decision in 1985 to cease defending the high price and the extraordinary success of shale-oil production in the USA after 2008. But the bonanza could also end due to depletion of the booming resource, as happened with Australian gold in the 1860s (Davis, 1995), or because of technical innovation (e.g. the developments in the German chemical industry that made guano redundant), or due to an emerging commodity surplus as the high price attracts new producers to the market (e.g. in the case of coffee). Precautions are then clearly needed to avoid the problems faced by Nigeria in the 1980s and 2010s. Even if the bonanza continues, policy may be desirable to prevent an accentuation of dualist development, with a poor hinterland existing beside the booming and rich commodity sector.

In an initial step, the policy remedies all involve the removal of a substantial part of the profits from the booming sector. This reduces its expansion. Taxation is the obvious instrument. Constraints on investment in new capacity may be an additional policy measure to prevent the emergence of monoeconomy extremes. Removal of profits will reduce the inflationary pressures, an inherent part of the disease, by limiting the conspicuous consumption and waste that is often connected with new riches.

A follow-up policy step involves the use of the funds extracted from the booming sector. There are basically two options. First, they can be employed for subsidizing the tradable sector so as to assure its survival. And second, they may be placed in reserves to carry the nation through after the bonanza has ended. Both of these have inherent problems. Subsidization requires a complex selection of activities to be supported, and there is a risk that uneconomic choices will be made. Most would agree that subsidization of wheat production in the desert of Saudi Arabia to an extent that yields export surpluses (United Nations, annual b) is going a bit too far. That is easy. In other cases, the borderline between appropriate and faulty selection in this area may be harder to agree upon. Sterilizing the bonanza proceeds through the establishment of funds to be used in lean days may be appropriate for short-run cyclical stabilization, as noted above. For the longer-run purposes considered here, funding surpluses created by the commodity industry risks becoming politically explosive. There will be strong temptations to spend immediately. A considerable degree of political maturity is needed for this instrument to be used as intended.

Economic purists may well assert that Dutch disease simply involves an optimal reallocation of resources toward the most rewarding activities and activist government policies to prevent such reallocation are always undesirable. That seems to be an exaggeration and to abstract from the inflexibilities and frictions that always characterize real economies, and especially underdeveloped ones.

Recent empirical studies reveal some of the vagaries of Dutch disease. Harding and Venables (2013) performed a study of 43 natural resource exporting countries from 1970 to 2006 and find that a US$1 increase in natural resource exports is associated with a fall of roughly US$0.75 in non-resources exports, out of which manufactures represent the major share (US$0.46). Ismail (2010) analyses oil-exporting countries and comes to the conclusion that an apparently permanent increase in oil prices impacts negatively on manufacturing output. Thus, there is some recent evidence that natural resource exports crowd out manufacturing, which implies a risk of stagnation – in other words – Dutch disease. However, Allcott and Keniston (2018) estimate the local economic effects of natural resource booms in the USA between 1969 and 2014 and find, on the contrary, that manufacturing industries have benefited from oil and gas resource booms. Recent evidence from Norway points in the same direction (Bjørnland et al., 2019). This literature thus suggests that the phenomenon of Dutch disease as such may not be that serious, at least in more developed countries (e.g. the USA and Norway) that, however, despite their resource wealth are not defined as monoeconomies.

To conclude: Yes, Dutch disease can cause serious economic problems, especially to poor monoeconomies. And yes, it can be avoided by cutting any tendencies for a resource bonanza in the bud. But it is hard to imagine the government that would make such a choice. The temptations and potential benefits of a resource boom are simply too valuable to be missed. The policy adviser's role is clearly limited to issuing early warnings against the risks and pointing to the measures whereby the problems are reduced. Possibly, the introduction of funds that absorb some of the resource bonanza during commodity booms and their distribution after commodity prices have fallen is a way for governments to reduce the risks associated with Dutch disease.

Resource Curse

The resource curse is related to, yet distinct from Dutch disease. According to its proponents (Auty, 2001; Gylfason, 2002; Sachs and Warner, 2001), the curse afflicts economies heavily dependent on the minerals and fossil fuels sectors. Such dependency, it is claimed, slows economic growth and social progress compared to that of other countries at corresponding levels of economic development. The dislocations caused by Dutch disease are seen as one important reason for the deficient performance of the mineral-dependent country group.

Why should the mineral-rich countries exhibit inferior development performance? One reason is the detriments of extreme dualism following from a resource bonanza and its ensuing social tensions. Another is the painful need for macroeconomic reallocation and the instability caused by volatile mineral markets. The mineral rent is not an undivided blessing. Where this rent is large, it is often wasted on conspicuous consumption or publicly financed "white elephants" with no economic prospects under competitive conditions. Furthermore, large rents (e.g. in diamonds and oil) often trigger unproductive corruption and give rise to destructive internal strife resembling that encountered in the production and trade of narcotics. In all these instances, the negative relationship is an indirect one. The presence of mineral dependence gives rise to social tensions, deficient governance, instability, conspicuous consumption and so on more frequently than when such dependence is absent. There is nothing wrong with the mineral sector as such. But when these effects occur, they tend to result in slower growth.

As noted in Chapter 4, the internal and international conflicts over high oil resource rents, a particular aspect of the resource curse, have arrested capacity development in a number of oil-producing nations, in some cases even resulting in capacity shrinkage, thus contributing to the extraordinary price performance of this commodity.

While there is reasonably general agreement that the growth-retarding problems listed above do occur in mineral-dependent economies (Davis and Tilton, 2005), a number of other studies have rejected the generality of the resource-curse case. Some of these have been unable to replicate the negative development conclusions for the mineral country group in aggregate. Davis (1995) compares 22 mineral and fossil fuel economies with 57 non-mineral ones in developing countries between 1970 and 1991 to conclude that the former performed much better both in terms of per capita growth and the human development index. This conclusion holds even when the fossil fuel country group is separated out. Maddison's (1994) monumental study covering 1913–1950 concludes that resource-rich countries such as Canada, Finland, Sweden, the USA and Latin America as a whole had much faster growth than resource poor ones, for example Japan, Korea and Asia more generally. Maxwell (2004) adds Chile after 1980 to the successful high-growth mineral economies. A World Bank (2002) study does find a negative worldwide correlation between mineral dependence (fossil fuels not included) and economic growth in developing and transitional economies in the 1990s, but this difference disappears when comparison is made on a regional basis. A majority of the mineral-dependent countries in Africa and Latin America did grow faster that the non-mineral group in each continent.

In more recent years the resource-curse paradox, as defined by its proponents, has been increasingly questioned for a number of different reasons (see Stevens, 2015 for a thorough literature review on the resource curse). One of these arguments has already been discussed in relation to export instability, that is, that it is not resource abundance per se that is the cause of the resource curse rather it is volatility in terms of trade (driven by volatile commodity prices) that drives this paradox (Blattman et al., 2007; Cavalcanti et al., 2012; van der Ploeg and Poelhekke, 2009; 2010). Other studies (Alexeev and Conrad, 2009; Brunnschweiler and Bulte, 2008; Ding and Field, 2005) argue that if resource abundance (natural resource wealth)is used instead of resource dependence (income share of natural resource exports) when assessing the effect of natural resources on growth the resource-curse paradox disappears.

Another strand that questions the resource curse argues that the empirical findings on this matter are indeed very sensitive to the period under investigation (Wright and Czelusta, 2004; Stijns, 2005; Haber and Menaldo, 2011; Ross, 2012). Thus, in periods with depressed commodity prices the occurrence of the resource curse is much easier to detect compared to situations when commodity prices are booming. Ross (2012) studies oil-producing countries and points to the fact that many of the earlier studies on the resource curse were related to the period between 1970 and 1990, when, according to the numbers he provides, real oil prices fell considerably.

Thus, alternative definitions, data sources and methodologies are claimed be the causes to the contradictory findings of the studies on the resource curse, and the thesis that one exists has not been definitively proven (see e.g. Papyrakis, 2017; van der Ploeg and Poelhekke, 2017). The subject matter of economic development is complex, and a 50-year old quote by Charles Kindleberger (1958) is apposite: "Anyone who claims to understand economic development in toto or to have found the key to the secret of growth, is almost certainly wrong." It could be that the resource curse is no more than a chimera. Wright and Czelusta (2004) may have hit the head of the nail in the title of their study, "The Myth of the Resource Curse." However, Stevens et al. (2015) argue that the resource curse is indeed both alive and active, as many natural resource dependent countries have not succeeded in diversifying their economies away from the extractive industry. This is posed as a serious risk, especially now that the most recent commodity boom has come to an end.

12.5 Exchange Rate Policies in Monoeconomies

The main purpose of a standard exchange rate policy is to keep the domestic currency (e.g. peso) at an equilibrium level, defined as the dollar price for a peso that assures a balanced current account. An overvalued currency (more dollars per peso) regularly results in a current account deficit. Overvaluation often follows from peso inflation that is higher than dollar inflation. The current account deficit can be remedied through a devaluation that stimulates export demand by reducing the dollar export prices and discourages imports by making them more expensive in peso terms. Conversely, an undervalued currency (fewer dollars per peso) typically yields a current account surplus, which can be symmetrically overcome through an appreciation of the peso.

The market conditions for the leading commodity – not relative rates of inflation – are the main drivers of current account imbalance in monoeconomies. Years of high commodity prices will ordinarily yield a sizable current account surplus, indicating an undervalued peso, and just as years of low prices will yield a deficit, indicating overvaluation. Is an exchange rate policy aiming at a balanced current account appropriate for economies whose dominant exports experience strong price fluctuations over the business cycle? The policy rule would require currency appreciation during the boom and devaluation during recession, not a very convenient policy stance since it would destabilize conditions for other economic sectors.

Monoeconomies are special, and not only because of their high dependence on a single commodity export. They are invariably also small economies. Size regularly involves economic diversification, so large monoeconomies are uncommon.

The small size has a bearing on the exchange rate policies. Monoeconomies face numerous intricate problems in their efforts to stabilize the current account and their choice of exchange rate policies. There are no straightforward solutions to these problems. The economies' small size has a bearing on these issues. One effect of devaluation is that all import prices, including the prices of imported inputs in commodity production, will rise. The change in competitiveness after devaluation is dependent on reduced payments in terms of dollars to the domestic factors of production. But the domestic share of total production costs will be quite limited, given the smallness of the economy. Devaluation must then be quite sizable to have a perceptible impact on competitiveness. Furthermore, any gain in competitiveness is hard to maintain over time, since small trade-dependent economies will find it hard to resist inflationary pressures after devaluation. Domestic factors will demand compensation for the increased cost of imports, especially where trade has a heavy weight in total consumption. If compensation is granted, the initial competitive improvement will be depleted. The need for new devaluation rounds will then arise, until the government succeeds in the difficult task of containing the upward price pressure coming from domestic labor and capital, which may not be easy.

A standard exchange rate policy would also have an adverse effect on international stability for the dominant commodity, and on its non-devaluing exporters. Devaluation during recession will lower the monoeconomies' supply curve, so the market price will weaken even more than it did due to recession in cases where the devaluing countries represent a significant share of total supply. Lesser volumes will therefore be sold at even lower prices by diversified producers as a result of the monoeconomies' exchange rate policy. The obverse will occur in consequence of the monoeconomies' currency appreciation during a boom. In this way, the exchange rate policy will accentuate the commodity price movements and destabilize export earning for other suppliers. For this reason too, the standard exchange rate policy advice may not be appropriate in the case of monoeconomies.

If the commodity business cycle is short and regular, a more appropriate, prudent policy might be to establish foreign exchange reserves of sufficient size to carry the country through the commodity cycle. Reserves buildup would then conveniently occur during the boom, with a subsequent drawdown during recession. A related though somewhat less prudent alternative would be to rely on borrowing from, for example, the IMF or from private international financial markets.

We claim that borrowing from the IMF or the international market is less prudent because experience has shown that the commodity cycle is not as short and regular as suggested above. Most commodity prices experienced substantial declines in real terms throughout the 1980s, and they then remained depressed until the boom of the 2000s decade.

A monoeconomy that borrowed in the 1980s to overcome the problems caused by commodity price declines in the expectation of a price recovery in the near future would have lost all its credit facilities due to an extreme indebtedness long before the prices improved. The extended commodity price depression was certainly a contributory factor to the international debt crises of the 1980s and 1990s that involved many commodity-exporting nations. By encouraging capacity expansion in the commodity sector, international borrowing along with the expectation of an impending price recovery probably prolonged the period of low commodity prices. Eventually, devaluations became unavoidable, as the indebted commodity-dependent nations tried to come to grips with their persistent current account deficits. Ironically, this too suppressed commodity prices, through the mechanisms explored above.

It is reasonable to assume that we will experience a similar development also in the decade after the most recent, somewhat prolonged, commodity boom that ended in 2014. Contemplating the depressed situation for many commodity prices, there is little evidence that prices will improve anytime soon, so borrowing from international markets to overcome the price decline will be a doubtful investment.

12.6 Conclusion: A General Case for Economic Diversification?

This chapter has surveyed the problems that confront monoeconomies and other countries that are heavily dependent on commodity production and exports. The discussion of commodity instability, generation of public revenue, Dutch disease, the resource curse and exchange rate policies in this country group clearly suggests that the problems they experience have a particular character and require special solutions. But while the one-sidedness of the commodity-dependent economies clearly involves risks, the coverage of which warrants taking out insurance and paying the premium, the above analyses have definitely not established a general and unambiguous case for diversification.

After all, commodity dependence is often the result of competitive advantage that normally yields above-normal returns to the commodity sector. These yields may well be more than adequate to cover the cost of instability and other monoeconomy problems. Obversely, part of the resource rents contained in the above-normal returns will be forgone when the country diversifies out of its reliance on commodities.

It is true that the global demand for many commodities has trend growth rates that are slower than for the aggregate of manufactures. Slow demand growth per se need not involve disadvantage. The market for the output of a monoeconomy can expand briskly if the supply from other sources stagnates. Besides, high profits can be earned even when demand is stagnant.

Chapter 5 revealed that the aggregate price index for commodities has tended to lag behind that for manufactures. This, too, does not by itself constitute a case against commodity specialization for countries that benefit from a strong comparative advantage. Besides, the profitability of commodity production can well be maintained in the face of falling prices, if technical advancement reduces the cost of production in equal or greater measure.

Commodity dependence does not constitute a general trap into technical or other backwardness. Contrary to frequent perceptions, commodity production often requires as much advanced technology and human skills as manufacturing. Modern agriculture and mining make heavy use of microbiology, electronics and the highly qualified labor that goes with these techniques.

Large and profitable primary commodity production, both agricultural and mineral, holds a prominent place in the economies of prosperous nations such as Australia, Canada, Norway, Sweden and the United States. This production would be even greater if the resource base permitted. The markets or governments would force a contraction of the raw materials industries if they were unprofitable or otherwise socially undesirable.

On these grounds, we conclude that a heavy concentration on commodity production in a national economy is not detrimental per se. Diversification out of a commodity sector that has lost its competitive advantage and superior profitability is certainly warranted. But it is much harder to find tenable arguments for a recommendation to, say, Zambia or Venezuela, both heavily dependent on the exports of a few raw materials, that they should reduce their commodity reliance by a greater emphasis on manufacturing.

References

Acemoglu D, S Johnson, J A Robinson and Y Thaicharoen (2003), "Institutional Causes, Macroeconomic Symptoms: Volatility, Crises, and Growth", *Journal of Monetary Economics*, vol. 50, no. 1.

Adämmer P, M T Bohl and C Gross (2015), "Price Discovery in Thinly Traded Futures Markets: How Thin Is Too Thin?" Working Paper 39, University of Münster, Germany.

Adelman M (2002), "World Oil Production and Prices", *Quarterly Review of Economics and Finance*, vol. 42.

Adelman M and C Watkins (2005), "US Oil and Natural Gas Reserve Prices, 1982–2003", *Energy Economics*, vol. 27.

African Union (2009), *Africa Mining Vision*, February, www .africaminingvision.org/amv_resources/AMV/Africa_Mining_Vision_Eng lish.pdf.

Aguilera R F and M Radetzki (2014), "The Shale Revolution: Global Gas and Oil Markets under Transformation", *Mineral Economics*, vol. 26, no. 3.

Aguilera R F and M Radetzki (2016), *The Price of Oil*, Cambridge University Press, Cambridge.

Aguilera R F, J E Tilton, R G Eggert and G Lagos (2009), "Depletion and the Future Availability of Petroleum Resources", *The Energy Journal*, vol. 30, no. 1.

Aharoni Y (1982), "The State Owned Enterprise: An Agent Without a Principal", in L Jones et al. (eds.), *Public Enterprises in Developing Countries*, Cambridge University Press, Cambridge.

Alexeev M and R Conrad (2009), "The Elusive Curse of Oil", *Review of Economics and Statistics*, vol. 91, no. 3.

Alhajji A F and D Huettner (2000), "OPEC and Other Commodity Cartels: A Comparison", *Energy Policy*, vol. 28.

Allcott H and D Keniston (2018), "Dutch Disease or Agglomeration? The Local Economic Effects of Natural Resource Booms in Modern America", *Review of Economic Studies*, vol. 85.

Alquist R and O Gervais (2013), "The Role of Financial Speculation in Driving the Price of Crude Oil", *The Energy Journal*, vol. 34.

Anderson K (2013), "Trade Barriers and Subsidies: Multilateral and Regional Reform Opportunities", in B Lomborg (ed.), *Global Problems, Smart Solutions: Costs and Benefits*, Cambridge University Press, Cambridge.

Anderson K and W Martin (eds.) (2006), *Agricultural Trade Reform and the Doha Development Agenda*, World Bank, Washington DC.

Anderson K and S Nelgen (2012), "Agricultural Trade Distortions during the Global Financial Crisis", *Oxford Review of Economic Policy*, vol. 28, no. 1.

Anderson K, G Rausser and J Swinnen (2013), "Political Economy of Public Policy: Insights to Distortions to Agricultural and Food Markets", *Journal of Economic Literature*, vol. 51, no. 2.

Areddy J T, D Fickling and N Shirouzu (2010), "China Denies Halting Rare-Earth Exports to Japan", *Wall Street Journal*, September 23.

Ates A and G H K Wang (2005), "Information Transmission in Electronic Versus Open-Outcry Trading Systems: An Analysis of US Equity Index Futures Markets", *Journal of Futures Markets*, vol. 25.

Auty R M (ed.) (2001), *Resource Abundance and Economic Development*, Oxford University Press, Oxford.

Auty R M (2003), "The Geopolitics of Mineral Resources", UNCTAD, Geneva.

Baffes J and T Haniotis (2010), "Placing the 2006/08 Commodity Price Boom into Perspective", Policy Research Working Paper 5371, World Bank.

Bagattini G Y (2011), "The Political Economy of Stabilisation Funds: Measuring their Success in Resource-Dependent Countries", IDS Working Paper 356, Institute of Development Studies.

Bairoch P (1965), "La baisse des couts des transports et le développement économique", *Révue de l'Institut de Sociologie*, vol. 2.

Barnett H J and C Morse (1963), *Scarcity and Growth: The Economics of Natural Resource Availability*, Resources for the Future, Washington, DC.

Bauer A (2018), Upstream Oil, Gas and Mining State-Owned Enterprises, Extractive Industries Transparency Initiative, September.

Behrman J R (1987), "Commodity Price Instability and Economic Goal Attainment in Developing Countries", *World Development*, vol. 15, no. 5.

Bentley R W (2006), "Global Oil and Gas Depletion", *IAEE Newsletter*, second quarter.

Bessler W and D Wolff (2015), "Do Commodities Add Value in Multi-asset-Portfolios? An Out-of-Sample Analysis for Different Investment Strategies", *Journal of Banking and Finance*, vol. 60.

Bina C and M Vo (2007), "OPEC in the Epoch of Globalization: An Event Study of Global Oil Prices", *Global Economy Journal*, vol. 7, no. 1.

Bjørnland H C, L A Thorsrud and R Torvik (2019), "Dutch Disease Dynamics Reconsidered", *European Economic Review*, vol. 119.

Blattman C, J Hwang and J G Williamson (2007), "Winners and Losers in the Commodity Lottery: The Impact of Terms of Trade Growth and Volatility in the Periphery 1870–1939", *Journal of Development Economics*, vol. 82, no. 1.

Bodie Z and V I Rosansky (1980), "Risk and Return in Commodity Futures", *Financial Analysts Journal*, vol. 36, no. 3.

Bohi D R (1999), "Technological Improvement in Petroleum Exploration and Development", in R D Simpson (ed.), *Productivity in Natural Resource Industries: Improvement through Innovation*, Resources for the Future, Washington, DC.

Bomsel O (1994), *The Future of Mining Countries: New Strategies or the Restructuring of the State?*, UNCTAD, Geneva.

Borcherding T E, W W Pommerehne and F Schneider (1982), "Comparing the Efficiency of Private and Public Production: The Evidence from Five Companies", *Zeitschrift für Nationalökonomie*, vol. 89.

Borenstein I (1954), "Capital and Output Trends in the Mining Industries 1970–1984", Occasional Paper 45, National Bureau of Economic Research.

BP (annual), *Statistical Review of World Energy*, London, www.bp.com/en/global/corporate/energy-economics.html.

Bradsher K (2010), "Amid Tension, China Blocks Vital Exports to Japan", *New York Times*, September 22.

Brown C P (1980), *The Political and Social Economy of Commodity Control*, Macmillan, London.

Brunetti C, B Bükyüksahin and J H Harris (2016), "Speculators, Prices and Market Volatility", *Journal of Financial and Quantitative Analysis*, vol. 51.

Brunnschweiler C and E H Bulte (2008), "The Natural Resource Curse Revised and Revisited: A Tale of Paradoxes and Red Herrings", *Journal of Environmental Economics and Management*, vol. 55.

Campbell C J (1997), *The Coming Oil Crisis*, Multiscience Publishing, Brentwood.

Carattini S, S Kallbekken and A Orlov (2019), "How to Win Public Support for a Global Carbon Tax", *Nature*, vol. 565.

Cashin P and C J McDermott (2002), "The Long-Run Behavior of Commodity Prices: Small Trends and Big Variability", *IMF Staff Papers*, vol. 49, no. 2.

Cavalcanti T V D V, K Mohaddes and M Raissi (2012), "Commodity Price Volatility and the Sources of Growth", IMF Working Paper WP/12/12.

Center for International Securities and Derivatives Markets (2006), The Benefits of Commodity Investments, 2006 update, Isenberg School of Management, University of Massachusetts, Amherst.

Chazan G (2011), "UK Oil Tax Rise Drives Drillers to Norway", *Wall Street Journal*, June 29.

Chevallier J and F Ielpo (2013), *The Economics of Commodity Markets*, Wiley, West Sussex.

COCHILCO (2005), *Copper Statistics 1985–2004*, Chilean Copper Commission, Santiago de Chile.

Commodity Yearbook (1964), Commodity Research Bureau, New York.

Conover C M, G R Jensen, R R Johnson and J M Mercer (2010), "Is Now the Time to Add Commodities to Your Portfolio?" *Journal of Investing*, vol. 19.

Cooper R N and R Z Lawrence (1975), "The 1972–75 Commodity Boom", *Brookings Papers on Economic Activity*, vol. 6, no. 3.

Corden M (1984), "Booming Sector and Dutch Disease Economics: Survey and Consolidation", *Oxford Economic Papers*, vol. 36, no. 3.

Crain M W and J Devlin (2003), "Nonrenewable Resource Funds: A Red Herring for Fiscal Stability?", paper presented at the annual meeting of the American Political Science Association, August 27, Philadelphia, PA.

Crowson P (1987), "The Global Distribution and Availability of Mineral Resources", paper presented to a symposium on mining and petroleum at the Delft University of Technology, November 3–4.

Crowson P (1998), *Minerals Handbook 1998–99*, Mining Journal Books, London.

Crowson P (2006), "Mineral Markets, Prices and the Recent Performance of the Minerals and Energy Sector", in P Maxell (ed.), *Australian Mineral Economics: A Survey of Important Issues*, Monograph 24, Australasian Institute of Mining and Metallurgy, Carlton, Victoria.

Cuddington J and D Jerrett (2008), "Super Cycles in Real Metal Prices?" *IMF Staff Papers*, vol. 55, no. 4.

Cyert R and J March (1992), *Behavioral Theory of the Firm*, Blackwell, London.

Darmstadter J, P D Teitelbaum and J G Polach (1971), *Energy in the World Economy: A Statistical Review of Trends in Output, Trade and Consumption since 1925*, Resources for the Future, Washington, DC.

Das A (2012), "Who Extracts Minerals More Efficiently – Public or Private Firms? A Study of Indian Mining Industry", *Journal of Policy Modeling*, vol. 34.

Davis G (1994), *South African Managed Trade Policy: The Wasting of a Mineral Endowment*, Praeger, New York.

Davis G (1995), "Learning to Love the Dutch Disease: Evidence from the Mineral Economics", *World Development*, vol. 23, no. 10.

Davis G and J Tilton (2005), "The Resource Curse", *Natural Resources Forum*, vol. 29.

Davis J, R Ossowski, J Daniel and S Barnett (2001), "Stabilization and Savings Funds for Nonrenewable Resources: Experience and Fiscal Policy Implications", IMF Occasional Paper 205, International Monetary Fund, Washington, DC.

Dempsey N, G Bramley, S Power and C Brown (2011), "The Social Dimension of Sustainable Development: Defining Urban Social Sustainability", *Sustainable Development*, vol. 19, no. 5.

Desjardins J (2018), "China's Staggering Demand for Commodities", World Economic Forum, March 7, www.weforum.org/agenda/2018/03/china-s -staggering-demand-for-commodities.

Deuskar P and T C Johnson (2011), "Market Liquidity and Flow-Driven Risk", *Review of Financial Studies*, vol. 24, no. 3.

Dillard D (1967), *Economic Development of the North Atlantic Community*, Prentice Hall, New York.

Ding N and B C Field (2005), "Natural Resource Abundance and Economic Growth", *Land Economics*, vol. 81.

Dobbs R, J Oppenheim, F Thompson, S Mareels, S Nyquist and S Sanghvi (2013), Resource Revolution: Tracking Global Commodity Markets, MacKinsey Global Institute, September.

Dobozi I (1987), "Emergence, Performance and World Market Impact of the State Mining Companies in Developing Countries", Studies on Developing Economies 123, Institute for World Economics, Budapest.

Eggert R (2013), "Mining, Sustainability and Sustainable Development", in P Maxwell (ed.), *Mineral Economics*, 2nd ed., Australasian Institute of Mining and Metallurgy, Carlton, Victoria.

EIA (2013), Technically Recoverable Shale Oil and Shale Gas Resources: An Assessment of 137 Shale Formations in 41 Countries outside the United States, Energy Information Administration, Washington DC, June.

EIA (annual), *Annual Energy Outlook*, Energy Information Administration, Washington DC.

Enerdata (annual), *Global Energy Statistical Yearbook*, Grenoble, France.

Erb C B and C R Harvey (2006), "The Strategic and Tactical Value of Commodity Futures", *Financial Analysts Journal*, vol. 62.

European Commission (2019a), "The Common Agricultural Policy at a Glance", https://ec.europa.eu/info/food-farming-fisheries/key-policies/c ommon-agricultural-policy/cap-glance_en#howitspaidfor.

European Commission (2019b), "EU–Japan Trade Agreement Enters into Force", press release, European Union, January 31, 2019.

Everingham, J-A (2012), "Towards Social Sustainability of Mining: The Contribution of New Directions in Impact Assessment and Local Governance", *Greener Management International*, vol. 57.

Exxon (1980), World Energy Outlook, New York, December.

EY (2015), "Riding the Silk Road: China Sees Outbound Investment Boom – Outlook for China's Outward Foreign Direct Investment", Ernst & Young, March.

Faber M (1982), "Some Old and New Devices in Mineral Royalties and Taxation", in *Legal and Institutional Arrangements in Mineral Development*, Mining Journal Books, London.

Fatás A and I Mihov (2005), "Policy Volatility, Institutions and Economic Growth", CEPR Discussion Paper 5388.

Fattouh B, L Kilian and L Mahadeva (2013), "The Role of Speculation in Oil Markets: What Have We Learned So Far?", *The Energy Journal*, vol. 34.

FCA (2014), Commodity Markets Update, Financial Conduct Authority, February.

FIA (annual), "Annual Trading Statistics in Futures and Options Market", www.fia.org/exchange-volume-reports.

Fidler C and M Hitch (2007), "Impact and Benefit Agreements: A Contentious Issue for Environmental and Aboriginal Justice", *Environments: A Journal of Interdisciplinary Studies*, vol. 35, no. 2.

Financial Times (2015), "Opec Agrees to Keep Oil Output High in Battle for Market", June 5.

Floyd R H, C S Gray and R P Short (1984), "Public Enterprise in Mixed Economies, Some Macroeconomic Aspects", IMF Discussion Paper, Washington DC.

Fouquet R and P Pearson (2006), "Seven Centuries of Energy Services: The Price and Use of Light in the United Kingdom (1300–2000)", *The Energy Journal*, vol. 27, no. 1.

Frank J and P Garcia (2011), "Bid-Ask Spreads, Volume, and Volatility: Evidence from Livestock Markets", *American Journal of Agricultural Economics*, vol. 93.

Friedman M (1969), "In Defense of Destabilizing Speculation", in *The Optimum Quantity of Money and Other Essays*, Macmillan, London.

Gallagher K P and A Irwin (2014), "Exporting National Champions: China's Outward Foreign Direct Investment Finance in Comparative Perspective", *China & World Economy*, vol. 22, no. 6.

Gately D (1984), "A Ten-Year Retrospective: OPEC and the World Oil Market", *Journal of Economic Literature*, September.

Gately D (2011), "OPEC at 50: Looking Back and Looking Ahead", conference, National Energy Policy Institute, Tulsa, Oklahoma, April 18.

Ghosh A and J Ostry (1994), "Export Instability and the External Balance in Developing Countries", IMF Working Paper 94/8-EA.

Ghosh S, C L Gilbert and A J Hughes Hallet (1987), *Stabilizing Speculative Commodity Markets*, Clarendon Press, Oxford.

Gilbert C L (1996), "Manipulation of Metals Futures, Lessons from Sumitomo", unpublished manuscript.

Gilbert C L (2010a), "Speculative Influences on Commodity Futures Prices, 2006–2008", United Nations Conference on Trade and Development, Discussion Paper 197.

Gilbert C L (2010b), "How to Understand High Food Prices", *Journal of Agricultural Economics*, vol. 61, no. 2.

Gilbert C L (2011), "International Agreements for Commodity Price Stabilisation: An Assessment", OECD Food, Agriculture and Fisheries Papers, no. 53.

Gilbert C L and C W Morgan (2010), "Food Price Volatility", *Philosophical Transactions of the Royal Society B*, vol. 365.

Gillis M (1980), "The Role of State Enterprises in Economic Development", *Social Research*, vol. 47, Summer.

Giraud P N (1983), *Géopolitique des resources minières*, Economica, Paris.

Goeller H E and A M Weinberger (1976), "The Age of Substitutability", *Science*, vol. 191.

Goldman Sachs (2005), "Commodity Sales: The Case for Commodities", New York, June.

Gooch E and F Gale (2018), China's Foreign Agriculture Investments, EIB-192, US Department of Agriculture, Economic Research Service, April.

Gordon R B, M Bertram and T E Graedel (2006), "Metal Stocks and Sustainability", *Proceedings of the National Academy of Sciences of the United States of America*, vol. 103, no. 5.

Gorton G B and K G Rouwenhorst (2006), "Facts and Fantasies about Commodity Futures", *Financial Analysts Journal*, vol. 62.

Greer L, S Lockie and J Rolfe (2010), "Regions in Transition: Regional Growth and Land Use in the Surat Basin, Queensland", Commonwealth Scientific and Industrial Research Organisation, Australia.

Greer R J (1994), "Methods for Institutional Investment in Commodity Futures", *Journal of Derivatives*, vol. 2, no. 2.

Griffin J (2009), *A Smart Energy Policy: An Economist's Rx for Balancing Cheap, Clean, and Secure Energy*, Yale University Press, New Haven, CT.

Griffin J and H Steele (1986), *Energy Economics and Policy*, Academic Press, Orlando, FL.

Grilli E R and M C Yang (1988), "Primary Commodity Prices, Manufactured Goods Prices and the Terms of Trade of Developing

Countries: What the Long Run Shows", *World Bank Economic Review*, January.

Guardian (2019), "US–China Trade: What Are Rare-Earth Metals and What's the Dispute?", May 29.

Guluzade A (2019), "Explained, the Role of China's State-Owned Companies", World Economic Forum, May 9.

Gylfason T (2002), "Mother Earth: Ally or Adversary?" *World Economics*, January–March.

Haase M, Y Seiler Zimmermann and H Zimmermann (2016), "The Impact of Speculation on Commodity Futures Markets: A Review of the Findings of 100 Empirical Studies", *Journal of Commodity Markets*, vol. 3.

Haber S and V Menaldo (2011), "Do Natural Resources Fuel Authoritarianism? A Reappraisal of the Resource Curse", *American Political Science Review*, vol. 105, no. 1.

Hamilton J D (2009), "Understanding Crude Oil Prices", *The Energy Journal*, vol. 30.

Hamilton J D and J C Wu (2015), "Effects of Index-Fund Investing on Commodity Futures Prices", *International Economic Review*, vol. 56, no. 1.

Hamilton M, J Barron and J Barnett (2019), "Saudi Arabia Crude Oil Production Outage Affects Global Crude Oil and Gasoline Prices", *Today in Energy*, US Energy Information Administration, September 23.

Harding T and A J Venables (2013), "The Implications of Natural Resource Exports for Non-Resource Trade", OxCarre Research Paper 103, Oxford Centre for the Analysis of Resource Rich Economies.

Heady D (2011), "Rethinking the Global Food Crisis: The Role of Trade Shocks", *Food Policy*, vol. 36.

Heap A (2005), "China: The Engine of a Commodities Super Cycle", Citigroup Global Markets Paper, March 31.Heisler K and S Markey (2013), "Scales of Benefit: Political Leverage in the Negotiation of Corporate Social Responsibility in Mineral Exploration and Mining in Rural British Columbia, Canada", *Society and Natural Resources*, vol. 26, no. 4.

Herfindahl O (1959), *Copper Costs and Prices 1870–1957*, Resources for the Future, Washington DC.

Hilson G and B Murck (2000), "Sustainable Development in the Mining Industry: Clarifying the Corporate Perspective", *Resources Policy*, vol. 26.

Hnatkovska V and N Loayza (2005), "Volatility and Growth", in J Aizenman and B Pinto (eds.), *Managing Economic Volatility and Crises: A Practitioner's Guide*, Cambridge University Press, Cambridge.

Holder M E, M J Thomas and R I Webb (1999), "Winners and Losers: Recent Competition among Futures Exchanges for Equivalent Financial Contract Markets", *Derivatives Quarterly*, vol. 6, no. 2.

Hotelling H (1931), "The Economics of Exhaustible Resources", *Journal of Political Economy*, vol. 39.

Humphreys D (2015), *The Remaking of the Mining Industry*, Palgrave Macmillan, New York.

Hurst L (2015), "Iron Ore Cartel Will Create a Monopoly on Bad Business", *Australian Financial Review*, May 17.

ICSG (annual), *Statistical Yearbook*, International Copper Study Group, Lisbon.

IEA (2001), *Oil Supply Security: The Emergency Response Potential of IEA Countries in 2000*, International Energy Agency, Paris.

IEA (2004), *Analysis of the Impact of High Oil Prices on the Global Economy*, International Energy Agency, Paris.

IEA (2005a), *Resources to Reserves*, International Energy Agency, Paris.

IEA (2005b), "Fact Sheet on IEA Oil Stocks and Emergency Response Potential", International Energy Agency, Paris.

IEA (2006), *Medium-Term Oil Market Report*, International Energy Agency, Paris.

IEA (2007), *Oil Supply Security: Emergency Response of IEA Countries 2007*, International Energy Agency, Paris.

IEA (2014a), *Coal Information 2014*, International Energy Agency, Paris.

IEA (2014b), *Medium-Term Oil Market Report*, International Energy Agency, Paris.

IEA (2014c), *Energy Supply Security: Emergency Response of IEA Countries 2014*, International Energy Agency, Paris.

IEA (2018), *Costs and Benefits of Emergency Stockholding*, Insight Series 2018, International Energy Agency, Paris.

IEA (annual), *World Energy Outlook*, International Energy Agency, Paris.

IEA (monthly), *Oil Market Report*, International Energy Agency, Paris.

IHS (2012), America's Energy Future: The Unconventional Oil and Gas Revolution and the US Economy, Englewood, CO, USA, October.

IHS (2018), The Shale Gale Turns 10: A Powerful Wind at America's Back, strategic report, IHS Markit, London, UK, July.

IMF (1982), *Financial Statistics Year Book*, International Monetary Fund, Washington, DC.IMF (2019), "IMF Standby Credit Facility", factsheet, www.imf.org/external/np/exr/facts/scf.htm.

IMF (biannual), *World Economic Outlook*, International Monetary Fund, Washington DC.

INSG (annual), *World Nickel Statistics Yearbook*, International Nickel Study Group, Lisbon.

International Tin Council (annual), *Statistical Yearbook*, London.

International Tin Council (monthly), *Monthly Statistical Bulletin*, London.

Irwin S H and D R Sanders (2011), "Index Funds, Financialization, and Commodity Futures Markets", *Applied Economic Perspectives and Policy*, vol. 33, no. 1.

Irwin S H and D R Sanders (2012), "Financialization and Structural Change in Commodity Futures Markets", *Journal of Agricultural and Applied Economics*, vol. 44, no. 3.

Ismail K (2010), "The Structural Manifestation of the 'Dutch Disease' in Oil-Exporting Countries", IMF Working Paper 10/103.

ITC (2010), *Market Access, Transparency and Fairness in Global Trade: Export Impact for Good 2010*, International Trade Center, Geneva.

Iwarson T (2006), *Investering i råvaror*, Handelsbanken Capital Markets, Stockholm.

Jacks D S (2013), "From Boom to Bust: A Typology of Real Commodity Prices in the Long Run", National Bureau of Economic Research, Working Paper 18874.

Jacks D S, K H O'Rourke and J G Williamson (2011), "Commodity Price Volatility and World Market Integration since 1700", *Review of Economics and Statistics*, vol. 93, no. 3.

Kahn M (2013), "Natural Resources, Nationalism, and Nationalization", *Journal of the Southern African Institute of Mining and Metallurgy*, vol. 113, no. 1.

Keynes J M (1933), "National Self-sufficiency", *Yale Review*, Summer.

Keynes J M (1936), *The General Theory of Employment, Interest and Money*, Harcourt, New York.

Keynes J M (1974), "The International Control of Raw Materials" (A UK Treasury Memorandum dated 1942), *Journal of International Economics*, no. 4.

Kharas H (2010), "The Emerging Middle Class in Developing Countries", OECD Development Centre Working Paper 285, OECD Publishing, Paris.

Kharas H and K Hamel (2018), "A Global Tipping Point: Half the World Is Now Middle Class or Wealthier", Brookings Institution, September 27.

Kilian L and T K Lee (2014), "Quantifying the Speculative Component in the Real Price of Oil: The Role of Global Oil Inventories", *Journal of International Money and Finance*, vol. 42.

Kilian L and D P Murphy (2014), "The Role of Inventories and Speculative Trading in the Global Market for Crude Oil", *Journal of Applied Econometrics*, vol. 29.

Kindleberger C (1958), *Economic Development*, McGraw Hill, New York.

Kingsnorth D J (2010), "The Challenges of Meeting Rare Earths Demand in 2015", in *Proceedings of the Technology and Rare Earth Metals Policy Conference*, Washington, DC.

Knittel C R and R S Pindyck (2016), "The Simple Economics of Commodity Price Speculation", *American Economic Journal: Macroeconomics*, vol. 8, no. 2.

Korinek J and J Kim (2010), "Export Restrictions on Strategic Raw Materials and Their Impact on Trade", OECD Trade Policy Paper 95.

Kowalski P, M Büge, M Sztajerowska and M Egeland (2013), "State-Owned Enterprises: Trade Effects and Policy Implications", OECD Trade Policy Paper 147.

Krugman P (2008), "More on Oil and Speculation", *New York Times*, May 13.

Kumar R and M Radetzki (1987), "Alternative Fiscal Regimes for Mining in Developing Countries", *World Development*, May.

Kuznets S (1966), *Modern Economic Growth, Rate, Structure and Spread*, Yale University Press, London.

Labys W C, A Achouch and M Terraza (1999), "Metal Prices and the Business Cycle", *Resources Policy*, vol. 25, no. 4.

Laherrere J (2011), "OPEC Quotas and Crude Oil Production", *The Oil Drum*, January 31, www.theoildrum.com/node/7363.

Landes D S (1980), "The Great Drain and Industrialization: Commodity Flows from Periphery to Center in Historical Perspective", in R C O Matthews (ed.), *Economic Growth and Resources*, vol. 2, *Trends and Factors*, Macmillan, London.

Loayza N V, R Rancière, L Servén and J Ventura (2007), "Macroeconomic Volatility and Welfare in Developing Countries: An Introduction", *World Bank Economic Review*, vol. 21, no. 3.

Lomborg B (2001), *The Skeptical Environmentalist*, Cambridge University Press, Cambridge.

Lowell J D (1970), "Copper Resources in the 1970s", *Mining Engineering*, April.

Lundgren N-G (1996), "Bulk Trade and Maritime Transport Costs: The Evolution of Global Markets", *Resources Policy*, vol. 22, no. 1/2.

Lynas Corporation (2011), *Chinese Rare Earth Export Quota Significantly Reduced for Second Half 2010*, July 9.

MacAvoy P (1982), *Crude Oil Prices as Determined by OPEC and Market Fundamentals*, Ballinger, Cambridge, MA.

MacBean A I (1966), *Export Instability and Economic Development*, Oxford University Press, Oxford.

MacBean A I and D T Nguyen (1987), *Commodity Policies: Problems and Prospects*, Croom Helm, London.

Maddison A (1994), "Explaining the Economic Performance of Nations", in W Baumol, R Nelson and E Wolff (eds.), *Convergence of Productivity*, Oxford University Press, Oxford.

Maddison A (2007), *Chinese Economic Performance in the Long Run, 960–2030*, OECD, Paris.

Malkenes Hovland K (2013), "Norway Plans Rise in Taxes on Oil Entities", *Wall Street Journal*, May 5.

Malthus T R (1798), *An Essay on the Principle of Population*, reprinted in 1970, Penguin Books, Harmondsworth.

Marcel V (2006), *Oil Titans: National Oil Companies in the Middle East*, Brookings Institution, Washington, DC.

Markowski A and M Radetzki (1987), "State Ownership and the Price Sensitivity of Supply: The Case of the Copper Mining Industry", *Resources Policy*, March.

Martin W and K Anderson (2011), Export Restrictions and Price Insulation during Commodity Price Booms, *American Journal of Agricultural Economics*, vol. 94, no. 2.

Masters M W (2008), "Testimony before the Committee on Homeland Security and Governmental Affairs", United States Senate, May 20.

Maurice C and C W Smithson (1984), *The Doomsday Myth: 10,000 Years of Economic Crises*, Hoover Institution Press, Stanford, CA.

Maxwell P (2004), "Chile's Recent Copper Driven Prosperity", *Minerals and Energy*, vol. 19, no. 1.

McKenzie S (2004), "Social Sustainability: Towards Some Definitions", Working Paper Series 27, Hawke Research Institute, University of South Australia, Magill.

Meadows D H, D L Meadows, J Randers and W W Behrens III (1972), *The Limits to Growth*, Potomac Associates, Washington, DC.

Megginson W and J Netter (2001), "From State to Market: A Survey of Empirical Studies on Privatization", *Journal of Economic Literature*, vol. 39.

Metallgesellschaft (1984), "Pressmeldungen ueber die Metallmärkte", Frankfurt am Main, January.

Metallgesellschaft (annual), *Metal Statistics*, Frankfurt am Main.

Mikesell R F (1979), *New Patterns of World Mineral Development*, British-North American Committee, London.

Mikesell R F (1986), *Stockpiling Strategic Materials*, American Enterprise Institute for Public Policy Research, Washington, DC.

Mill J S (1848), *Principles of Political Economy*, vol. I, John W. Parker, London.

Miller B and M Sapozhnikov (2014), "Mechanisms for Commodity Trading", *Commodities Now*, October.

Mining Journal (1983), December 9.

MMSD (2002), *Breaking New Ground: Mining, Minerals and Sustainable Development*, report of the MMSD Project, Earthscan for International

Institute for Environment and Development and World Business Council, London.

Moffat K and A Zhang (2014), "The Paths to Social License to Operate: An Integrative Model Explaining Community Acceptance of Mining", *Resources Policy*, vol. 39.

Molchanov P (2003) "A Statistical Analysis of OPEC Quota Violations", Duke University, April.

Mudd G M (2010), "The Environmental Sustainability of Mining in Australia: Key Mega-Trends and Looming Constraints", *Resources Policy*, vol. 35, no. 2.

Murphy K (2012), "The Social Pillar of Sustainable Development: A Literature Review and Framework for Policy Analysis", *Sustainability: Science, Practice, and Policy*, vol. 8, no. 1.

Nicita A, M Olarreaga and P Silva (2018), "Cooperation in WTO's Tariff Waters?" *Journal of Political Economy*, vol. 126, no. 3.

Nordhaus W D (1997), "Do Real-Output and Real-Wage Measures Capture Reality? The History of Lightning Suggests Not", in T F Breshnan and R J Gordon (eds.), *The Economics of New Goods*, University of Chicago Press, Chicago, IL.

Nucleonics Week (1971), "Canada, Australia Move Forward Uranium Price, Processing Collaboration", May 13.

OECD (2014), *Export Restrictions in Raw Materials Trade: Facts, Fallacies and Better Practices*, OECD, Paris.

OECD (2019), *Agricultural Policy Monitoring and Evaluation 2019: OECD Countries*, OECD Publishing, Paris.

O'Faircheallaigh C (2010), "Aboriginal-Mining Company Contractual Agreements in Australia and Canada: Implications for Political Autonomy and Community Development", *Canadian Journal of Development Studies*, vol. 30, no. 1–2.

O'Faircheallaigh C (2013), "Community Development Agreements in the Mining Industry: An Emerging Global Phenomenon", *Community Development*, vol. 44, no. 2.

Oil & Gas Journal (2011), "OGJ100 Companies Report Higher Earnings, Output", *Oil & Gas Journal*, vol. 109, no. 17.

Ossowski R, M Villafuerte, P A Medas and T Thomas (2008), "Managing the Oil Revenue Boom: The Role of Fiscal Institutions", IMF Occasional Paper 260, International Monetary Fund, Washington, DC.

Paley W S (1952), *Resources for Freedom*, summary of vol. 1, The President's Materials Policy Commission, Washington, DC.

Papyrakis E (2017), "The Resource Curse – What Have We Learned from Two Decades of Intensive Research: Introduction to the Special Issue", *Journal of Development Studies*, vol. 53, no. 2.

Parsons R (2008), "We Are all Stakeholders Now: The Influence of Western Discourses of 'Community Engagement' in an Australian Aboriginal Community", *Critical Perspectives on International Business*, vol. 4, no. 2–3.

Pindyck R S (2004), "Volatility and Commodity Price Dynamics", *Journal of Futures Markets*, vol. 24, no. 11.

Pindyck R and J Rotemberg (1990), "The Excess Co-movement of Commodity Prices", *The Energy Journal*, vol. 100.

Pirrong C (2008), "Restricting Speculation Will Not Reduce Oil Prices", *Wall Street Journal*, June 11.

Poulton M M, S C Jagers, S Linde, D Van Zyl, L J Danielson and S Matti (2013), "State of the World's Nonfuel Mineral Resources: Supply, Demand and Socio-Institutional Fundamentals", *Annual Review of Environment and Resources*, vol. 38.

Prain R (1975), *Copper: The Anatomy of an Industry*, Mining Journal Books, London.

Prebisch R (1950), "The Economic Development of Latin America and Its Principal Problems, *Economic Bulletin for Latin America*, no. 7.

Radetzki M (1970), *International Commodity Market Arrangement: A Study of the Effects of Post-War Commodity Agreements and Compensatory Finance Schemes*, Hurst, London.

Radetzki M (1974), "Commodity Prices during Two Booms", *Skandinaviska Enskilda Banken Quarterly Review*, no. 4.

Radetzki M (1975), "Metal Mineral Resource Exhaustion: The Case of Copper", *World Development*, vol. 3.

Radetzki M (1976), "The Potential for Monopolistic Commodity Pricing", in G K Helleiner (ed.), *A World Divided: The Less Developed Countries in the International Economy*, Cambridge University Press, Cambridge.

Radetzki M (1981), *Uranium: A Strategic Source of Energy*, Croom Helm, London.

Radetzki M (1985), *State Mineral Enterprises: An Investigation into Their Impact on the International Mineral Markets*, Resources for the Future, Washington, DC.

Radetzki M (1990a), *A Guide to Primary Commodities in the World Economy*, Blackwell, Oxford.

Radetzki M (1990b), "Long Run Factors in Oil Price Formation", in L A Winters and D Sapsfords (eds.), *Primary Commodity Prices: Economic Models and Policy*, Cambridge University Press, Cambridge.

Radetzki M (1995), "A Scrutiny of the Motives for Hard Coal Subsidies in Western Europe", *Resources Policy*, no. 2

Radetzki M (2001), *The Green Myth: Economic Growth and the Quality of the Environment*, Multiscience Publishing, Brentwood.

Radetzki M (2002), "Is Resource Depletion a Threat to Human Progress? Oil and Other Critical Exhaustible Materials", paper presented at the Ninth International Energy Conference and Exhibition, Energex 2002: Energy Sustainable Development – A Challenge for the New Century, Krakow, May 19–24.

Radetzki M (2006), "The Anatomy of the Three Commodity Booms", *Resources Policy*, vol. 31.

Radetzki M (2008), *A Handbook of Primary Commodities in the Global Economy*, Cambridge University Press, Cambridge.

Radetzki M (2013a), "The Relentless Progress of Commodity Exchanges in the Establishment of Primary Commodity Prices", *Resources Policy*, vol. 38.

Radetzki M (2013b), "The Perseverance of the Ongoing Metal and Mineral Boom", *Mineral Economics*, vol. 25.

Radetzki M and S Zorn (1979), *Financing Mining Projects in Developing Countries*, Mining Journal Books, London.

Radetzki M, R Eggert, G Lagos, M Lima and J Tilton (2008), "The Boom in Mineral Markets: How Long Might It Last?", *Resources Policy*, vol. 33.

Ramey G and V A Ramey (1995), "Cross-country Evidence on the Link between Volatility and Growth", *American Economic Review*, vol. 85, no. 5.

Resources for the Future (1987) *Resources for Freedom*, 35th anniversary edition, Washington, DC.

Reuters (2014), "Saudis Block OPEC Output Cut, Sending Oil Price Plunging", November 28.

Reuters (2019), "Russia Agrees with Saudi Arabia to Extend OPEC+ Oil Output Deal", June 29.

Ross M (2012), *The Oil Curse: How Petroleum Wealth Shapes the Development of Nations*, Princeton University Press, Princeton, NJ.

Rowe J W F (1965), *Primary Commodities in International Trade*, Cambridge University Press, Cambridge.

Rutten M, L Shutes and G Meijerink (2013), "Sit Down at the Ball Game: How Trade Barriers Make the World Less Food Secure", *Food Policy*, vol. 38.

Sachs J and A Warner (1999), "The Big Push: Natural Resource Booms and Growth", *Journal of Development Economics*, vol. 59.

Sachs J and A Warner (2001), "Natural Resources and Economic Development: The Curse of Natural Resources", *European Economic Review*, vol. 45.

Schmitz J A (2004), "Privatization's Impact on Private Productivity: The Case of Brazilian Iron Ore", Research Department Staff Report 337, Federal Reserve Bank of Minneapolis.

Shah S and B W Brorsen (2011), "Electronic vs. Open Outcry: Side-by-Side Trading of KCBT Wheat Futures", *Journal of Agricultural and Resource Economics*, vol. 36.

Shiller R (2000), *Irrational Exuberance*, Princeton University Press, Princeton, NJ.

Simon J (1996), *The Ultimate Resource*, Princeton University Press, Princeton, NJ.

Simpson R D (ed.) (1999), *Productivity in Natural Resource Industries: Improvement through Innovation*, Resources for the Future, Washington, DC.

Singleton K J (2014), "Investor Flows and the 2008 Boom/Bust in Oil Prices", *Management Science*, vol. 60.

Singer H (1950), "The Distribution of Gains between Investing and Borrowing Countries", *American Economic Review*, vol. 40.

Skidelsky R (1996), *The Road from Serfdom: Economic and Political Consequences of the End of Communism*, Allen & Lane, London.

Smith J L (2005), "Inscrutable OPEC? Behavioral Tests of the Cartel Hypothesis", *Energy Journal*, vol. 26, no. 1.

Solomon F, E Katz and R Lovel (2008), "Social Dimensions of Mining: Research, Policy and Practice Challenges for the Minerals Industry in Australia", *Resources Policy*, vol. 33, no. 3.

Stein J L (1981), "Destabilizing Speculation Activity Can Be Profitable", *Review of Economics and Statistics*, vol. 43.

Stevens P (2015), "The Resource Curse Revisited – Appendix: A Literature Review", Royal Institute of International Affairs, Chatham House.

Stevens P, G Lahn and J Kooroshy (2015), "The Resource Curse Revisited", Royal Institute of International Affairs, Chatham House.

Stijns J C (2005), "Natural-Resource Abundance and Economic Growth Revisited", *Resources Policy*, vol. 30, no. 2.

Stratfor (2018), "State-Owned Enterprises Are a Hard Habit China Doesn't Want to Break", *Worldview Stratfor*, November 7. https://worldview .stratfor.com/article/state-owned-enterprises-are-hard-habit-china-doesnt -want-break

Sugawara N (2014), "From Volatility to Stability in Expenditure: Stabilization Funds in Resource-Rich Countries", IMF Working Paper WP/14/43.

Suopajärvi L, G A Poelzer, T Ejdemo, E Klyuchnikova, E Korchak and V Nygaard (2016), "Social Sustainability in Northern Mining Communities: A Study of the European North and Northwest Russia", *Resources Policy*, vol. 47.

Svedberg P and J Tilton (2006), "The *Real*, Real Price of Non-renewable Resources", *World Development*, vol. 34, no. 3.

Tang K and W Xiong, (2012), "Index Investing and the Financialization of Commodities", *Financial Analysts Journal*, vol. 68.

Telser L G (1981), "Why There Are Organized Futures Markets", *Journal of Law and Economics*, vol. 24.

Tilton J (1992), "Mineral Wealth and Economic Development: An Overview", in J Tilton (ed.) *Mineral Wealth and Economic Development*, Resources for the Future, Washington, DC.

Tilton J (2003), *On Borrowed Time? Assessing the Threat of Mineral Depletion*, Resources for the Future, Washington, DC.

Tilton J (2006), "Outlook for Copper Prices – Up or Down?" *Mining Engineering*, August.

Tilton J (2014), "Cyclical and Secular Determinants of Productivity in the Copper, Aluminum, Iron Ore and Coal Industries", *Mineral Economics*, vol. 27.

Tilton J and H Landsberg (1999), "Innovation, Productivity, Growth and the Survival of the US Copper Industry", in R D Simpson (ed.), *Productivity in Natural Resource Industries*, Resources for the Future, Washington DC.

Tilton J and B Skinner (1987), "The Meaning of Resources", in D McLaren and B Skinner (eds.), *Resources and World Development*, John Wiley, New York.

UNCTAD (1976), *Handbook of International Trade and Development Statistics*, United Nations, New York.

UNCTAD (1981), "Processing and Marketing of Phosphates: Areas for International Cooperation", TD/B/C. IIPSC/22, United Nations.

UNCTAD (1987), "Commodity Export Earnings Shortfalls", TD/B/AC.43/5, Geneva, July.

UNCTAD (1999), "The World Commodity Economy: Recent Evolution, Financial Crises, and Changing Market Structures", TD/B/COM.1/27, Geneva.

UNCTAD (2003), "Back to Basics: Market Access Issues in the Doha Agenda", UNCTAD/DITC/TAB/Misc9, Geneva.

UNCTAD (2012a), The Iron Ore Market 2011–2013, United Nations Conference on Trade and Development, Geneva.

UNCTAD (2012b), *Excessive Commodity Price Volatility: Macroeconomic Effects on Growth and Policy Options*, United Nations, Geneva.

UNCTAD (2019), *State of Commodity Dependence 2019*, United Nations, Geneva.

UNCTAD (annual a), *Review of Maritime Transport*, United Nations, New York.

UNCTAD (annual b), *Handbook of Statistics*, United Nations, New York.

UNCTAD (annual d), *Trade and Development Report*, United Nations, New York.

UNCTAD (monthly), *Monthly Commodity Price Bulletin*, United Nations.

UNEP (2010), Metal Stocks in Society, Scientific Synthesis, International Panel for Sustainable Resource Management, United Nations Environment Programme, Nairobi.

United Nations (2014), *Millennium Development Goal 8: The State of the Global Partnership for Development*, United Nations, New York.

United Nations (annual a), *Statistical Yearbook*, New York.

United Nations (annual b), *International Trade Statistics Yearbook*, New York.

United Nations (monthly), *Monthly Statistical Bulletin of the United Nations*, New York.

USAID (2013), "Economic Effects of Indonesia's Mineral-Processing Requirements for Export", study produced by Nathan Associates Inc. for the US Agency for International Development, Jakarta, April.

US Bureau of Mines (1986), *South Africa and Critical Materials*, Division of Minerals Policy Analysis, Bureau of Mines, US Department of the Interior, Washington DC, July.

US Census (2019), Foreign Trade 2018, www.census.gov/foreign-trade/bal ance/c5700.html#2018.

US Department of Commerce (2018), "Secretary Ross Releases Steel and Aluminum 232 Reports in Coordination with White House", February 16, www.commerce.gov/news/press-releases/2018/02/secretary-ross-releases-steel-and-aluminum-232-reports-coordination.

USGS (annual), *Mineral Commodity Summaries*, United States Geological Survey, Washington, DC.

Valenzuela E, D van der Mensbrugghe and K Anderson (2009), "General Equilibrium Effects of Price Distortions on Global Markets, Farm Incomes and Welfare", in K Anderson (ed.) *Distortions to Agricultural Incentives: A Global Perspective, 1955–2007*, Palgrave Macmillan, London; World Bank, Washington, DC.

van der Ploeg F and S Poelhekke (2009), "Volatility and the Natural Curse", *Oxford Economic Papers*, vol. 61, no. 4.

van der Ploeg F and S Poelhekke (2010), "The Pungent Smell of 'Red Herrings': Sub-soil Assets, Rents, Volatility and the Resource Curse", *Journal of Environmental Economics and Management*, vol. 60, no. 1.

van der Ploeg F and S Poelhekke (2017), "The Impact of Natural Resources: Survey of Recent Quantitative Evidence", *Journal of Development Studies*, vol. 53, no. 2.

van Eyden R, M Difeto, R Gupta and M E Wohar (2019), "Oil Price Volatility and Economic Growth: Evidence from Advanced Economies Using More Than a Century's Data", *Applied Energy*, vol. 233–234.

Varian H (2014), *Intermediate Microeconomics: A Modern Approach*, 9th ed., W.W. Norton & Co., New York.

Vedavalll (1977), "Market Structure of Bauxite/Alumina/Aluminium, and Prospects for Developing Countries", *World Bank Commodity Paper*, no. 24.

Vernon R (1983), *Two Hungry Giants: The United States and Japan in the Quest for Oil and Ores*, Harvard University Press, Cambridge, MA.

Wälde T (1984), "Third World Mineral Development: Recent Issues and Literature", *Journal of Energy & Natural Resources Law*, vol. 2.

Wårell L (2014a), "Trends and Developments in Long-Term Steel Demand: The Intensity-of-Use Hypothesis Revisited", *Resources Policy*, vol. 39.

Wårell L (2014b), "The Effect of a Change in Pricing Regime on Iron Ore Prices", *Resources Policy*, vol. 41.

WBMS (2014), *World Metal Statistics Yearbook 2014*, World Bureau of Metal Statistics, London.

WCED (1987), *Our Common Future*, World Commission on Environment and Development, Oxford University Press, Oxford.

Wenar L (2008), "Property Rights and the Resource Curse", *Philosophy & Public Affairs*, vol. 36, no. 1.

Widerlund A, B Öhlander and F Ecke (2014), *Environmental Aspects of Mining*, pre-study report, Luleå University of Technology.

Will M G, S Prehn, I Pies and T Glauben (2016), "Is Financial Speculation with Agricultural Commodities Harmful or Helpful? A Literature Review of Current Empirical Research", *Journal of Alternative Investment*, vol. 18, no. 3.

Williams M L (1975), "The Extent and Significance of the Nationalization of Foreign-Owned Assets in the Developing Countries", *Oxford Economic Papers*, vol. 27.

Williamson J G (2008), "Globalization and the Great Divergence: Terms of Trade Booms and Volatility in the Poor Periphery 1782–1913", *European Review of Economic History*, vol. 12.

World Bank (1994), "Market Outlook for Major Primary Commodities", Report 814/94.

World Bank (2002), *Treasure or Trouble? Mining in Developing Countries*, Washington, DC.

World Bank (2011), *Overview of State Ownership in the Global Minerals Industry*, Extractive Industries for Development Series 20, Washington, DC, May.

World Bank (2018a), Commodity Markets Outlook, The Changing of the Guard: Shifts in Commodity Demand, World Bank Group, October.

World Bank (2018b), *Impacts on Global Trade and Income of Current Trade Disputes, July*, MTI Practice Note 2, Washington, DC.

World Bank (2018c), *Global Economic Prospects: Broad-based Upturn, But for How Long?*, Washington, DC.

World Bank (2019a), *Commodity Markets Outlook: Food Price Shocks: Channels and Implications*, Washington, DC.

World Bank (2019b), Agriculture, Value Added (% of GDP), https://data.worldbank.org/indicator/NV.AGR.TOTL.ZS.

World Bank (annuala), *World Development Report*, Washington, DC.

World Bank (annualb), *Commodity Trade and Price Trends*, Washington, DC.

World Bureau of Metal Statistics (annual), *World Metal Statistics Yearbook*, London/Hertfordshire.

World Steel Association (annual), *Steel Statistical Yearbook*.

Wright G and J Czelusta (2004), "The Myth of the Resource Curse", *Challenge*, vol. 47, no. 2.

WSJ (2016), "Barrel Breakdown", *Wall Street Journal*, April 15, http://graphics.wsj.com/oil-barrel-breakdown.

WTO (2012), *China – Measures Related to the Exportation of Rare Earths, Tungsten and Molybdenum – Request for Consultations*, WT/DS431/1, March 15.

WTO (2014), *China – Measures Related to the Exportation of Rare Earths, Tungsten and Molybdenum – Reports of the Panel*, WT/DS431/R, March 26.

WTO (annual), *World Trade Statistical Review*, Geneva.

Yan L and P Garcia (2017), "Portfolio Investment: Are Commodities Useful?", *Journal of Commodity Markets*, vol. 8.

Zambian Mining Yearbook (various issues), Kitwe.

Zhu X (2012), "Understanding China's Growth: Past, Present, and Future", *Journal of Economic Perspectives*, vol. 26, no. 4.

Index

Acemoglu, D, 101
acid drainage, 178–179
Adämmer, P, 143–144
additional profits taxes, 272–273
Adelman, Morris, 164
Africa
  foreign aid to, 21
  as net importer, 38–41
agricultural products
  GDP linked to, 65
  mineral products distinguished from, 30
  tariff escalation for, 69–70
agricultural sector
  of China, 64
  commodity boom in, 127
  in developing countries, 228
  in Europe, 23
  Kuznets on, 7–8
  lobbies for, 58
  in Nigeria, 279
  protectionism in, 46, 54–56
  share of, in GDP, 8
  state ownership of, 228
  trade liberalization of, 65–66
  in United States, 46
Aguilera, R F, 88
Allcott, H, 280–281
Alquist, R, 158–159
aluminum, tariffs on, 61–62
Anderson, K, 55, 61, 65
APEF. See Association of Iron Ore
  Exporting Countries
Asia
  commodity booms and role of, 123–124
  economic development in, 24–26
  emerging, 24, 27
  exports of, 44
  foreign aid to, 21

GDP of, 124–125
imports of, 44
natural resource demand
  in, 24–26
Asia-Pacific market, 132–135
Association for the Study of Peak Oil, 164–165
Association of Iron Ore Exporting
  Countries (APEF), 220
Ates, A, 136
auctions, 107
Auty, R M, 239

back-stop resources, 93–94
backwardation, 140, 145–146
Baffes, J, 127
Bagattini, G Y, 267
Bairoch, P, 13
Baltic dry index, 17
bauxite, 67–68, 216
  producer cartels, 215–217
Belt and Road Initiative, 252
Bessler, W, 152–153
bilateral agreements, 110
  of Soviet Union, 21
bilateral contracts, commodity price
  formation and, 108–109
biofuels, 73–74
biomass, 74
Blattman, C, 262
Bloomberg Commodity Index, 151–152
Borcherding, T E, 249–250
BP, 72, 73–74, 90
Bretton Woods system, 122
Brorsen, B W, 136
Brunetti, C, 158–159
bubbles, speculative, 156–157, 158–159
buffer stocks, 263–264

bulk transportation technology, 14–15, 45–46
business cycle, 285

call options, 141
Cashin, P, 103
Caspian basin, 87
CFF. *See* Compensatory Financing Facility
CFTC. *See* Commodity Futures Trading Commission
Chevallier, J, 138
Chicago Board of Trade, 132–135
Chicago Mercantile Exchange (CME), 132–136
China, 1–2, 11–12, 128–129
 agricultural sector of, 64
 as consumer, 3, 47
 demand from, 17–18
 global GDP share of, 50–51, 125
 industrialization of, 50
 as net importer, 38, 45–52, 108–109
 population of, 24
 rare earth metals in, 193
 soybean consumption of, 62
 state ownership in, 252–253
 tariffs of, 54–55
 trade liberalization in, 23
 US trade imbalance with, 58, 185
 value-added taxes in, 70
 WTO joined by, 61
China Development Bank, 244–245
China Export-Import Bank, 244–245
Chinese Bao Steel, 108–109
chromium, 190
CIPEC. *See* Intergovernmental Council of Copper Exporting Countries
CIS. *See* Common Independent States
climate change, 89–90
 greenhouse gases in, 178–179
Club of Rome, 104, 161, 163
CME. *See* Chicago Mercantile Exchange
coal, price evolution of, 76, 88–89
cobalt, 110, 192
Codelco, 148, 243, 249
Coffee Agreement, 21
collective action, 19
colonialism, 19, 235–236
commercial energy, at primary stage, 51

Commitment of Traders (COT), 157
commodity booms, 1–2, 25–26, 174, 180–181, 278–279
 in agricultural sector, 127
 Asia during, 123–124
 commodity prices in, 99, 120
 defining, 116–119, 128
 demand increased by, 278
 duration of, 118–119
 economic growth patterns during, 118, 124, 125–126, 128
 end of, 279–280
 food prices and, 66–67, 127
 historical, 120–121, 122–123
 inflation during, 122, 123–124
 macroeconomic conditions for, 117–118
 raw materials in, 121
 super cycles of, 118–119
 taxation and, 280
commodity dependence, 286, 287
 of developing nations, 257
 measurement of, 256–260
 of monoeconomies, 256–260
 on oil products, 259
commodity exchanges, 110, 130–160
 actors on, 147–154
 commodity optimal functioning on, 136–137
 commodity price formation and, 106–107
 excluded commodities on, 137
 functions of, 138–146
 hedges in, 147–149
 impacts of, 159–160
 instruments, 138–146
 new arrivals on, 137
 objectives of, 147–154
 open outcry systems of, 135–136
 price formation on, 143–145, 155–160
 proliferation of, 130
 in twentieth century, 132–135
Commodity Futures Trading Commission (CFTC), 157
commodity groups
 characteristics of, 28–33
 classifications of, 29–31
 defining, 28–30
 export evolution by, 33

commodity groups (cont.)
  price elasticity of demand of, 32
  storage and classification of, 31
Commodity Index Fund, 151–152
commodity markets, 276–277
  complacency and function of, 11–12
  financial investors in, 151–154
  speculators in, 149–151
  transportation costs and emergence
    of, 12–18
commodity prices, 1–3
  alternative trading arrangements in
    formation of, 106–112
  auctions and formation of, 107
  bilateral contracts and formation of,
    108–109
  capacity utilization and, 92
  closures and reopenings impacting,
    96
  in commodity booms, 99, 120
  commodity exchanges and formation
    of, 106–107
  cost relationship to, 97–98
  cycle length for, 285–286
  declines in, 285–286
  demand contributing to, 99–100
  exchange rates and, 114–115
  factors determining, 91–95
  indices, 117, 122–123, 125
    in constant money, 76, 120
    energy, 123
    manufactures, 105
  instability of, 95–101
  international economy and,
    33–38
  long-run price determination, 92–93,
    101–106
  Mill on, 104
  monopolistic, 95
  peaks in constant dollars, 120
  producer-dictated, 109–110
  public-policy impacting, 96
  quotations, 112–114
    currency in, 112
    delivery place in, 113
    measurement units in, 112
    product quality and, 112–113
    stage of processing and, 112–113
    time of delivery and, 113
  resource depletion and, 167

  short-run price determination,
    91–92, 94, 98–101
  speculators and, 155–159
  supply contributing to, 100
  supply disruptions and, 186
  transfer pricing and formation of,
    109–110
  transparency in, 109
  in unregulated competitive markets,
    91
  user-driven, 109–110
  volatility of
    commodity booms caused by, 99
    economic growth and relationship
      to, 100
    history of, 98–99
    uncertainty caused by, 100
commodity processing, 67–71
Commodity Research Bureau, 151–152
commodity supply, traded
  provenance and destination of,
    38–45, 52
  by region, 39–40
Common Agricultural Policy (CAP), 23
Common Independent States (CIS), 41
communism, 22
Compensatory Finance Schemes, 263,
    265–266
Compensatory Financing Facility
    (CFF), 266
complacency, commodity market
    functioning and, 11–12
concessional lending, 57
conflicts, 81–83
  oil production and, 81
contango, 140, 145–146
  defining, 145–146
Cooper, R N, 157–158
copper, 51, 95–96
  producer cartels, 219–221
  variable costs, 96
  in Zambia, 248–248
corporate taxes, 79
costs
  commodity price relationship to,
    97–98
  of extraction of oil, 173
  of nationalization, 238
  oil production, per barrel, 173
  of price stabilization, 269

resource depletion and evidence
 from, 168–173
transportation, 12–18
variable, of copper, 96
COT. *See* Commitment of Traders
Crain, M W, 267
currency, in commodity price
 quotations, 112
CVRD, 108–109
Czelusta, J, 283–284

Dalian Commodity Exchange, 132–135
Davis, G, 267, 282–283
demand
 from China, 17–18
 commodity booms and, 278
 in emerging world, 24–25
 income elasticity of, 105
 for industrial commodities, 50–51
 for iron ore, 31
 for metals, 47
 natural resource, 24–26
 price stabilization with variable, 264
 for rare earth metals, 12
 for raw materials, 99–100
 stagnation of, 47
 for steel, 11
 for uranium, 219
dematerialization
 in advanced economies, 182
 economic development as process of,
  10–11
Dempsey, N, 179–180
Department of Agriculture, US,
 113–114
Deuskar, P, 158–159
developing countries, 235
 agricultural sector in, 228
 commodity dependence of, 257
 economic growth in, 229–230
 foreign direct investment for, 196
 GDP of, 270
 nationalization in, 211, 232–236
 postcolonial period in, 235–236
 state ownership in, 251
 sustainability in, 177
Devlin, J., 267
direct payments, 57
discontinuities, 175
Doha Round, 54, 55

domestic installations, 57
domestic output, 198–199
Dutch auctions, 107
Dutch disease, 277–281
 empirical studies on, 280–281
 history of, 277–278

economic development, 26
 in Asia, 24–26
 as dematerialization process, 10–11
 primary commodities in, 6–12
 productivity in, 9
 in South Korea, 11
economic growth
 commodity booms and patterns of,
  118, 124, 125–126, 128
 commodity price volatility and
  relationship to, 100
 in developing countries, 229–230
 export instability slowing, 262
 resource curse and, 80
 state-owned enterprises and,
  229–230
Economic Partnership Agreement, 23
Ecuador, 78
Eggert, R, 176
EIA. *See* Energy Information
 Administration
electricity, 73, 182
electronic trading, 136
emerging world, 1–2
 demand in, 24–25
 primary commodity markets and,
  25–26
energy consumption, global, 72
 by source, 73
Energy Information Administration
 (EIA), 85, 87, 90
energy price index, 123
energy raw materials, 72
energy sector, state ownership of,
 228–229
Engel's Law, 29–30
environment
 climate change and, 89–90
 fracking and concerns about, 85
 mineral extraction consequences for,
  178–179
equity ownership, 231
ETFs. *See* exchange traded funds

Eurex, 143–144
Europe
   agricultural sector in, 23
   imports in, 13
   industrialization of, 13–14
Everingham, J-A, 179
exchange rates
   commodity prices and, 114–115
   goals of, 284
   in monoeconomies, 284–286
exchange traded funds (ETFs), 152
Extractive Industries Transparency
      Initiative, 254–255
exhaustibility, 175–176
Exogenous Shocks Facility, 266
exports, 20
   of Asia, 44
   of Australia, 44
   evolution of, by commodity groups,
      33
   instability
      economic growth slowed by, 262
      in monoeconomies, 260–269
      savings for prevention of, 268–269
   net, from Latin America, 38–41
   oil, 44
   primary commodity values
      as global, 35
   restrictions on
      arguments for, 59–60
      detriments of, 60–61
      in international commodity trade,
         58–61
      of minerals, 59–60
      subsidies as, 59
   of Russia, 44–45
   shares of world, 42–43
   in supply disruptions, 187
   of United States, 44
   values of, 34, 36
   voluntary restraints on, 56–57
Exxon, 90, 165–166

Fatás, A, 101
Fattouh, B, 158–159
FIA. *See* Futures Industry
      Association
financial crisis of 2008, 17–18
   international trade following, 18
financial investors, 151–154

fiscal revenue extraction, 269–277. *See
   also* taxes
fishing, 8–9
food
   aid, 21
   commodity boom and prices of,
      66–67, 127
   supply, 12
foreign aid, 21
foreign direct investment, 70–71, 244
   for developing countries, 196
   nationalization of, 235–236
   outward, 244–245
   in state-owned enterprises, 244–245
foreign exchange reserves, 268–269
forward contracts, 139
fossil fuels, 72. *See also specific types*
   abundance of, 83–89
   dominance of, 74–77
   global GDP share of, 75
   output values of, 75
fracking, 88
   environmental concerns raised by, 85
Frank, J, 136
freight rates, 12–13, 14–15
futures contracts, 138–141, 150
   margins in, 139
   volume of, 131
Futures Industry Association (FIA), 130

Gaddafi, 81–83
Garcia, P, 136, 154
Gately, D, 225
GDP. *See* gross domestic product
Gecamines, 242–243
Germany, 190
Gervais, D, 158–159
Ghana, 45, 70
Ghosh, S C, 260–261
Gilbert, C L, 127, 158, 265
Gillis, M, 240, 241
Global Dairy Trade, 107
globalization
   defining, 12–13
   of natural gas market, 15
   primary commodities impacted by,
      16–17
golden share, 231
Goldman Sachs, 151–152, 153
government greed, 79

oil prices and, 77–78
government officials, 1–2
the Great Depression, 19, 119, 184,
    214–215
greenfield capacity, 126–127
greenhouse gases, 178–179
Grilli, E R, 102, 103, 166–167, 212
gross domestic product (GDP)
    agricultural product assistance linked
        to, 65
    agricultural sector share of, 8
    annual growth of, 126
    of Asia, 124–125
    calculation of, 28–29
    Chinese share of global, 50–51, 125
    of developing countries, 270
    fossil fuels share of global, 75
    mining share of, 8
    primary sector and, 9, 28–29
    utility share of, 8
*A Guide to Primary Commodities in the
    World Economy* (Radetzki), 1

Haase, M, 158–159
Hamel, K, 25
Hamilton, M, 158–159
Haniotis, T, 127
Harding, T, 280–281
hedges
    in commodity exchanges, 147–149
    long, 149
    for price stabilization, 268
    short, 147–148
Hilson, G, 179
Hnatkovska, V, 101
Holder, M E, 143–144
horizontal drilling, 88
Hotelling rule, 165, 167
Hurricane Katrina, 202

ICE. *See* Intercontinental Exchange Inc.
IEA. *See* International Energy Agency
Ielpo, F, 138
IHS, 85–86
IMF. *See* International Monetary Fund
IMF Commodity Prices, 114
imports, 203
    of Asia, 44
    assurance measures, 198
    China and net, 38, 108–109

dependence on, 186
    in Europe, 13
    licenses, 56–57
    net, to Africa, 38–41
    quotas, 56–57
    rich world dependence on, 45–52
    supply disruptions and economy of,
        186–188
    tariffs, 56, 61–63
    US dependence on, 19
income elasticity of demand, 105
India, 11–12
    mining in, 250–251
    population of, 24
indigenous people, 180
industrial commodities
    consumption of, 48–49, 53
    falling demand for, 50–51
industrialization
    of China, 50
    of Europe, 13–14
    of United States, 47
inflation, during commodity booms,
    122, 123–124
Intercontinental Exchange Inc. (ICE),
    132–135, 136, 144
Intergovernmental Council of Copper
    Exporting Countries (CIPEC),
    212, 220
Intergovernmental Panel on Climate
    Change, 89
international commodity agreements,
    22, 263
international commodity trade
    commodities and, 33–38
    export restriction growth in, 58–61
    measurement of restrictions in,
        63–67
International Energy Agency (IEA), 74,
    87, 90, 170
    members of, 201–202
    oil stockpiles of, 201–202
    on supply disruptions, 202
International Monetary Fund (IMF),
    24, 168–170, 261, 266
    IMF Commodity Prices, 114
International Standard Industrial
    Classification (ISIC), 28–29
International Tin Agreement, 140
International Tin Council, 20

international trade, 26
    after financial crisis of 2008, 18
    global production volume and,
        36–38
    United States' role in, 115
International Trade Center, 69–70
intrinsic value, 141
Iranian Revolution, 201–202
Iran–Iraq war, 192, 202
iron ore
    demand for, 31
    producer cartels, 219–221
Irwin, A, 136, 158–159
ISIC. *See* International Standard
        Industrial Classification
Ismail, K, 280–281
Iwarson, T, 153

Jacks, D S, 100, 103
Jamaica, 215–217
Japan, 46, 47, 69–70
Johnson, S, 158–159
joint sharing arrangements, 198

Keniston, D, 280–281
Keynes, J M, 184, 262
Kharas, H, 25
Kilian, L, 158–159
Kim, J, 61
Kindleberger, C, 283–284
Korean conflict, 20
Korinek, J, 61
Kowalski, P, 254
Kuznets, S, 7
    on agricultural sector, 7–8

Latin America, 21, 44
    as net exporter, 38–41
Lawrence, R Z, 157–158
Lee, T K, 158–159
liberalization. *See* trade liberalization
light, price of, 182
liquid natural gas (LNG), 15–16,
        85–86
LME. *See* London Metal Exchange
LNG. *See* liquid natural gas
loan write-offs, 57
Loayza, N, 101
lobbies, agricultural sector, 58
Lomé conventions, 266

London Metal Exchange (LME), 62,
        132–135, 140
long hedges, 149
long-term contracts, 196–197

MacBean, A I, 260–261
Mali, 70
Malthus, T, 161
manufactures price index, 105
margins, in futures contracts, 139
market power, 209
marketing boards, 267–268
Martin, W, 55
Masters, M, 157–158
Maurice, C, 161
Maxwell, P, 282–283
MBD, 83
McDermott, C J, 103
McKenzie, S, 179
Megginson, W, 249–250
metals. *See also* rare earth metals
    demand for, 47
    index, 76
    operating cash costs for, 169, 170
    strategic, 188
Mexico, 78
middle class, global size of, 24–25
Mihov, I, 101
Mill, J S, 104
mineral products, 71
    agricultural products distinguished
        from, 30
    environmental consequences of
        extraction of, 178–179
    export restrictions on, 59–60
    extraction of, 180
    index, 76
    as national patrimony, 232–235
    population density and, 46
    royalties on, 275–276
mineral sector
    dependence on, 282–283
    expansion of, 276
    international markets of, 253–255
    monoeconomies, 282–283
    privatizations in, 250
    rent in, 247–248
    state ownership in, 228–229,
        232–245
mining, 7, 14–15

in India, 250–251
share of, in GDP, 8
state ownership of, 232–234
monoeconomies, 257, 258–259,
    261–262
  commodity dependence of, 256–260
  exchange rate policies in, 284–286
  export instability in, 260–269
  fiscal revenue extraction in, 269–277
  mineral sector, 282–283
  oil, 259
  resource curse in, 281–284
monopolistic prices, 95
Morgan, C W, 158
Morocco, 217–218
multilateral contracts, 21
Murck, B, 179
Murphy, K, 158–159, 179
MUV index, 121, 123–124
  World Bank on, 102

national standards, 56–57
nationalization, 227. *See also* state
    ownership
  in developing countries, 211,
    232–236
  of foreign direct investment, 235–236
  managerial inexperience after,
    238–239
  of oil industry, 23, 224
  setting-up costs of, 238
natural gas. *See also* shale gas
  globalization of market for, 15
  liquid, 15–16, 85–86
  price evolution of, 76
  regional prices of, 16
  US production of, 15–16, 84–85
natural resource demand, 24–26
Nelgen, S, 61
Netter, J, 249–250
New York Mercantile Exchange
    (NYMEX), 110, 132–135, 144
New Zealand, 8–9
Nguyen, D T, 260–261
Nidera, 245
Nigeria, 279
nonrenewable resources, 176–178
  social sustainability and, 179–180
  sustainability and, 178–179
Nordhaus, W, 89, 182, 183

Norilsk Nickel, 110
North Sea, 50
  depletion in, 79
  oil production in, 79
Norway, 8–9
  corporate taxes in, 79
nuclear utilities, 219
NYMEX. *See* New York Mercantile
    Exchange

OECD. *See* Organisation for Economic
    Co-operation and Development
OFDI. *See* outward foreign direct
    investments
oil, crude
  production increases in, 172–173
  shipment of, 67–68
oil crises, 188
oil exports, 52
  world, 44
oil industry, 8–9
  monoeconomies, 259
  nationalization of, 23, 224
  privatization in, 251
  profits of, 80
  resource curse and, 80
  state ownership of, 229
  supply disruption in, 190,
    192, 193
oil output, 74, 75
oil prices, 22, 33–34, 77
  decline in, 170, 279
  on energy price index, 123
  evolution of, 77–83
  government greed and, 77–78
  macroeconomics of, 77–83
  reserve, 168
  rises of, 75
oil production. *See also* shale oil
  cartels in, 77
  commodity dependence on, 259
  conflicts and, 81
  costs per barrel, 173
  depletion and, 81
  extraction costs, 173
  IEA stockpile of, 201–202
  in North Sea, 79
  OPEC and world output of, 224
  reserves, proved, 230
  resources, 172

oil production (cont.)
  in Russia, 79
  shale, 85
  in US, 84–85
OPEC. *See* Organization of Petroleum
    Exporting Countries
operating cash costs, for metals, 169,
    170
options, 141–142, 150
  call, 141
  holders of, 141
  issuers of, 141
  put, 141, 148
  volume of, 131
Organisation for Economic Co-
    operation and Development
    (OECD), 38, 61, 64–65
Organization of Petroleum Exporting
    Countries (OPEC), 23, 77, 78,
    170, 205, 215
  capacity expansion of, 224
  decline of, 243
  history of, 221–225
  new strategic partnership of, 223
  as producer cartel, 221–225
  on quotas, 223
  resource curse in, 224–225, 243
  royalties utilized by, 272
  world oil output and, 224
Ossowski, R, 267
Ostry, J, 260–261
outward foreign direct investments
    (OFDI), 244–245
over-the-counter (OTC) swaps,
    151–152
overvaluation, 284

Paris Agreement, 89, 90
Peak Oil, 77, 174
Petrobras, 229–230
Petroleum Exporting Countries, 195
Petronas, 244
Petroperu, 78
phosphate rock, 217–218
physical trade outlets, 142–143
Pindyck, R, 100
Poelhekke, S, 262
population density, 46
  mineral products and, 46
  of USA, 47

postcolonial period, 235–236
posted prices, 111
Prain, R, 229
Prebisch, R, 104–105
premium, 141
preservation, 31
price elasticity of demand, 207, 219
  of commodity groups, 32
  estimation of, 210
  for producer-cartel output, 208
price elasticity of outside supply, 212
price stabilization, 22, 145, 266–267
  from agreements, 263–264
  costs of, 269
  equilibrium levels for, 265–266
  government-expenditure volatility
    and, 267
  hedging as measure for, 268
  with variable demand, 264
  with variable supply, 264
primary commodities
  contraction over time in share of, 7
  defining, 6, 28–29
  in economic development, 6–12
  global export value for, 35, 36, 37
  globalization repercussions on,
    16–17
  markets, 1
    emerging world and, 25–26
    public intervention in, 19–24
  prices of, 2–3
  significance of, 7
  systematic data on, 7
  world export shares of, 42–43
  world production of, 37
primary sectors
  GDP and, 9, 28–29
  secondary sectors compared with,
    28–29
primary stage, commercial energy at, 51
primary supply, 32
private investors, 274
privatization, 22, 249–252
  in mineral sector, 250
  in oil industry, 251
producer cartels
  bauxite, 215–217
  copper, 219–221
  defining, 205
  formal preconditions for, 205–209

iron ore, 219–221
market intervention by, 207
in 1970s, 214–225
in oil production, 77
OPEC as, 221–225
phosphate rock, 217–218
preconditions for, 209–214
price elasticity of demand for output
  of, 208
profit maximization of, 206–207
success of, 205–209
uranium, 218–219
producer-dictated prices, 109–110
producer power, 211, 225–226
production chain, 99–100
productivity, 105–106
in economic development, 9
profit maximization, 111, 206
deviations from, 97
of producer cartels, 206–207
social responsibility and, 237
proportional rod, 231
protectionism, 26–27, 38, 185
in agricultural sector, 46, 54–56
goals of, 56–58
measurement of, 63–67
rationales for, 57
in raw materials, 54–56
in USA, 200
public ownership. *See* state ownership
public procurement, 57
put options, 141, 148

Qatar, 45
quotas, 221–222

Radetzki, M, 1, 3, 88, 119
railroads, 13
Ramey, G, 101
rare earth metals, 36–38, 60
in China, 193
demand for, 12
supply disruptions of, 193
rationing, 189
raw materials, 10–11, 13
in commodity boom, 121
demand for, 99–100
protectionism in, 54–56
rich world dependence on, 45–46
self-sufficiency in, 185

substitutions of, 189
Reagan, R, 22, 249–250
refrigeration, 13–14, 31
renewable energy, 73–74
future expectations for, 89–90
resource booms, 177–178
resource curse, 80
defining, 283–284
economic growth and, 80
in monoeconomies, 281–284
oil industry and, 80
in OPEC countries, 224–225,
  243
paradox, 283
quantification of, 81
volatility as feature of, 262
resource depletion, 161–163, 177
commodity prices and, 167
cost evidence on, 168–173
defining, 162–163
evidence of, 173–175
historical, 162
long-run price evolution and,
  165–167
in North Sea, 79
oil production and, 81
reserve availability and, 163–165
threats of, 180–183
unit price of unexploited resources
  and, 167–168
resource rent, 270, 271
royalties for extraction of, 272
taxation of, 270–271
revenue maximization, 206
Ricardian rents, 240–241
Ricardo, D, 104
risk aversion, 187
RMG Consulting, 232
Rowe, J W F, 212
royalties, 273, 274–275
advantages of, 272
defining, 271
on mineral products, 275–276
OPEC utilizing, 272
for resource rent extraction, 272
R/P ratios, 165
Russia. *See also* Soviet Union
exports of, 44–45
oil production in, 79
Rystad Energy, 173

Sachs, J, 263
Sanders, D R, 136, 151–152, 158–159
Second World War, 19, 20, 235
secondary sectors, primary sectors
    compared with, 28–29
secondary supply, 32
self-sufficiency, in raw
    materials, 185
Senegal, 70
Shah, S, 136
shale gas, 15–16, 85
    economic benefits of, 85–86
    global resources, 87
shale oil, 85
    economic benefits of, 85–86
    production increase, 172–173
shale revolution, 87–88
Shanghai Futures Exchange, 132–135
short hedges, 147–148
Simpson, R D, 171
Singer, H, 104–105
Singleton, K J, 158
SITC. *See* Standard International Trade
    Classification
Skinner, B, 171
Smith, A, 104
Smithson, C W, 161
social responsibility, 239
    profit maximization and, 237
social sustainability, 179–180, 183
socialism, 142, 232–235
Solomon, F, 179
Soviet Union, 22, 142
    ascent of, 19
    bilateral agreements of, 21
    collapse of, 222–223
soybeans
    Chinese consumption of, 62
    tariffs on, 62
S&P GSCI. *See* Standard & Poor's
    Goldman Sachs Commodity
    Index
speculators
    bubbles caused by, 156–157,
        158–159
    in commodity markets, 149–151
    commodity prices and, 155–159
    defining, 150
    destabilization caused by, 156
    objectives of, 150

STABEX, 266
Standard International Trade
    Classification (SITC), 29–30
Standard & Poor's Goldman Sachs
    Commodity Index (S&P GSCI),
    151–152
Standby Credit Facility, 266
State Owned Asset Supervision and
    Administration Commission,
    252
state ownership, 97, 227, 273–274
    of agricultural sector, 228
    characteristics of, 236–245
    in China, 252–253
    control under, 246–247
    in developing countries, 251
    economic growth and, 229–230
    of energy sector, 228–229
    enterprise, 231–232
    financial environment under,
        240–245
    firm behavior under, 236–237
    foreign direct investment in, 244–245
    inefficiencies of, 77
    international mineral markets and,
        253–255
    investment behavior under, 240–245
    mineral rent under, 247–248
    in mineral sector, 228–229, 236–245
    of mining, 232–234
    motivations for, 232–236
    national economy impacted by,
        245–253
    national goals and, 247–248
    of oil industry, 229
    operations under, 238–240
    principal–agent relation under, 246
    private sector compared to, 241
steam power, 13
steel
    demand for, 11
    South Korea use of, 11
    tariffs on, 61–62
Stevens, P, 283–284
strategic metals, 188
    US stockpiles of, 199–201
strike price, 141
subsidies, 57
    as export restriction, 59
substitutability, 181–182

Suez crisis, 14
Sugawara, N, 267
Sumitomo scandal, 144
Suopajärvi, L, 179
supply
    commodity prices impacted by, 100
    curves, 93–94, 95–96
    food, 12
    price stabilization with variable, 264
    primary, 32
    secondary, 32
    security of, 184–186
supply disruptions
    alleviation of, 192–202
    commodity prices and, 186
    domestic output and prevention of,
        198–199
    export concentration in, 187
    IEA on, 202
    import economy and, 186–188
    oil industry and impacts of, 190, 192,
        193
    of rare earth metals, 193
    severity of problems caused by,
        189–192
    substitution difficulties during, 187
    supplier relations and prevention of,
        196–197
    sustainability and, 186
sustainability, 161–163, 175–176,
        180–183
    in developing countries, 177
    economic, 176–178, 183
    nonrenewable resources and,
        178–179
    social, 179–180, 183
    supply disruptions and, 186
sustainable development, 175

Tang, K, 158
tariffs, 13
    on aluminum, 61–62
    of China, 54–55
    escalation, 67–71
        for agricultural products, 69–70
        counters to, 70–71
        in high-income OECD countries,
            69–70
        nominal and effective rates in, 69
    import, 56, 61–63

    on soybeans, 62
    on steel, 61–62
    of USA, 54–55
taxes
    additional profits, 272–273
    commodity booms and, 280
    corporate, 79
    resource rent, 270–271
    value added, 70
Thatcher, M, 22, 249–250
Tilton, J, 171, 176
tradability, 139
Trade Expansion Act of 1962,
        Section 232,
Trade Integration Mechanism, 266
trade liberalization, 23, 26–27, 54
    of agricultural sector, 65–66
    in China, 23
    reform of, 66
transfer pricing, 109–110
Trans-Pacific Partnership, 23
transportation, 26
    bulk, 14–15, 45–46
    costs, 16–17, 105
    global commodity markets and costs
        of, 12–18
    maritime, 17–18
    refrigerated ships and long-distance,
        13–14
    steam-power development and, 13
    technological revolutions in, 16–17
Trump, D, 61–62, 90, 185

UN Framework Convention on Climate
        Change, 89
UNCTAD. *See* United Nations
        Conference on Trade and
        Development
unexploited resources, 167–168
unit price, 30–31
    of unexploited resources, 167–168
United Kingdom, 79, 184–185
United Nations Conference on Trade
        and Development (UNCTAD),
        29, 70, 261–262
United Nations International Trade
        Center, 69–70
United Nations Statistical Office, 28–29
United States (US), 215–216
    agricultural sector in, 46

United States (US) (cont.)
Chinese trade imbalance with, 58, 185
exports of, 44
import dependence of, 19
industrialization of, 47
international trade role of, 115
natural gas production in, 15–16, 84–85
oil production in, 84–85
population density of, 47
protectionist policy in, 200
strategic metals stockpiles of, 199–201
tariffs of, 54–55
uranium
demand for, 219
producer cartels, 218–219
US. *See* United States
user-driven prices, 109–110
utilities, 8

Vale, 229–230, 243
Valenzuela, E., 65–66
value added tax (VAT), 70
van der Ploeg, F, 262
van Eyden, R M, 101
variable import levy, 56
VAT. *See* value-added tax
Venables, A J, 280–281
very large crude carriers, 67–68
voluntary export restraints, 56–57

Wang, G H K, 136
Wårell, L, 3, 17–18
Warner, A, 263
waste, 74
Western Mining Corporation, 110
white elephants, 281–282
Will, M G, 158–159
Williams, M L, 235–236
Williamson, J G, 101
Wolff, D, 152–153
World Bank, 67, 165–166, 228, 282–283
on MUV index, 102
World Bank Commodities Price Data (The Pink Sheet), 114
World Trade Organization (WTO), 29, 54, 60, 193
China joining, 61
Wright, G, 283–284
WTO. *See* World Trade Organization
Wu, J C, 158–159

Xiong, W, 158

Yan, L, 154
Yang, M C, 102, 103, 166–167, 212

Zaire, 192, 220
Zambia, 220
copper in, 248–248
ZCCM, 244
Zinc, Rio Tinto, 212

Printed in the United States
By Bookmasters